ICONS OF AMERICA

ICONS
OF
AMERICA

Edited by
Ray B. Browne
&
Marshall Fishwick

Popular Press

ISBN 0-87972-090-5 cloth
0-87972-091-3 paperback

Library of Congress Catalogue Card
Number 77-84917

Contents

Icons Of America

INTRODUCTION

Marshall Fishwick

The terrible winter of 1977 found America short on energy, but not on icons. Indeed, the craving for external expressions of internal convictions (one of the best basic definitions of icons) only grows as confidence in religion, economics, and politics dwindles. In various phases of the word's long use and alteration (the Greek root, *eikon*, means "image") icons have been, David Orr points out, "the most unintelligible of images: especially in a culture whose visual spectrum is intense, convoluted, diverse, and ubiquitous." Still icons do objectify deep mythological structure of reality, revealing basic needs which go from age to age, media to media, generation to generation. Cultural ciphers, these admired artifacts (some of our contributors insist they may be intangible) help us to decipher, to unlock, the mystery of our attitudes and assumptions. As objects they can be approached objectively; but those who believe in them also operate on an emotional level — the level of love and reverence. The real task is not merely to define icons, but to participate in the iconic life.

To do this one need merely to have a coke, play a pin ball or slot machine, pick up the telephone, turn on the tube, drive down to the corner drug store. Perhaps your car has a Virgin Mary on the dashboard — artifact, image, symbol, icon — plastic piety in the 1970's! Thus do old and new icons converge in our driveways.

3

Icons accumulate and alter meanings; they also lose them. The iconic Virgin Mary does not speak to the twentieth century as she did to the thirteenth. The swastika does not motivate European youth of the 1970's as it did those of the 1940's. Man carries meanings, not merely objects invested with meanings. The image precedes the idea in the development of human consciousness; the idea drives the image on to glory or oblivion.

In *Icon and Idea,* Herbert Read observes that "thinking in pictures" is the first stage of icon-making. The ensuing steps to the construction of icons were taken in the prehistoric period. All cultures invent icons. Freud spoke of "optical memory-residues — things as opposed to words." The mind is not so much a debating society as a picture gallery. We look with our eyes, see with our minds, make with our hands. Form and formula fuse. The word becomes flesh and dwells among us.

Icons are symbols and mindmarks. They tie in with myth, legend, values, idols, aspirations. Because of the great stress religion places on icons, some would limit icons to conventional religious images typically painted on a wooden panel.[2] We seek to revitalize the word and relate it to popular culture. Icons still move men, even when they are not recognized as such in supermarkets, discotheques, used car lots, and funeral parlors. They pop up on billboards, magazine covers, and TV commercials. Manna may still come from heaven; but much daily information flows through the Big Tube, which constantly flashes images and cools outer reality.

Icons traditionally connote fixity and permanence; but pop icons deal with the flux and impermanence of contemporary Protean Man. A style of self-process and simultaneity is emerging; icons, like everything else, adapt accordingly. Objects are the building-blocks; ideas the cement holding them together. Modern man is starved for ideas and objects that give coherence to electric-age culture. What he finds most acceptable, Robert Jay Lifton notes, are "images of a more fragmentary nature than those of past ideologies. These images, though often limited and fleeting, have great influence upon his psychological life."[3]

With all the changes icons are still omnipresent. The old process continues: history becomes mythology, mythology begets ritual, ritual demands icons. Concepts end up as creeds and icons. Careers of men as different as Buddha, Christ, Marx, Einstein, and Lenin confirm it. Heroes and icons survive because they function: when warm for devotion, when cool for companionship. They are literally indispensable in what Jacob Bronowski has chronicled so brilliantly in *The Ascent of Man* (1973).

Science "went iconic" with Heisenberg and Bohr — some would say, with Plato. Since then scientists have thought more like poets than technicians. "Thinking in pictures" is the very essence of icon making: what Sigmund Freud called "optical memory-residues." A new generation gets them not from crypts or cathedrals, but from billboards and supermarkets. Icons must reflect the change. The essays that follow show that they do.

A cluster of compatible words emerge — cipher, symbol, artifact, emblem, amulet, totem, allegory, charm, idol, image. Erwin Panofsky's pioneering *Studies in Iconology* (Oxford University Press, 1939), which begins by defining iconography as "the branch of art history which concerns itself with the subject matter of meaning of works of art, as opposed to their form." Then follows an involved abstract discussion on the distinction between meaning and form. Fourteen pages later we learn that the act of interpretation requires not only "pre-iconographical description (and pseudo-formal analysis) but iconographical analysis in the narrower sense of the word and iconographical interpretation in a deeper sense (iconographical synthesis)." This volume does not seek its synthesis in such high scholarship: instead, it looks at objects of everyday man, convinced that in a democracy, Uncle Sam's icons are by, of, and for Everyman.

Every age is compulsively creative. With each, mythology is transformed into history, history into life, and life into icons. Concepts and emotions become finally creeds and images, as Plato's Ideas, Kant's Categories, Jung's Archetypes and McLuhan's Media all illustrate. Pop icons are created by and mirrored in twentieth century life, as they have been in the life of all centuries.

Religious icons — surely the most powerful of all times past — remain in our secular times. For some people they still have power; for most of us they are dead. Diedrich Bonhoeffer, German theologian martyred in Hitler's Germany, sensed this when he wrote:

> Honesty demands that we recognize that we must live in the world as if there were no God. And this is just what we do recognize — before God! God himself drives us to this realization. He makes us know that we must live as men who can get along without Him.

We seem to survive without much pain in a world where God is dead. But we cannot exist without images. Living in the Secular City, we crave and therefore create the externalizations of our psychic environment. In post Bicentennial America the icon goes pop.

But as people never change basically, their icons remain essentially the same, as do the purposes to which they are put. Ancient Egyptian tombs were full of icons, mainly religious but also secular. There was a long record of sacred man-bearing objects throughout ancient history. Christianity continued the use of iconography. Icons used for prayer abounded in the early days of Christianity. "I have seen a great many portraits of the Saviour, of Peter and of Paul, which have been preserved up to our times," wrote Eusebius, Bishop of Caesarea in Cappadocia (265-340 A.D.). The catacombs were centers of icons, used by both the simple people as well as the ecclesiastical hierarchy. In Christendom, the meaning and language of icons have always been a strength. Key words were *legend, belief, sacred object, veneration.*

Icons are associated with age and class groups. They demand a cult, a lore, a spot of veneration. "All sacred things must have their place," Claude Levi-Strauss notes. "Being in their place is what makes them sacred. If taken out of their place, even in thought, the entire order of the universe would be destroyed." As the old order has changed, yielding place to the ever-new, the sacred spots for icons are no longer churches and monasteries but, in the new statements of man's beliefs and aspirations, on superhighways, television screens, and in discotheques. Still central to them, however, wherever they are placed, is their objectifying something near man's essence.

Deep in the forests of present-day icons can we find bases for new definitions and implications? Today, as always in the past, men want to make sense out of the universe. That "sense" must be made in the context of present time, place and belief. Even "natural" facts such as birth, growth and death are reacted to in a "cultural" fashion.[4] Every style that develops is complete in itself and *sui generis,* of its own order. Former styles are no longer viable because they are not ours. Iconologically the consequences are profound and traumatic.

The mainstream of iconology in our time — because of its dissemination through the mass media — is the popular stratum of our culture. Because of its position, therefore, it has received severe criticism. Elitist critics Dwight Macdonald and Edmund Wilson have long preached that those elements in our lives that are esthetically satisfying are aristocratic and for the minority. Other elements — those catering to and acceptable by the majority—are esthetically deficient and therefore contemptible. Though this condescending attitude is still popular among some esthetes, it is being powerfully roughed up by such sensitive and sensible critics as Susan Sontag:

> What we are getting is not the demise of art, but a transformation of the function of art. Art, which arose in human society as magical-religious operation, and passed over into a technique for depicting and commenting on secular reality, has in our own time arrogated to itself a new function — neither religious, nor serving a secularized religious function, nor merely secular or profane . . . . Art today is a new kind of instrument, an instrument for modifying consciousness and organizing new modes of sensibility.

Many critics today agree with philosopher Abraham Kaplan: popular art although not yet arrived at esthetically great accomplishment has great potential and is working toward considerable success.

Esthetically great or small, satisfying or terrifying, however, surely the most irrefutable statement about popular art — and therefore icons — could be a paraphrase of Samuel Johnson's contradiction of the philosopher Berkeley's belief of the Ideal. Dr. Johnson merely kicked a rock. All we need do is hold up an icon.

We need to devise new criteria and categories for intrinsic

meanings. Profiting from Erwin Panofsky's creative work we should apply the same serious analysis to the current American Renaissance that was used for the Italian and French period. This would involve not only surface data (identification, description, authentication) but interior qualities (evaluation, interpretation, significance).

Most of all, it would involve an intensive reappraisal of the thingness of things (for our purposes, the iconness of icons). Filling the space-time continuum, haunting our dreams, things determine not only our lives but our fantasies. Primitive man wrestles with life's raw stuff, stone and wood, until he develops a technology. And as cultures have a technology, so do they have a history.[5]

Thus objects in general, and icons in particular, are the building blocks of reality. They are sensitive indicators of who we are, where we come from, where we intend to go. Long after an individual has died, and even his language and culture have disappeared, artifacts remain. By digging into the earth, men known as archaeologists uncover the story of the past. Things form the solid basis of our understanding and concern for millions of human beings who preceded us. Archaeology plus imagination equals historical insight.

Dynamos, telephones, cameras, film, printing presses, plastic discs, picture tubes: are these icons not the essence of popular culture? Have they not shaped the mass media which carries the message?

The thingness of things has fascinated the liveliest intellects since Aristotle's time. A conscious interest in what Lewis Mumford calls (in *Art and Technics*) "the go of things" has been such an obvious major factor in history that one posits and predicates it in every period, event, sequence. Yet how few people in the academy know how to deal with — even to describe or classify — the artifacts that make things go. Having defined artifact as "a thing made by man purposefully, so that he transforms materials already existing" he goes back to his notes and his lecture.

There is ample evidence to support Professor Harold Skramstad's article "American Things: A Neglected Material Culture."[6] Some readers were surprised to find him single out "New Journalist" Tom Wolfe for special praise, since

Wolfe "demonstrates how insights from a study of new artifact forms are able to increase our understanding of present
day American civilization."

More frequently praised is Professor James Harvey Robinson, whose "New History" (now over 50 years old) insisted
that we study "not only the written records, but the remains
of buildings, pictures, clothing, tools, and ornaments."[7] A
promising start was made in the mid-twenties in the twelve-
volume *History of American Life* series edited by Arthur M.
Schlesinger and Dixon Ryan Fox in which some attention
was paid to "non-literary remains and physical survivals."
T. J. Wertenbaker's volumes on *The Middle Colonies* and
The Puritan Oligarchy made use of material culture. But
when Caroline F. Ware edited *The Cultural Approach to History* for the American Historical Association in 1940, neither
her introduction nor the 36 essays describing the so-called
new tools of the cultural historian had a word to say about
the historic artifact.

Research Opportunities in American Cultural History
(1961) edited by Frances McDermott calls attention to many
important possibilities, but none involves a study of artifacts.
A look at *Documents in American Civilization* suggests how
an idea of the historian can be illustrated by an artist, rather
than how the work of an artist or artisan can lead the historian to a new idea.

The American Historical Association, having in 1934
created a Conference on Historic Sites and Monuments, and
in 1939 added a Special Committee on the Preservation and
Restoration of Historic Objects to its standing committee on
Historical Source Materials, discontinued both in 1947. In
1962 the AHA tabled a motion made in the Council to create
a new committee on historic sites. The only session devoted
to material culture as such by the AHA was at its 1964
annual meeting, and by the Organization of American Historians at its 1972 annual meeting. *Word*-people simply don't
know how to handle *images* and *icons*. Historians, for better
or worse, have decided to put all their bluechips on words.
One measurable result is declining enrollments, mounting unemployment, and a major effort to plead the historians'
case: in words.

The iconologist must find a point of significant beginning. This involves not only structure analysis between arts but configurational analysis of the total *gestalt*. Understanding criticism and scholarship must catch up with performance. Since today's poets and artists are (as they have always been) joint bearers of a central pattern of sensibility, it must be explored.

The pattern is not easily found. What our book does is cover partially the vast sweep of iconology and study in depth certain examples in man's life today. Instead of dismissing objects of our increasingly mechanized, trivialized and standardized world as contemptuous, it argues that they must be treated seriously as the stuff from which a new style has evolved.

Does it offend you to think that a TV picture tube, a pin ball machine, or a plastic Jesus is in a grand tradition? The Greeks had their mythological metaphors, the Romans their biographical archetypes, the early Christians their hagiography. They fade into history. But like the snows of yesteryear, they had their season and fulfilled their purposes. Today our pop icons are standing in place and serving a purpose. They are *us*. In the 1380's all experience found visual form in a single metaphorical system. Will this be true in the 1980's?

This second edition of our essays on icons finds the evidence in flux, and the answers moot. Interest in popular icons (as in all aspects of popular culture) has not only expanded, but exploded, in the last decade. We have included new topics and subjects, inside a whole new framework. David Orr, a classical archeologist, and Gregor Goethals, an art historian, root an investigation of recent centuries in ancient ones. Dennis Mann and Christopher Geist suggest how buildings, sites, and monuments set parameters not only for our civilization, but the icons which intertwine with it.

After this preparation we look closely both at objects and people who partake of the iconic. "To see our contemporary icons as being only objects," Professor Brauer writes, "is to cut off from our understanding the study of the cultural significance of people who have affected our experience in iconographic ways." We then move to even newer territory and interpretation in the essay, "Iconic Modes." Valerie

Carnes insists that fashion belongs here: for fashion forms a "visible, popular iconology, revealing much about our values, attitudes, and assumptions." The iconology takes on special visibility in certain "movements" (Black Power, Women's Lib, Gay Liberation) and at certain places (Wall Street, The Pentagon, Las Vegas, "in" beaches). The "bestsellers" on Waikiki are not paperback books, but Aloha shirts, Puka shell neckware, and imported T-Shirts. National boundaries of popular culture are gone forever. Everywhere, in the global mode, people munch on "icon sandwiches" from the ever-changing menu.

All of which suggests that we are (or soon will be) engulfed in iconic culture. Nostalgia will fuel it: vestigial remains of the Southern Plantation and Western Romance will haunt us, authors Earl Bargainnier and Michael Marsden argue. There will be new elements, perhaps even requiring a new vocabulary. In our latter chapters you will encounter words (like *Comicons* and *Academicons*) that are entirely new to you. Soon there may be a new word — *culticons* — to characterize the new territory which we have attempted to scout. Such words, and certain ideas these essays propose, may seem far-fetched, even nonsensical. How better to end our introduction than by quoting the wise words of Alfred North Whitehead: "The nonsense of today is the truth of tomorrow."

NOTES

[2]See for example, Leonid Ouspensky and Valdimir Lossky, *The Meaning of Icons* (Basel, Otto Walter, 1952).

[3]Robert Jay Lifton, "Protean Man," *Partisan Review,* Winter, 1968, p. 47. William Zinssen's *Pop Goes America* (New York, 1966) pursues the same theme.

[4]See Myron Bloy, *The Crisis of Cultural Change* (1965). He defines technology as the "mind-set" which has become the "Objective spirit" of the Western World.

[5]This whole area is explored by John A. Kouwenhoven. See *Made in America* (1948), reprinted as *The Arts in Modern American Civilization* (1960).

[6]The article, which appeared in the Spring 1973 issue of *American Quarterly,* contains a helpful bibliography.

[7]I am indebted here to research and conversation with Dr. E. McClung Fleming, of Winterthur Museum.

Words ensnare, perhaps enslave us. A main argument of this essay has been that words cannot adequately deal with the realm of images; yet we conclude with a list of additional *words* to be consulted and reverenced. Many of these books contain few or no illustrations; none contains a single three-dimensional object. If I cannot solve this paradox (and contradiction), I at least want to identify it.

Here, then, are my suggestions for further reading:

Bronowski, Jacob, *The Ascent of Man* (Boston: Little Brown, 1973)

Calas, Nicolas and Elena, *Icons and Images of the Sixties* (New York: Dutton, 1971)

Fishwick, Marshall, *Parameters of Popular Culture* (Bowling Green: Popular Press, 1974)

The New Journalism (Bowling Green: Popular Press, 1976)

Gowans, Alan, *Images of American Living* (Philadelphia: Lippincott, 1964)

Huxley, Aldous, *Brave New World* (London: Faber, 1930)

Kouwenhoven, John, *Made in America* (New York: Holt, 1948)

Lasareff, Victor, *Russian Icons* (New York: UNESCO, 1962)

McLuhan, Marshall, *Understanding Media: The Extensions of Man* (New York: McGraw Hill, 1964)

Oupensky, Leonid and Lossky, Vladimir, *The Meaning of Icons* (Basel: Otto Walter, 1952)

Panofsky, Erwin, *Studies in Iconology* (New York: Oxford University Press, 1939)

Rosenberg, Harold, *The Tradition of the New* (New York: Dutton, 1959)

Thompson, W.I., *At the Edge of History* (New York: Harper & Row, 1971)

White, Edward M., *The Pop Culture Tradition* (New York: Norton, 1973)

The Icon in the Time Tunnel

David Gerald Orr

From the first periods of settlement in the New World until well into our own century, the realistically depicted image has had an importance and impact that is difficult to measure. Our modern visual spectrum is so intense, convoluted, diverse, and ubiquitous, that we tend to forget that we are not distantly removed from a time when practically any rendered image was rare and even marvelous.[1] Expensive to obtain, difficult to produce, and narrow in subject material, images were nonetheless important focii for the projection of cultural statements, religious conceptions, and occasionally, political policy. Yet today — drive a car, go to the city, turn on the TV, and you are swamped with a complex barrage of visual patterns, some novel, most ancient, and those few significant ones intensively charged with power; a real modern assemblage of what the ancient Romans called "numina".[2]

Icons are the most significant and ambivalently, the most unintelligible of images.[3] Icons can recur over centuries and in various media — stone, wood, metal, steel, cardboard, styrofoam, — and can be found at various times in all parts of the globe. Their meaning can change with each reoccurrence, e.g. the cross and the eagle, but their form survives. Dennis Williams[4] has mused how a post-nuclear holocaust art historian would approach the problem of classification and cultural identification of the cross and how its iconic force would have to be assessed. Its cruciform shape would have survived the vagaries of style and the idiomatic expression of

13

many groups scattered throughout the world; a central focus which had run unchanged through a gamut of bewildering regional interpretations.[5] Williams differentiated between the "iconic reference" (general characteristics common to all renderings of the theme in a given society) which introduces "style"; and the nuances of "idiom" (spatial distribution and regional adaptation). Yet, to Williams, it is the iconic power of the cross which moves meaning to viewer without reference to aesthetics of the vagaries of idiomatic expression.[6] Even if the wooden cross found in the House of the Bicentenary in ancient Herculaneum had not been solidly attributed to an early first century A.D. Christian cult in Campania, its force as a visual expression is still dramatically similar to the modern Italian house shrines still present in great numbers in the Bay of Naples area.[7] Moreover, the word lararia by which these shrines were called, at least in the ancient sources of the late Roman Empire, has passed into the Neapolitan dialect as a term which describes the house shrines of modern Campania.[8] Both use the iconic power of the cross as physical links in the establishment and permeation of a long tradition. The aesthetic qualities of both are clearly secondary to the iconic transfer of meaning.

The creation of tridimensional symbols, tangible images as opposed to thoughts and words, invariably conveys vitality. Vitality is the great property of prehistoric art; as, for example, the isolation in time and space of painted animals. These types of forms are visualizations of formidable natural animated power.[9] Especially in religious ritual, where icons were continuously employed, the visual image of vitality was constantly attempted, in order to prevent the conventional symbol from lapsing into the product of a rigidly imitative and purely rote process. Read[10] comments on this problem of the symbolic image when he states that it tends to be "conventionalized, systematized, and commercialized." Thus the ancient Pompeian painted on the stuccoed surfaces of his domestic house shrine, the gathering place for all of his traditional memories, tutelary powers and gods in a rather conventionalized canon of symmetrical composition and rigidly controlled postures.[11] Yet, no two Pompeian shrines are even remotely similar in their color, detail, portrait quality, and execution. Vitality, individuality, and a fierce familial loyalty, coupled with a flexible set of formal obligations had dictated otherwise. The "worksmanship of risk"[12] also assisted in the attainment of a vital, if regular, ritual group of images. Similarly, the pop icons of our contemporary life are constantly being evolved and manipulated, redesigned and reshaped, as our industrial and scientific society races to perfect and replace its visual world.[13]

Although this essay does not seek to discuss the numinous aspect of art; i. e., the relationship of magic to religion and the role of symbols as attributes of divinity, some note of this historic quality of icons should be made. An excellent learning ground for this function of icons can be found in the religious art of the late Roman and early Byzantine cultures. The Christian debate over the use of sculpted and painted images of the saints and Christ serves as a vivid testator of Christianity's great dilemma; the melding of eastern religious concepts of spirit with the material culture of the Graeco-Roman Mediterranean world. Bishop Leontius defended the practice of religious images in Christianity by stating: "We do not say to the Cross or to the icons of the Saints, 'You are God.' For they are not gods but opened books to remind us of God and to His honor set in our churches and adored."[14] The eighth century attempt to limit and even terminate the use of icons in the Christian ritual reflected primarily the influence of eastern religious and cultural institutions, such as Islam.[15] Leo III (717-740) sought to abolish the image of Christ in the church; thereby limiting its province to the spiritual world and correspondingly stressing the use of the imperial portrait, thus transferring the iconic idea to the physical world of Byzantine politics. The icon of "emperor-ness" would thus reinforce Leo's attempts to reunify the Mediterranean and Byzantine hegemony. The end result was a schism and a serious religious crisis involving the entire empire.[16] The worshipper who for centuries had touched god through image felt threatened. The problem was resolved partially by the Council of Nicaea in 787 which among other things stated that "reverence" and "true worship" were different commodities and that: ". . the honor which is paid to the image passes on to that which the image represents, and he who shows reverence to the image shows reverence to the subject contained in it."[17] The historical Christ is visualized, and identified in historic time, and the power of Christ thus appears to have flowed to objects in much the same way as numen came to the lararia painting of the Romans. For Christianity, this crisis captured the real intellectual and social dilemma of the religion. Christian images today bleed, sweat, change colors, and otherwise clearly demonstrate their linkage with divine power. Many Greek, Roman, and even Egyptian images did the same thing. Two ideas permeated the Iconoclast Movement (726-843 A.D.) in the Eastern Roman Empire. One was the quality of image worship and its ritual exploitation, and the other was the intellectual discussion of the very legitimacy of religious art (suggested by the teachings of Islam, the rival to Christianity's control of the Mediterranean). There was, accordingly, a taste for ornamental secular works also during this period and some Iconoclast emperors possessed impressively executed figural works of art including a throne which was covered with metal birds which sang and metal lions which roared.[18] Non-representational art powerfully generated by Islam was nonetheless incapable of shattering the tight bond which generations of Christians had formed between god and man through icons. These figural representations, however rudely executed, maintained the traditional feelings of Christianity in thousands of one-to-one iconic transfers of meaning.

This drives us resolutely into the hidden nooks of icon meaning; a meaning banded with ringlets of magic. Icons are images, sacred objects, storehouses of traditional lore, and in religious ritual, the inspirer of veneration. Panofsky's idea[19] that icons are geared to meaning, not form, is mandatory in any understanding of the branch of art history called iconography. Icons consistently reinforce meaning by the repetitious visual bombardment of the observer with ideas encapsulated in consistent form. Our simple exemplum of the Roman house shrine and its modern counterpart in Calabria demonstrates this point effectively and conclusively. Niches in the walls of Calabrian farm houses still occur regularly like the niches in ancient Roman houses: only the cult image has been changed. The niche and its religious community of objects powerfully intrude into the Italian home; constantly comforting, warning, reminding, converting, and reaching. Cosmetically and historically altered, the famililial niche continues to provide a basic domestic service—unchanged through two millenia.

Icons are also indispensable for societies structured on sharply defined sets of military criteria. The military regimen, as it appeared, for example, in the late Roman Empire after the middle of the third century A.D. dictated finely honed ritual patterns for living. A man's military situation bound him to rank and file, crumbled individual names into military units, and fractured independent action into great blocks of uniformity; an ordered society, efficient and disciplined, prepared and fit, yearning for universality in thought, government, and religion. Out of the infinitely complex matrix of the mid-third century Mediterranean arose an ordered, well-regulated, and symmetrically structured state heirarchy.[20]

The emperor, on top of the bureaucratic pyramid, was god himself on earth, the apex of a new order of temporal stability. The emperor image (icon) becomes a devotional picture. His visage vividly illustrates the move from individuality to regularity, from autonomy to typlification. The emperor adopts a common "holy type" and its form departs little from one ruler to the next.[21] His image is that of real power on earth, a secular icon which attempts to demonstrate the divine essence of the state; as Ammianus Marcellinus reveals in his description of Constantius II: "the emperor was not a living person but an image".[22] As the western Roman world disintegrated in the fourth and fifth centuries, the iconic image of the emperor was fixed straight ahead, calm, impassive, secure, an island of temporal and spiritual permanence. Young nations with no inherited iconography also can benefit from the example cited above. Just as the Roman imperial portrait attempted to bring order from chaos, the early visual images employed by Federal America sought to create legitimacy and normality from classical Greece and Rome. The American eagle benefitted from centuries of European acceptance as an icon of political strength and military authority. The eagle's incredibly rich legacy, derived from Hellenistic Greece and later used as a military symbol by Republican Rome, was welcomed in the early American Republic. In the face of such iconic tradition, what chance had Franklin when he advanced an indigenous American bird, the turkey? The visual trappings of Greece and Rome formed a great reservoir of political imagery for the new nation and were especially valuable in their reflection of the young republic's military posture. Liberty caps and poles, laurel wreaths, togas, and festoons, proclaimed the New Order of the Ages and the New Constellation in the heavens.[23] Like Caesar, Washington was Pater Patriae, and was so portrayed in the iconography of early Federal America. Also, like Caesar, his death was foretold by astral signs and his apotheosis was even depicted in engravings and paintings. While Washington led his troops in the guise of Cincinnatus, many of his lieutenants vied for the epithet Cato (Addison's play, *Cato*, popular all through the Revolutionary War in the colonies, was even performed at Valley Forge). Classical names were also used topically to refer to new programs and policies. Thus fostered, the cult of antiquity in early America produced in the late eighteenth and early nineteenth century a whole series of icons. The Greek Revival style in American building created icons, e. g. the classical image of the American Bank, as initially represented by Strickland's Second Bank in Philadelphia (1818-1824). Even works of industry and technology took on symbolic values when they were couched in the fashionable elements of antiquity. Both of the first two municipal waterworks of Philadelphia were carefully conceived classical structures: the Center Square Pumping Station (1798-1800) evoking the Pantheon and elements of the Doric Order and the later Fairmount Waterworks (1812-1822) reflecting the Roman temple form.[24] Since both waterworks doubled as civic and social centers, the classical treatment connoted *polis* and early Republican Rome to the beholders. The Center Square Pumping Station served as a theatrical backdrop to Fourth of July celebrations etc., while the Fairmount Waterworks even provided galleries for the use of Sunday and holiday stollers. When the first illuminating gas plant was built in the 1830's it was furnished with giant cast iron Doric column smokestacks, iron Greek treasury gas meters, and even a Colosseum like gas holder.[25]

How iconic are the great American sports' arenas? The first Yale Bowl in New Haven, Connecticut, was a clear copy of the Colosseum, the Flavian Amphitheater, in Rome. The Houston Astrodome, its modern spinoff, serves as a vehicle for spectacles in much the same manner as the Colosseum. Its sophisticated scoreboard and astroturf are paralleled by the complex subterranean rooms and elevators of the Roman arena; its dome completes a development begun by the Colosseum's *nautae* (sailors) who laboriously manned the great awning which provided shade to the Roman spectators. Both of the great arenas were engineered to control mobs and both are forms whose great scale testifies to their cities' pride and achievement. Just as the Colosseum splendidly served as a coin type in ancient Rome, the Astrodome now can be seen emblazoned on T-shirts, bumper stickers, and beverage glasses. Will the Astrodome replace the Colosseum in the ancient medieval poem:?

> As long as the Astrodome stands, America will stand
> When the astrodome falls, America will fall,
> When America falls, the world . . . .

A quick return to the early Federal period of American history is instructive in the study of those special values and ritual matrices which seem to give birth to icons. Our own hagiography and mythology were developed by the use of a whole series of icons. Fleming[26] and others have described the broad spectrum of forms and media used in expressing the *Genius Americae* in the period 1770-1850. The personification of Liberty, closely patterned after Roman prototypes, underscores those qualities of tradition, acceptance, and familiarity, which new nations so desperately long for. Parson Weems' biography of Washington was part and parcel of an American Plutarch from whose pages all sections and classes of the New Republic could be enlightened. Washington's role as hero can be traced from early nineteenth century Latin biographies to Appalachian folk songs which encourage young boys to emulate his deeds. Washington's visual statements broadly based in popular, elitist, and vernacular culture served as *summas* which expressed the simple virtues of the new nation. Apotheosis scenes of Franklin and

Washington in heaven together with Liberty, Columbia, and other Neo-Classic personifications, humorous by today's standards, were originally rather serious in their attempt to provide a traditional basis to the heroes of the young republic. Even though Washington complained about his sculpted portrait bust having the togate trappings of antiquity; most Americans did not.[27] It seemed safer and indeed more practical to state the young nation's ideals within the visual limits set by the 18th century's conception of antiquity.

Forms and objects intrinsically charged with meaning diachronically react in many diverse ways. Things are not merely things: they are distinct capsules of meaning. The Parthenon, early in its history, became an icon for the ancient city of Athens, an objective manifestation of the ideals of the Greek Polis. Its carefully planned composition, its sculptural programs, its symmetry and Eurhythmy, its visual expression of order and balance, and its ritual role in one of the chief religious festivals of the city of Athens, created its power as icon. The late Doric Greek temple expressed as the Parthenon was subsumed in an associative force which distorted its meaning into an icon of Greek temple-ness. Throughout centuries of western artistic evolution the Parthenon was a tridimensional box from which countless formal heritages were extrapolated. The Parthenon became the archetypical Greek temple, although it clearly was not that in fact. Originally the Parthenon had heavily depended on centuries of antecedental development. By the eighteenth century its iconic value was not diminished by the ruined and imperfect state caused by neglect and decay. Indeed, the qualities suggested by organic decay and the insuperable will of Hellenic values expressed in its shattered friezes and ragged columns exerted a particular kind of force. Stuart and Revett, among others, disseminated the Parthenon form in the eighteenth century through their source books, which found their way into the private libraries of European and American worthies. Temple-ness was no longer embodied in the Greek idea of a dark home for the cult statue or even the civic shrine of the polis. American architects like William Strickland used the Parthenon form iconically as a strong visual image of balance, permanence, and national stability. Pierced by large windows, carved up internally into functional spaces, and dominated by a barrel vaulted banking hall, the Second Bank by Strickland reshaped the Parthenon's temple-ness into something dramatically different. The "Greek Ideal" archaeologically evoked by the Second Bank was part and parcel of the new nation's neo-classic iconography. Perhaps the ultimate evolution of the temple icon was reached when wooden classic porticoes and pediments wrapped around dwelling places and American vernacular housing received archaeologically derived Greek temple frontons. Greek temples in the early nineteenth century framed waterworks and gasworks, as we have seen, as well as train stations, bridges, and even municipal comfort stations. Radical and innovative in the late eighteenth century, the classical Greek temple by the end of the nineteenth century connoted rigid resistance to change. Architectural archetypes such as the Greek temple form expressed by the Parthenon, the porticoed cylinder and dome structure embodied by the Pantheon, and the fluid plastic vaulted style exemplified by the Baths of Caracalla, all dramatically reappeared in the American landscape. The Greek temple is ubiquitous and the Pantheon can also be experienced in practically every urban center; its monumental statements found in the library at Columbia University and the rotunda in Jefferson's University of Virginia. McKim, Mead, and White's Penn Station in New York City (now demolished) once magnificently recalled the vast vaulted expanses of the Baths of Caracalla in Rome.

Monumental visual icons like those mentioned above play important roles in American towns since they show clearly the passage of historic time. They externalize our own quest for cultural identity. They tower above us as firm commitments to aspirations and ideals. Respect for this kind of visual icon in order to maintain cultural identity, the changing vagaries of aesthetics and taste, and the historic thrust of buildings through time, must be reestablished. Icons must not embarrass or confuse, they must remind and reinforce. This power to remind is probably the key to the real meaning of icons. Yet despite this power, visual icons, whether popular, folk or elitist, must be preserved from the threats of high wastage. What institutions are data-banking television commercials or commercial advertising? Who is making an effort to logically and consistently archive vernacular icons? Ironically, many icons of our own experience are ephemeral by nature and should be recorded. The alternative is a great cultural loss to generations of future historians and "iconographers."

NOTES

[1] For example, Seventeenth Century New England theocracy tended to reject all forms of religious painting. This attitude had a long lasting impact on American art. See John W. McCoubrey, *American Art 1700-1960* (Englewood Cliffs: Prentice-Hall, 1965), p. 3.

[2] For numen see R. M. Ogilvie, *The Romans and their Gods* (London: Chatto and Windus, 1969), pp. 13 and 123.

[3] Williams, Denis, *Icon and Image* (New York: New York University Press, 1974), pp. 4-46. See also *in passim* F. Boas, *Primitive Art* (New York, Dover, 1955), M. Focillon, *The Life of Forms in Art* (New York: 1948), E. Gombrich, *Art and Illusion,* rev. edn, (London: Phaidon, 1962), and Roger Fry, *Vision and Design* (London: Chatto and Windus, 1920).

[4] Williams, *op. cit.,* pp. 6-8.

[5] Herbert Read, *Icon and Idea* (Cambridge: Harvard University Press, 1955), pp. 17-34.

[6] Williams, *op. cit.,* p. 8.

[7] Joseph J. Deiss, *Herculaneum: A City Returns to the Sun* (New York: Thomas Crowell Co., 1966), pp. 65, and 68.

[8] In Italian, *larario.*

[9] Read, *op. cit.,* p. 24.

[10] *Ibid.,* p. 34. See also, Arnold Hauser, *The Social History of Art,* Volume 1, (New York: Knopff, 1951), pp. 37-43.

[11] George K. Boyce, *Corpus of the Lararia of Pompeii* (Rome: American Academy in Rome, 1937).

[12] David Pye, *The Nature and Art of Workmanship* (Cambridge: Cambridge University Press, 1968), p. 22.

[13] Marshall McLuhan, *The Mechanical Bride* (Boston: Beacon Press, 1967). See also David Manning White, "Mass Culture in America: Another Point of View" included in Bernard Rosenberg and David Manning White, *Mass Culture, The Popular Arts in America,* (Glencoe: The Free Press, 1957), pp. 13-21, and Craig Gilborn, "Pop Iconology: Looking at the Coke Bottle", included in Ray Browne and Marshall Fishwick, *Icons of Popular Culture* (Bowling Green: Bowling Green University Press, 1970), pp. 13-28.

[14] J. M. Hussey, *The Byzantine World* (New York: Harper and Bros., 1961), pp. 30-31.

[15] H. P. Gerhard, *The World of Icons* (New York: Harper and Row 1971), pp. 9-40. See also David Talbot Rice, *Byzantine Art* (Hammondsworth: Penguin, 1968), pp. 20-22.

[16] Rice, *op. cit.,* pp. 20-22. See also Williston Walker, *A History of the Christian Church* (New York: Charles Scribner's Sons, 1959, revised edition), pp. 148-150, and 189.

[17]Williston, *op. cit.*, p. 149. See also David and Tamara Talbot Rice, *Icons and their History* (Woodstock: Overlook Press, 1974), pp. 10-11.

[18]David Talbot Rice, *op. cit.*, p. 21.

[19]Erwin Panofsky, *Studies in Iconology* (New York: Oxford University Press, 1939).

[20]H. P. L'Orange, *Art Forms and Civic Life in the Late Roman Empire* (Princeton: Princeton University Press, 1965), pp. 3-8. See also Ranuccio Bianchi Bandinelli, *Rome: The Late Empire* (New York: George Braziller, 1971), pp. 1-41.

[21]L'Orange, *op. cit.*, pp. 122-125.

[22]Ammianus Marcellinus 16. 10.

[23]E. McClung Fleming, "Symbols of the United States: From Indian Queen to Uncle Sam", included in Ray Browne *et al.* eds., *Frontiers of American Culture* (Purdue University Studies, 1968), pp. 1-24. See also Hugh Honour, *The New Golden Land* (New York: Pantheon Books, 1975), pp. 138-160. See also Fleming's further studies on the American Image as Princess in *Winterthur Portfolio II* (1965), pp. 65-81, and III (1967), pp. 37-66.

[24]Center Square Pumping Station: See David G. Orr, "Center Square Pump House" in *Philadelphia: Three Centuries of American Art* (Philadelphia: Philadelphia Museum of Art, 1976), pp. 188-189.

Fairmount Water Works: H. D. Eberlein, "The Fairmount Water Works, Philadelphia" *Architectural Record,* 62 (July 1927), pp. 57-67.

[25]D. Orr and H. Levy, "History of the Philadelphia Gas Works" Historic American Engineering Record, Washington D. C. Copy on file.

[26]See above, n. 23.

[27]James Thomas Flexner, *George Washington and the New Nation: (1783-1793)* (Boston: Little, Brown and Company, 1969), pp. 25-26.

Sacred - Secular Icons

Gregor Goethals

The term *icon* has its roots in the Greek word for "image," *eikon,* and for general usage it simply designates visual or pictorial representation. However, *icon* is also a term that refers to a special kind of image, an image intended to put us in relationship to the sacred.[1] This concept of icon as sacred image does indeed transform the word so significantly that even our casual use of the term trades upon its religious meaning and function. While conscious of the strict meaning of the term in Eastern Orthodoxy and in Western Christian thought and while aware of the obvious differences in our theological and cultural situations, we nevertheless find it convenient to use. When we designate certain images and objects as "icons," we are really asserting that these images and objects are extraordinary in that they embody particularly important values or even some residue of the sacred. Otherwise, why not simply use the word "image"? "Icon" suggests the power of certain images to convey important values or sacred elements in our culture. Clearly its continued use indicates our interest in questions that go beyond a formal and aesthetic examination of images and objects.

Aware of the vast differences between traditional forms of Christianity and contemporary secular culture, we accept — even cultivate — the overtones of religious meaning that accrue to the word "icon." What lies behind this impulse to designate particular images and objects in contemporary culture as "icons"? Let me outline briefly three residual functions of the "sacred image" found in some images of contemporary culture: (i) images as symbolizations of order that transcend the individual, (ii) images as evocations of questions and resolutions and (iii) images as concrete models of heroic human experience. In trying to find residual connections between traditional and modern sacred images, I do not wish to imply a correspondence of aesthetic qualities or a concentric profundity of theological world views. What I want to explore is the continuous use of visual images to embody and communicate values and their continuous power to shape our sense of self and our mental constructs of the world. My concern is to study similar functional elements of the traditional sacred images that seem to have been transposed to modern images. If we can identify some similarities of function, then we may begin to see the connections and contrasts between modern and traditional sacred images. More importantly, we may be able to understand better the power of many images in contemporary popular culture.

(i) Images as symbolizations of order

Traditional religious images in Western and Eastern Christianity have given to those who reflected upon them or participated in their presence a basic orientation to human experience. The faithful beholder was presented with a concrete, meaningful world through sacred images. Whether they made visual a sacred past or an anticipated sacred future, images provided the viewer with a sense of participation in that meaningful order. In the midst of elusive, capricious and uncertain events that characterize human experience, the viewer found in sacred images a reassuring "world" in which he could locate himself, get his bearings or renew a sense of his origin and destiny. Through images persons could relate to and participate in a larger process of events that transcended private and particular moments in time. Images could assuage the sense of isolation, meaninglessness or aloneness. Although the sacred events represented were "outside" the immediate, transitory world of the observer, the images provided the faithful with contexts in which to place his own present experience. They were visual explanations of a larger symbolic order of time and space that helped to make sense of the ordinary world and to relate it to that larger process.

The symbolization of a meaningful order which transcends the individual is one of the most important roles of the traditional sacred image. But the role of images as symbolizations of order is not confined to traditional religious images or pre-modern experience. Today, just as in the past, persons need to locate themselves in a larger symbolic order or process. The fact that contemporary American culture is dramatically pluralistic does not negate the desire to link an individual with other individuals. Indeed, the heightened sense of pluralism in American society may actually increase the need to orient oneself and one's values within a significant symbolic order. Within this complex pluralism contemporary images, especially those of popular culture, provide us with a number of meaningful "worlds."

One major difficulty in discerning analogous functions of sacred images in our own culture is that we are so saturated with images and our images are so convincing (especially photography, film and television) that we become "unaware" of their role and ontological status as *image*. Consider, for example, what we think we know about the world, even the cosmos, after the multiple images of the television nightly news have sped past us for thirty minutes. Our identification of "image" with "reality" may be more prevalent than we think.

In order to understand this fundamental analogy between traditional and contemporary icons I would like to outline briefly three symbolic orders that have been important for Americans as they sought to understand their time and space in a larger context. These symbolic orders can be found in both high and popular images. I shall list them here only briefly, although each of these orders should be examined from decade to decade, artist to artist, in American culture.

The first symbolic order is that of the common life — family, neighborhood, city, nation. Although the range of interpretation is immense, images of the common life, especially that of the family, have been an important way of visualizing a meaningful order. This is especially true of advertising art. Think of the innumerable products that use the context of the family life to legitimate the product. Whatever sociological "reality" factors relative to marriage, divorce, family life, come to our consciousness through statistics and computers, it takes only a casual glance through any popular magazine to see the "family" presented as the "world" in which we locate ourselves, our appetites and possessions — from brownie mixes to television sets. In contrast to image makers in advertising, many museum artists, especially in the later twentieth century, take a more jaundiced view of the common life in all of its areas, whether family, city or nation. Whatever the range of interpretations, however, we need to explore the persistence of the symbolizations of the common life in American images from Currier and Ives to Norman Rockwell to Norman Lear, from George Bellows' *Cliff Dwellers* to Marisol's family groups.

A second symbolic order to be discerned in contemporary American images is that of science and technology. This order is particularly important in the twentieth century; however, even in the nineteenth century Horatio Greenough theorized that nature itself was the model for the development of functional forms and that the machine was man's effort to extend the principle of function. In the twentieth century the imagery of the machine and the preoccupation with all the objects and gadgets made possible by technology have provided a unique kind of symbolization of order — Charles Sheeler to Ernst Trova to the Six Million Dollar Bionic Man. The contemporary understanding of selfhood is hard to envision without scientific "truths" as context and without machines as adjuncts to our personality. We find comfort and a sense of fulfillment in the machines we become involved with. The world of science orients us to our origins and destiny; meanwhile in the in-between time, we exult in our machines.

A third, and a particularly deeply rooted symbolization of order for many Americans is that of nature. Whether in a calendar sunset or in a sophisticated Arthur Dove painting, American image makers have been able to identify with the times, spaces and processes of nature. The symbolic order of nature was essential to nineteenth century America. In the twentieth century, technology became autonomous. Today the order of nature is considered in terms of "trade-offs" between energy and environment, between the nurture of machines and man and the nurture of earth and its creatures. However, in spite of the degree to which the American public has adapted its rhythms to the beat of an urban environment, the order of nature still seems to evoke primary loyalties from many of us. The ecological crisis has forcefully brought the symbolization of the natural environment back into the forefront of popular advertising images, from "natural" foods to the "natural" men and women of cigarette ads. Consult any magazine. One recent ad for the U.S. Army shows two young men in uniform leisurely browsing in a lush natural environment: a paradoxical use of the natural order for recruitment into a technological military life.

(ii) Images as evocations of questions and resolutions

The traditional sacred image located the individual in a world that transcended his present one. But, the traditional sacred image also evoked questions which today might be considered "heavy" by some or, by others, irrelevant. Those questions which emerged from traditional sacred images asked about eternal life, salvation, action toward one's neighbor, justice and on and on. Whatever comfort the beholder might find in images regarding his origin or end, there were nitty-gritty problems for the in-between. Thus sacred images were often moralistic and persuasive. Individuals could learn to cope with moral questions through sacred images of the past by attending to them seriously, by experiencing their presence or by contemplating the mythic actions represented. Images were not, of course, the only means for communication about human action, but in pre-modern societies visual images played an informative, perhaps awesome, role in articulating the virtues and vices of human action. Remember, for example, the many marvelous sculptures at Vézelay that worried St. Bernard, who felt that the monks would study them rather than their books.

There is a remnant of this traditional role of sacred images present even in a secular society. Is there any commercial that does not sooner or later pose a question and/or propose a resolution? The dramatic tone of voice and the seriousness with which images represent various "problems" could, if we did not understand the language, be addressing the heavy questions of salvation, morals, and justice.

It almost seems as though the traditional "serious" questions were reappearing in some new guise. Questions once related to significant human action in the sphere of morals seem to have been transformed into a new type of "serious" question: Milder? Less dandruff? Cover up the gray? Ring around the collar? The questions and jingling resolutions have become a kind of modern visual catechism through these "icons."

Is it possible that some of the success of contemporary advertising can be attributed, in part, to its discovery and promotion of new public questions and resolutions, however trivial? Do the commercials, frothy as they appear to be, catch our attention because they cater to our human habit of raising questions and finding resolutions? If our culture has ignored or dismissed more imponderable questions, do these questions about body odor and the weekly wash camouflage, or even satisfy, our need to raise questions related to the more mysterious and complex human experiences?

The endless, mindless questions and answers presented in publicity images may witness in a fractured, sometimes pathetic, way to the persistent human compulsion to raise questions and cope with life's processes. They also reflect the profound metamorphosis from Questions to questions, from the mysteries and miracles of traditional sacred truths to the mysteries and miracles of modern detergents. This metamorphosis of questions and resolutions is accompanied by a metamorphosis of both images and faith: from gods to goods, from salvation to soaps.

(iii)   Images as concrete models of heroic human experience

A third major function of icons was to present models. It is related to the previous functions of (1) providing a basic orientation to a symbolic order and (2) raising questions and presenting resolutions within that order. The human figures depicted in the sacred narratives provided models for human activity for those who seriously attended these images. One cannot overstate the human hope and comfort provided by such models. The notion that someone is able to cope or deal with life in an extraordinary and exemplary way provides comfort and inspiration to a boring and disillusioned existence. The figures in the traditional icons, whether sacred personages mediating grace or humble persons receiving grace, were luminous as models. Both held out a special kind of hope. Whether or not individuals stood a chance of such grace, the models nurtured the hopes and aspirations for exemplary action or grace. Saints and heroes took on a special power as representative figures that offer, at the least, a vicarious experience for less privileged human kind.

This residual element of heroic models which is present in popular icons may perhaps be the one most apparent to us. We have now a sophistication that permits us to acknowledge the need for heroes and saints. The psychological power of the saint or hero witnesses to the power of empathy and identification in a most deeply felt, personal way. It is an opportunity for the magic of *likeness,* the conviction of an individual that what he wants to be is possible. The path has been made; one has been there before. A reporter recently thrust a microphone in front of a small boy, "Why do you like Mark Fidrych?" With no hesitation, the boy burst forth: "He's like me." Models, however idealized, falsified, or glamorized, have been an important aspect of the imagery of popular culture. While much of modern high art has been pre-occupied with formal problems and the representation of private realities, popular images have consistently zeroed in on exemplary types, from movie stars of the 20's and 30's to hard hat and superbowl heroes in the 70's. Contemporary advertising has been sensitive to the demands for models in minority groups. All such changing patterns are evidence of the power of the traditional sacred image to affect the individual through the lure and mystery of likeness to a model.

Comparisons and contrasts

The functions of traditional icons have been considered in an effort to understand better some of the power of images today. Paradoxically, the United States, with such deep roots in a protestantism that has been most uncertain and unwilling to use sacred images, has in the twentieth century developed a culture with an unbelievable proliferation of images, particularly in mass media and publicity. It is especially important, therefore, to underscore certain fundamental differences between our use of the word "icon" and its traditional usage and concept as a sacred image in both Eastern and Western Catholic Christendom.

First, our icons differ most dramatically from those in Eastern Orthodoxy. In that tradition the form of the icon is determined by strict formulae for visual representation and fabrication of the image. The image is sacred because of the manner and circumstances under which it is made. Secondly, in both Eastern and Western Christianity the subject matter or motifs of the sacred images are derived from sacred scriptures or from narrative traditions about heroes and saints of the faith. The images present or represent persons and events from a sacred history. Past, present and future are linked through the revelations of sacred scripture, and images issue from these revelations. A third distinction derives from the context in which sacred images are placed. Traditionally icons were to be contemplated in special places — churches, shrines and sacred sites. While individuals often had icons in homes, the public places of worship were part of a long process of development of communal liturgical spaces.

In contrast to the traditional sacred images, our contemporary icons differ sharply in all three respects: stylistic traditions and techniques, iconography, and context. First, in the making of contemporary images we depend upon a constantly changing, almost kaleidoscopic experience of styles and techniques. Our sense of style and aesthetic power has recently been synchronized with the technological development within media. The imagination of the contemporary image maker is programmed into a variety of techniques that would boggle the mind, if not offend the sensibilities, of the traditional icon maker. The technical expertise and conceptualization that go into a one-minute television commercial take us into an entirely different world from that of a traditional icon.

Secondly, our iconography follows no single scriptural or iconographical tradition. Our icons are often part of the free enterprise, competitive frenzy of contemporary publicity images. The images that "catch on" and become popular are frequently attuned to the deeply felt sentiments that transcend the individual and offer persons a larger whole with which they can identify. I attempted earlier to outline briefly three general areas of these sentiments: our common life, science-technology, and nature — all basic symbolic orders within the American environment. But these are intermingled and interpreted in a variety of ways. There really is no single sacred tradition to which our image makers turn. Finally, there are no sacrosanct and exclusive sacred sites in which our icons are placed. When there are so many images competing for our contemplation and attention, they burst out into all of the spaces in which we move. Our "sacred images" roam freely, exuberantly, and aggressively through streets, highways, subways, television channels, museums, theme parks and sports arenas. In some sense there is no place to hide, no place to escape our images unless we literally seek out the desert places.

The differences between the traditional icons and modern icons are indeed so profound that one wonders at this point why we continue to use the word at all to refer to contemporary images. Do we continue to use it because we still have an interest in what a society considers sacred? Do we still have an interest in how the "sacred" is communicated?

To pursue further the analogies between traditional sacred images and modern sacred images involves a reevaluation of the concept of the "sacred" itself and a hard look at our loyalties and values in contemporary culture. A discussion of the contemporary concept of the sacred goes beyond the scope of this introduction, but it is here, I think, that we begin our study. It is the key to our understanding of contemporary icons. We cannot reflect in detail about this now, but it is possible to indicate the direction in which thoughts and speculations are moving.

Contemporary American society is characterized by its religious pluralism. Within that pluralism, there is, of course, a continuity of the major religious institutions which use images as they have been used in centuries past. However, for our understanding of the contemporary icon we need especially to discern in American society the loyalties and faiths which exist outside of institutional religions. H. Richard Niebuhr has put it succinctly: "Faith as human confidence in a center and conserver of value and as human loyalty to a cause seems to manifest itself almost as directly in politics, science, and other cultural activities as it does in religion."[2] If we can think about the sacred in Weberian terms of the need to make sense out of reality or the need for a basic orientation and principle of meaning in our lives, then we can discern the religious loyalties that abound in our lives: from professional sports, to adoration of the machine, to the private communal realities that make life bearable. What is important for understanding the common link between the old and new "sacred image" is that both kinds of icons embody centers of values which "offer objective realities from which and for which our selves live as valued and valuing beings."[3]

What I am suggesting is that a serious study of popular icons will lead us sooner or later into a study of that which a society finds sacred. We can postpone the discussion, but that is where we are headed when we use the word icon. *Icon* is a word that has become encrusted with a variety of traditional and contemporary interpretations. We have to use it with qualifications and caution. We use it in the face of our culture-bound obtuseness or our inability to perceive some of its earlier mysteries. But, however darkly we perceive those mysteries, it still seems to be the most fitting word to use when we try to understand the power that images exert over us to reveal and shape our loyalties and faiths.

NOTES

[1]For a very clear statement about the nature and significance of the icon in Eastern Orthodoxy see Chapter 1, "The Orthodox Icon," in Ernst Benz, *The Eastern Orthodox Church* (New York, Anchor Books, 1963). Icons in the Eastern tradition were not simply representations but were "manifestations of the heavenly archetypes . . . . The countenance of Christ, of the Blessed Virgin, or of a saint on the icons was therefore a true epiphany, self-made imprint of the celestial archetypes. Through the icons the heavenly beings manifested themselves to the congregation and united with it." (p. 6)

The reader interested in Eastern Orthodox images will also find a very useful discussion of Byzantine icons in Otto Demus's book, *Byzantine Mosaic Decoration: Aspects of Monumental Art in Byzantium* (Boston, Boston Book & Art Shop, 1955). In his discussion of the icon Demus also emphasizes the special kind of identity between the image and its sacred archetype and the consequent reciprocal relationship between viewer and image. "In Byzantium the beholder was not kept at a distance from the image; he entered within its aura of sanctity, and the image, in turn, partook of the space in which he moved. He was not so much a 'beholder' as a 'participant.' While it does not aim at illusion, Byzantine religious art abolishes all clear distinction between the world of reality and the world of appearance." (p. 4)

In the Western Catholic tradition images did not have this same kind of identity with the prototype. The emphasis was placed on representation and narrative, rather than presentation of the sacred through the image. For an excellent analysis of the differences between the Eastern and Western Catholic traditions, see Edwyn Bevan, *Holy Images* (London, George Allen & Unwin Ltd., 1940). In the Western Latin tradition homage paid to the images can be thought of as passing through the material symbols to the persons for whom the symbol stands. (p. 152) The controversy in Western theology of images has centered on the ontological status of the material symbol itself and the relationship between the image and its archetype. As long as no supernatural power is thought to be residing in images, the use of images to call up recollections, ideas or emotions is acceptable even among some Protestants. (p. 169) However, the Catholic traditions, both East and West, have made the greatest use of sacred images, although their interpretations of the status and the homage due the image differ. While the distinctions are very complex, often confusing, Bevan concludes that "images in the Latin West have never had the place in religion which wonder-working icons have had in Greek and Russian Christianity." (p. 157) As Bevan observes, the controversial question is whether or not the images are charged with a quasi-personal supernatural power. (p. 177)

[2]H. R. Niebuhr, *Radical Monotheism in Western Culture,* New York, Harper, 1960, p. 64.

[3]Niebuhr, p. 22.

Architectural Icons: The Best Surprise Is No Surprise

Dennis Alan Mann

Introduction

Children are marvelous sources for inspiration. Their casual, innocent remarks about what they see often dislodge the blinders that academic disciplines protectively build around themselves. As an 'academic' myself this point is constantly reiterated when I travel with my own family. Our last trip took us through the Smoky Mountains on the way to the North Carolina shore. As we drove through southeastern Kentucky and eastern Tennessee, the landscape presented itself in all its magnificence. Green, lush, rolling foothills gradually built towards the mist-shrouded mountains beyond. Narrow valleys appeared and disappeared as the highway wound out of Knoxville and headed gracefully toward Gatlinburg. Although the conversation in the front seat between my wife and me seldom strayed from the splendor of the natural landscape, the silence in the backseat, where our two children, eight and five, had established a temporary junkyard was suspicious. It led me to believe that they were either busying themselves sorting through their magazines and crayons or had dozed off, lulled to sleep, unmoved by the beauty around then. But as soon as we entered Gatlinburg, I found out otherwise. Suddenly they were wide awake and peering out of all the windows simultaneously. They couldn't believe the richness that lay before them; shops, lights, signs, trinkets, and souvenirs flowing out of a barrage of storefronts. There were motels of every type and style, rides up and down the mountainsides, and the streets were mobbed with busy tourists; all the activity was overwhelming. Oh what splendor the environment held for them.

Of course Gatlinburg, with its familiar franchises and hard-sell commercialism, was immediately recognizable to them as *some place*. It was a stereotype and since America is filled with thousands of similar environments, instantly recognized, understood and accepted. I remember that it used to be a standing joke among architects that no matter which Howard Johnson's Restaurant you stopped at, you always knew where the john was. Holiday Inn advertises "The best surprise is no surprise," and you're never lost when you're on the interstate.

What is of great interest to many who study the built environment, whether they are archeologists digging among the ruins of ancient civilizations or contemporary scholars sorting through the vast wasteland of our urban environment, is the relationship between the built world and the cultural values that generated its built-form. By being more perceptive about our buildings, as students of American culture, we might be able to make more accurate inferences about the values that are dominant in our society; when we can better understand our value system (or systems), as students of our architectural environment, we might be more capable of designing buildings which have significance within our own culture.

That's the point about children. They're not misled by academic ideals, theoretical pretensions or detached observations. In spite of all of my incantations about the beauty of the natural environment, the kids weren't for one minute fooled. What turns them on is the human activity, the thoughts of shopping, and the visual excitement of Myrtle Beach, Panama City, Atlantic City, Surf City and all the similar commercial environments in America. Even the commercial strip in most of our suburbs, which apparently is incomprehensible to architects, is paradoxically recognized, understood, and appreciated by children. But don't misunderstand the point. I'm not implying that the majority of society responds to the physical environment in the same manner as a child. Quite the contrary. What all of society responds to is that which satisfies their own predispositions and what does that most successfully is what is most easily recognized and understood.

Perception

Psychologists tell us that our responses to space are primarily learned. Early studies by Swiss Psychologist Jean Piaget[1] show that a child learns to construct his world through a gradual recognition of objects which he locates in space. His world is built through similarities. He learns to connect recognized *things* to particular *places* and thus build a comprehensible spatial *totality* — a concept of space. As he becomes more sophisticated and as his perceptive faculties become sharper he learns to distinguish between similar things. Put simply, he becomes capable of identifying differences among similarities. Thus, because of this collected-over-time cognitive knowledge, people are better able to move about in the environment with comfort and security. And in addition, when an environment reinforces social needs, it can logically be considered superior to one that subverts social expectations. It is also generally accepted that the environment serves as a physical setting for thoughts of action.[2] People are able to act in relation to their environment because they have some plan in mind. This plan enables us to carry out our daily activities and to intuitively and consciously program our behavior. Basically, in carrying out these plans, we orient to (or attend to) *objects* and we interact with people. When we orient to objects we tend to select those which are familiar and those which are the most familiar are those which are the most common to the contemporary American scene, for logically, if we see enough of certain types of things we grow used to expecting them. For instance, because we know how a city is structured when we're low on gas we know about where to look for a gas station.

No matter who we are or what our tastes might be we cannot avoid the built world. It continually surrounds us, we move through it, satisfy our needs and desires by it and within it, and we change and modify it when necessary. It represents a collective human agreement, an agreement towards a way of life which prefers in America, at least, privacy, anonymity, individual freedom, leisure, and consumerism over community life, class solidarity, and social interaction.[3]

Symbols and Icons

Without trying to split hairs or meditate the variety of distinctions made between symbols and icons[4] we shall assume for the purpose of this essay that symbols are signs that stand for ideas (truth, beauty, and goodness) and icons are signs which have certain properties that the object it denotes also possesses.[5] The generic category is "sign" and the specific categories are, in this case, symbols and icons. This does not imply that objects are either symbols or icons but can have both symbolic and iconic relationships to that which they denote.

For instance, the golden arches on a McDonald's billboard (fig. 1) could be interpreted as playing at least a dual role. As

Fig. 1 Top The arches as pure icon

Bottom McDonald's billboards

a symbol they would function as an "M" and thus refer to all McDonald's restaurants. As an icon they would, because they share the characteristics of the golden arches *on* McDonald's restaurants, refer directly to the restaurants themselves. Symbols are not objects but about ideas and, according to Susanne Langer, are "the vehicle for the conception of things."[6] Here, conception is used synonomously with idea.

An icon on the other hand is less esoteric. It has far more mimetic qualities and represents what it denotes more directly. It reminds us of all similar objects but does not necessarily suggest a higher meaning. If it does suggest a higher meaning, it tends to be more immediate and direct. Icons, in the case of architecture, are objects which are *about other objects.* They are fixed mental images and can be quite literally interpreted.[7] Although their forms might have been established for one reason, they have come to be identifiable for a totally different reason. For instance, White Castle Hamburger shops don't inspire us to reflect on the ideologies that existed in medieval England, but only remind us of similar places which serve similar hamburgers. It is this idea that leads Geoffrey Broadbent to suggest that

> People know what to expect from Iconic design because they
> have already experienced its kind.[8]

He continues this thought when applied directly to architecture by noting

> . . . . one knows what the building is going to be like in terms
> of architectural quality; the appearance will not be a shock
> to anyone and one can visualize how it will look in context.[9]

Since buildings we are interested in here serve more as icons than symbols, we might investigate those in particular that result from our penchant for consumerism, leisure and fantasy. These inclination manifest themselves, for example in the pseudo-vernacular architecture that gathers around interstate interchanges, in building façades and what they objectify and in the territorial imperative resulting in the decomposition of our lives into specific types of activities, which in turn result in single purpose environments that serve only one segment of our lives. The architectural icons that occur because of these choices are uniquely twentieth-century American. Although we can make comparisons between these icons and those which exist in the treasure house of architectural history, we must recognize that they are part of a life-style unknown in any other era and non-existent within any other culture. There appears to be a dominant trend in America towards leisure, fantasy and consumerism and the architectural icons that arise from this trend can be examined in light of their significance to our culture. In general, they can be shown to be only reincarnations of similar ideas that have existed in other cultures and they can be evaluated on the basis of similarities (what they share in common formally) and differences (how they might "look" the same but "mean" different). By analyzing our architectural icons within a cultural framework we can better grasp the "realities" of ourselves and our physical environment.

Pseudo-Vernacular Icons

The interstate system in this country has very rapidly become the main route by which most of us travel from place to place, both locally, regionally and nationally. It not only serves as a physical linkage network but it has also become one of the main methods for cognitively organizing our environment.[10] In addition, the interstate has been one of the key factors, along with the automobile of course, in the development of an architecture which has grown to directly serve the needs of mobile Americans.

Beginning in the late 1950's and extending through the 1960's the commercial activity spawned by the interstate system came under attack from many directions. Peter Blake's *God's Own Junkyard* was highly critical of all the rank commercialism that gathered around the fringes of the city. Commercialism generated by a general increase in wealth during the peacetime years of the Eisenhower and Kennedy Administrations and commercialism made possible by the rapid growth of new highways extending out from the cities. Typical of this continuing criticism is the accusation by John Robinson that private enterprise shows

.... its ugly face (on the highway). Not only are there

commercial entrepeneurs who crowd as closely as possible to
the roadside to hawk their wares with blatant advertising and
structures but the billboards whose users try to sell from a distance,
and the unlovely tangle of utility wires and poles . . . .[11]

The criticism that abounded during those years came primarily from those who have contended that the tastes of the
public should be raised to a higher (and more aesthetic
they said) level. And most of the commercial activity that
grew around the interchanges was characteristically garish,
showy and visually chaotic. But historically commercial
trade has always flourished around transportation routes.
Major cities grew up around trade routes in Europe and Asia.
In America, first the rivers and then the railroads acted as key
determinants not only for the location of cities but also as
generators for new commercial developments around port
and depot locations. Why should we expect different results
today?

Meanwhile, the public remained indifferent to the visual
clutter caused by the commercialization of the highway.
Their main concern was the availability of goods and services
that had previously required a tedious trip to the central
business district. Now everything was accessible. Much like
the open market places in the rest of the world, the interchange became a new marketplace with all the vitality and
activity that marketplaces generate. Within that vitality lay
an architecture unacceptable to the critics but of great value
to the public.

Critical judgment, though, is usually post facto and normally ignores the popular approval or disapproval of those
for whom the object is being created. How often can we cite
instances of an expressway being contructed on an unde-
veloped edge of the city and then, ten years later discover
that a satellite city has grown up around its interchange with
local feeder roads. Northland Shopping Center outside of Detroit and Tri-County Shopping Center north of Cincinnati
are excellent examples of this growth phenomenon. Even in
rural America, complete new commercial developments have
grown up around the interstate exit and the old U.S. Highway. In time, the stability of the old town was destroyed and
a new vitality flourished around the interchange. The new

architecture that was built there was made to serve the automobile and the conveniences of a consumption society. The criteria of stability and permanance that generated the town architecture could not compete with the needs of a more mobile society.

And out on the strip all hell was breaking loose. Drive-Ins, drive-throughs, drive-bys-the picture is the same the country over. Once you've seen one you've nearly seen them all. A kind of pseudo-vernacular architecture, plastic and temporary, sprang up almost overnight.

It's more often a question of style rather than differentiation. Differentiation and variety occurred when each business was family owned and was in and of itself unique. A restaurant along the highway in Peoria was not at all like a similar family owned restaurant in Flagstaff. Today's economics and the growth of franchise business has, for all practical purposes, run individual operations off the main drag. They can't compete in land values, in national or local advertising campaigns, in the lower cost of products due to large scale purchasing and production, or in the ability to afford the higher rents in the more popular and modern shopping centers. Thus what we see everyplace tends to be the same. The pseudo-vernacular of McDonalds, Exxon, Long John Silver, Midas Muffler or Piggly Wiggly appears everywhere (fig. 2). And each of their products are exactly alike and reliable — we can depend on that. So it follows that architecturally they should be identifiable as what they are. That is precisely what an icon is: easily identifiable, about itself and bearing a direct resemblance to something familiar. Thus they are a good guarantee of commercial success.

Because these icons are, by definition, recognizable, the chaos that some say exists, actually doesn't — at least not in the minds of those who experience those environments. They're not chaotic because what is visually occurring around us is expected. The interstate and its connecting highways are not only the generator of the activity but also the ordering agent, the connective tissue. What we see when we exit, no matter where we exit, are familiar artifacts. Our world is ordered and we feel secure. Thus one of the functions of an icon as a part of culture is to reinforce this sense

Fig. 2   White Castle, Cincinnati, Ohio

of security. Icons are integral to culture.

Facades

Studying façades is another way of delving into the various iconic qualities of buildings. Architectural history is rich with examples of buildings whose faces have been modified over the years. Giving a building a "face lift" often means completely renovating the exterior with little or no regard for the interior distribution of spaces or activities. This often results in buildings with no formal, functional, or symbolic relationship between the interior and exterior. These contradictions, contrasts, and conflicts are treated on a broad historical basis by Robert Venturi in *Complexity and Contradiction in Architecture*. One conclusion he reaches is

> Since the inside is different from the outside, the wall—the point
> of change — becomes an architectural event.[12]

The exterior wall — the face of the building — is, in fact, the wall of the street. The façade, then, has a dual role at least: it encloses the space of the building (as well as holding up the floors and keeping out the weather) and it encloses the space of the street. In its role as the wall of the street it also has two responsibilities: it carries on the continuity of the street (or disrupts that continuity by serving as a kind of architectural exclamation point) and it serves as an identifiable image for the institution that it serves. It is this second role that gives the façade its iconic qualities. A well known historical example of these roles is the facade of San Carlo Alle Quattro Fontane (fig. 3) in Rome designed by Francesco Borromini and constructed between 1662 and 1667. Sigfried Giedion describes the exterior wall of San Carlo in ebullient terms, emphasizing the movement and flow of the forms which he says

Fig. 3   San Carlo Alle Quattro Fontane Florence, Italy Borromini, architect

.... embodies a conception which was of great influence on
the time that followed. Not merely a single form but the whole
wall has been translated into undulating movement . . . .[13]

In this case Giedion is describing form about form. Nonetheless, it is an iconic treatment of a façade built independent of and nearly thirty years later than the cloister and interior of the church.

Since we have defined icons as being objects which refer to themselves, or to other objects with similar qualities, it follows that this line of thinking could, from time to time, lead architects to design buildings which refer to themselves. Peter Eisenman, for instance, claims to design buildings which are about "Architecture." He is quoted in a *Newsweek* article as saying, "My houses aren't shaped for client's needs." In fact, most architectural history focuses on the building itself and, by removing it from its cultural context, treats it as a treasured icon (fig. 4).

Fig. 4   House 11   Peter Eisenman, architect

Fig. 5 Santa Maria Novella Florence, Italy Alberti, architect

Fig. 6 San Lorenzo Florence, Italy Brunelleschi, architect

Indeed, as suggested in the above two examples, architects often have their own icons which they tend to perpetuate regardless of cultural trends. But the majority of our buildings exist within the public realm and have not been designed by architects. For instance, Santa Maria Novella in Florence, (fig. 5) constructed during the Medieval Period, clearly shows the façade, constructed during the Renaissance, as a separately conceived entity, much like San Carlo, when compared with San Lorenzo, also in Florence (fig. 6). Everyone *knew* what the facade should look like. The only question was whether or not they could afford the front and the only judgment to be made following its construction was how well it was accomplished compared to other existing models (Cathedral of Santa Maria Del Fiore).

The tendency to treat facades as the most important element of a building has become far more prolific today. Each retail establishment in a shopping center has its own façade (fig. 7). If it is a national chain, the façade is essentially pre-

Fig. 7   Hickory Farms storefront Northgate Mall   Cincinnati, Ohio

designed and its primary purpose is to distinguish that chain from its competitors. When a new commercial establishment occupies a vacated space, a new façade appears.

Today, façades describe exactly what the building is. Commercial façades visually detail quite concretely the nature of the activities and services that we can expect to find within the building itself. They are specific and literal and do not attempt to lead the observer into a state of "euphoristic detachment from the concerns of life" as architecture for the sake of architecture might be expected to do. Architecture is not "simply the highest form of pure ornament" (Spengler), a search for pure form (Mies Van der Rohe) or the "masterly, correct, and magnificent play of masses brought together in light" (Le Corbusier) but it is also an artifact, or icon, if you will, which should not deter us from identifying it with a specific institution. It could be called "an artifice in aid of the retention of the image in the mind."[15] As a memory image, it then connects us back to the original artifact to which it refers.

Rustler Steakhouses (fig. 8) are multiple facades laid up against a solid concrete block shell. They are actually not unlike the false fronts that were constructed in many western towns one hundred and fifty years ago. Homebuilders magazines, as Venturi suggests, display different exterior styles on essentially the same plan. Whether the style you prefer is English Tudor, western ranch, French colonial or Cape Cod contemporary, you can find a style in these magazines to suit your taste. Both facades and complete style wrappings display iconic relationships since they refer to themselves and to the model which generated them. Thus in the case of the French colonial model it would bear an iconic relationship to a French colonial house.

One discovers in many urban areas a continuous one-story line of storefronts which, as they extend along the street, provide a unified pattern of mercantile activity, regardless of the type, size, or style of building that exists above. Most often these facades show little direct stylistic relation to the buildings to which they have been wed. They are designed with the intention of describing to the passerby what products or services are available within. When they formally bear

Fig. 8   Rustler Steakhouse   Cincinnati, Ohio

Fig. 9   Vine Street contrast Cincinnati, Ohio

a direct relationship to the products sold, then it can be said that they have an iconic relationship; products to façade.

A case in point is the excellent contrast found on Vine Street in Cincinnati (fig. 9), a porno shop and a church supply store, each appropriately decorated with the elements that call to mind what each building is about. Dark colors, gaudy lights, titillating glimpses of peep shows and suggestive phrases are haphazardly composed on the street façade of the porno shop while the church supply store sedately exposes little other than its pure virgin white clapboard siding with a humble window filled with religious artifacts. The contrast as they exist side by side, of sin and salvation is unique but the point isn't. Clearly, people, as creatures of habit, learn to identify types of buildings with a familiar 'look' with the content of those buildings. Churches look like churches. Houses look like houses. Schools look like schools. And porno shops look like porno shops. Façades only function as all buildings do when viewed as icons. They communicate.

The Territorial Imperative

At a more complex scale our inclination to divide our lives into discrete chunks as well as an increase in disposable income has led to a phenomenal growth in leisure environments, recreation environments and fantasy environments. We are all familiar with Las Vegas, Reno, Tahoe, Miami Beach, Myrtle Beach, Atlantic City, Old Town (Chicago), German Village (Columbus), Yellowstone, Sun City (Arizona), Marco Island (Florida), Disneyland, Kings Island, and Disneyworld. From time to time they have been paid homage to by the architectural press. Occasionally they are praised ("You Have To Pay For The Public Life", Charles Moore, *Perspecta 9/10*[16]) and occasionally they are analyzed with an eye towards application (*Learning from Las Vegas*, Robert Venturi and Denise Scott Brown).[17] More often, however, they are viewed with rancor and disdain (*God's Own Junkyard*, Peter Blake).[18] Still it is not how architects view these environments that has significance for us here, since as stated earlier, architects have their own icons to which they tend to religiously adhere. It's no wonder that architects give awards to their own buildings.

Now the idea of group territory is a broad and complex concept that has its roots not only in studies of territoriality as it applies to animal behavior (Hall, Calhoun, Ardrey)[19] but also in behavior setting studies (Sommer, Spievak)[20], and human ecology and ecological psychology (Barker).[21] What is often discovered in these studies is the human need to clearly define territories which have a particular function and which are seldom multifunctional.

These places are physically identifiable, highly legible, and fully comprehendible and define, architecturally, a specific place (domain). We can immediately call to mind many of these places that we know from experience. They are often about *leisure* (a recreation center surrounded by a golf course both of which surround a small man-made lake, about *recreation* (a neighborhood swim club surrounded by a fence with its tennis courts and bath-house appendages) and about *fantasy* the various ". . . lands" that line the highways around tourist areas or the completely self-sufficient environments like Disneyworld, which offer a release from the tensions of life). We all instantly recognize these places when we see them and immediately understand what pleasures and frustrations and conveniences and costs they offer. They have become icons of the Leisure State as they proliferate around the country. They act as reminders and reinforcers of a way of life that we, as a society, have come to value. They are images of an imagistic way of life and of the atomistic existence that we, as a society, seem to prefer. Whether or not we agree that the decomposition of the whole city and our own lives into such discrete parts and the physical classifications of certain functions into distinct territories is acceptable to our own ideals and aspirations is not important. It is a reality and it is what we are presently disposed to. It serves as a reminder that we exist some place.

Where once villages dotted the landscape and, because of their size, could be visually and psychologically grasped, we now find vast urban and metropolitan developments. It is not unusual for the visitor as well as the dweller to not only lose orientation but also find that he has no sense of place — that he lacks a kind of intuitive grasp of the uniqueness of an environment. Now if we combine this need for identity of place with the previously mentioned inclination to divide our lives into a variety of life styles, each replete with its own symbols and its own life-times, with particular places suited for each event within these life-times, it is clear to see why we build ersatz walls around each place. These ersatz walls, when viewed iconically, are concretized architecturally in many different ways. In the inner city public housing clearly segregates those who are economically immobile into brick and concrete jungles, while in the suburbs the middle class surround their apartment complexes with brick walls and gatehouses.

Those complexes are described in most editions of the Sunday paper. The housing section of the paper calls our attention to new developments with names like "Pixley Mews," "Becket Ridge," "Landon," "Oxford Hills," and "The Commons." Architecturally, each development has its own distinguishing features. These include an harmonious use of materials, similarity of form, common landscaping and often a gate and partial wall to inform the visitor that he is penetrating claimed territory. Expand this description to include retirement communities, vacation communities, second home communities, leisure communities, high rise developments, hillside condominiums, ranchettes, beach front developments and ski villages and it becomes clear now we have created icons of our image of the good life while at the same time defining again that village that once dotted the landscape.

A case in point can be demonstrated by the advertisements for home sites for the "Beckett Ridge" development north of Cincinnati. It reads

> Now there's a perfect setting for your dream home - a custom
> home site in one of three prestigious villages at Beckett Ridge:
> 'Tall Tree,' 'The Forge,' and 'Ironwood' 22

On another page the development of "Crooked Tree" advertises a community of country homes set on 580 rolling acres where you have all the values of the country with shopping and recreation just minutes away. Crooked Tree, according to the ad, is a restricted new residential community dedicated to a rural family environment.23 Again and again, the image is conjured of sacred territory with children frolicking in the woods while I play the back nine before dinner.

For the less affluent, apartment complexes identify their territory as "nestled in the park," "special places for special people," "an adult oriented community with land, spaciousness and convenience" and other similar descriptions which point out how living in that particular place will give the dweller something to identify with. Clearly, identification with a place, although semi-imaginary, is worth a great deal today.

While the coke bottle and the plastic Jesus-on-the-dashboard are icons at one scale, the result of translating claimed territory into real images of living, at a larger scale, also serves to illustrate our investigation of popular icons.

At a still larger scale, the following city, described by a former student, paints a picture which idealizes the iconic view of territory concretized.

> The city of Sophronia is made up of two half-cities. In one there
> is the great rollercoaster with its steep humps, the carousel with its
> chain spokes, the death ride with crouching motorcyclists, the big
> top with the clump of trapezes hanging in the middle. The other half
> of the city is of stone and marble and cement, with the bank, the
> palaces, the factories, the slaughterhouses, the schools and all the
> rest. One of the half-cities is permanent, the other is temporary and
> when the period of sojorn is over, they uproot it, dismantle it, and
> take it apart, transplanting it to the vacant lots of another half-city.
> And so every year the day comes when the workman remove the
> marble pediments, lower the stone walls and the cement pylons,
> take down the ministry, the monument, the docks, the petrol refinery,
> the hospital (and) load them on trailers to follow from stand to stand
> their annual itinerary. Here remains the (other) half — Sophronia
> of the shooting galleries and the carousels, the shout suspended
> from the cart of the headlong roller coaster; and it begins to count
> the months, the days it must wait before the caravan returns and a
> complete life can begin again.[24]

Conclusions

People understand buildings at many levels. The four-function model (Hillier, Musgrove and O'Sullivan, 1972) suggests that buildings do at least four things: modify space, modify climate, modify behavior, and modify symbols.[25] This only touches on the concrete and deterministic functions of buildings. In addition buildings have as many esoteric qualities as concrete qualities. They act as cultural symbols as well as symbols of self,[26] they describe institutional power and authority, they remind us of the past, and from time to time point to the future. For instance *Architectural Forum,* June 1972, in an article entitled "Walt Disneyworld" describes Disneyworld in Florida as one of the most technically advanced "cities" in the world.[27] It could be viewed as perhaps the first 21st century city in America.

In addition to buildings casting a glance towards the future, one of their most important social roles is that of reinforcing existing codes.[28] Over time we learn to recognize buildings for what they do (function), for their relative beauty (form) and for what they signify (meaning). It is in the latter interpretation that buildings serve as icons. And it is in this iconic (as well as symbolic) role that, until only recently, has so little attention been paid. Investigative work in other cultures (Ardalan, Chang, Nietschke, Alexander)[29] have shown how built form can be entirely subsumed by culture as a whole. Anthropological studies have shown that often religious values, social structure, cosmic and world views, family organization, technological order (what is useful) and moral order (what is right) appear as direct translations in the architecture of that culture. In each of these cases the most important prerequisite has been the studies which describe the culture itself. Each culture must be understood for its unique qualities. Certainly America has a complex system of root cultures but no culture has ever emerged quite like this one. Consequently we cannot judge our artifacts based on remote standards, universal standards or imported standards but only on those which we agree to be culturally specific. And those standards change!

The challenge then lies in our ability to recognize stable structures amidst change and for those involved in the process of building to learn *from* the environment around them. As Alan Gowans has been saying for many years, form-finding should precede form-making.[30] The study of buildings for their iconic value will continue for many years but as I have implied above a greater significance for those interested in popular culture will be placed on buildings which appear to be generated by the American life style.

NOTES

[1]Christian Norberg-Schulz, *Existence, Space and Architecture* (Cambridge: MIT Press, 1971). p. 17.

[2]*Ibid,* p. 10.

[3]Martin Pawley, *The Private Future (New York: Random House, 1974.)*

[4]See the variety of treatises on the subject, particularly *An Introduction To The Philosophy of Charles S. Peirce* by James K. Feibleman, *Signification and Significance* by Charles Morris, *Studies in Iconology* by Erwin Panofsky and *Icon And Idea* by Herbert Read.

[5]Charles Morris, *Signification and Significance* (Cambridge: MIT Press, 1964) p. 68.

[6]Susanne K. Langer, *Philosophy In A New Key* (New York: Mentor, 1951), p. 61.

[7]Although Panofsky in *Studies In Iconology* p. 14-15 suggests three acts of interpretation of icons; (1) preiconographical description (formal), (2) iconographical analysis (images and allegories) and (3) iconographical interpretation (intrinsic meaning).

[8]Geoffrey Broadbent, *Design In Architecture* (John Wiley and Sons, London & New York 1973), p. 418.

[9]*Ibid,* p. 418.

[10]Kevin Lynch, *Image Of The City* (The Technology Press and Harvard University Press, Cambridge:, 1960) p. 96.

[11]John Robinson, *Highways And Our Environment,* p. 126.

[12]Robert Venturi, *Complexity and Contradiction in Architecture* (New York: Museum of Modern Art, 1966), p. 88.

[13]Sigfried Giedion, *Space, Time and Architecture* (Cambridge: Harvard University Press, 1962) p. 111.

[14]*Newsweek,* October 4, 1976, p. 66.

[15]Herbert Read, *Icon and Idea* (Cambridge: Harvard University Press, 1955), p. 24.

[16]Charles Moore, "You Have To Pay For The Public Life" in *Perspecta* 9/10, New Haven: The Yale Architectural Journal, 1965.

[17]Robert Venturi and Denise Scott Brown, *Learning From Las Vegas* (Cambridge: MIT Press, 1972).

[18]Peter Blake, *God's Own Junkyard* (New York: Holt Rinehart and Winston, 1964).

[19]See for instance Edward T. Hall *The Hidden Dimension,* John B. Calhoun "Population, Density and Social Pathology," *Scientific American,* Feb. 1962 and Robert Ardrey, *The Territorial Imperative.*

[20]See for instance Robert Sommer, *Personal Space* and Mayer Spivak, "Archetypal Place" in *Architectural Forum,* October 1973.

[21]See Roger Barker *Ecological Psychology.*

[22]Cincinnati Enquirer, Sunday November 17, 1976, "At Home" Section E-2.

[23]*Ibid.*

[24]Jeffrey Skeggs "Land of Signs" an unpublished paper written in January 1975.

[25]Bill Hillier, John Musgrove and Pat O'Sullivan "Knowledge and Design" *EDRA 3,* 1972.

[26]See Clare Cooper's essay "The House as Symbol of Self" in Jon Lang (ed.) *Designing For Human Behavior,* Dowden Hutchison and Ross, Stroudsburg, 1974, p. 130-146.

[27]*Architectural Forum,* June 1972 "Walt Disneyworld".

[28]Umberto Eco, "Function and Sign" in *VIA,* Publications of the Graduate School of Fine Arts, University of Pennsylvania, Vol. 2, p. 145.

[29]See for instance Nader Ardalan and Laleh Bakhtiar, *Sense of Unity* (The Sufi Tradition in Architecture), Amos Chang, *Intangible Content in Architectural Form,* Gunter Nietschke, "The Four Ages of Heaven" in *Architectural Design* Dec. 1974 or "Principles of Place-Making" in *Generated by Patterns,* the Center for Environmental Structure, Berkeley, Calif..

[30]Alan Gowans in a lecture entitled, "Towards a Humane Environment: First Principles for Architectural Design and History," Given April 7, 1976 at the University of Cincinnati.

Historic Sites and Monuments As Icons

Christopher D. Geist

Americans *use* their icons. The things of American culture establish the parameters of everyday life. Americans define their various roles within their communities and seek out status through the trappings of the material culture which surround them. The most significant (useful) of these artifacts are transformed into icons in the fullest sense of the term. The Riviera, the Volkswagen, the driftwood and glass coffee table, the Sony Trinitron, the antique wall phone, and the sculptured shag rug might be the icons pulled together by the middle class family on the make to define and proclaim its impending leap up the social ladder toward upper-middle class affluence.

There is, of course, a plethora of national symbols which loom up larger than life to characterize, define, and justify the face of modern America — the hot dog, the coke bottle, the football, the Bell Telephone System logo, the Golden Arches, and the "Big Wheel" toy are but a few examples. Icons of popular culture delineate everyday American culture and life in the here and now. A panorama of American cultural experience is to be discovered amidst the material artifacts which are elevated to icons. But what about the past? Do Americans have and use icons of history? Do Americans seek out icons to place their nation and culture in historic perspective? How do Americans view their past, and how complete is that vision? How accurate? In the wake of the Bicentennial celebrations it seems appropriate to examine our culture's icons of popular history and their use.

In an interesting but little-noticed work, historian Daniel J. Boorstin postulated that American history rushed from past to present so rapidly that few of the usual manifestations of human achievement were left upon the landscape.[1] Europeans, he noted, are surrounded by artifacts which represent their history — the great cathedrals, the Acropolis, the Colosseum, Versailles, Buckingham Palace, fortresses. Each succeeding generation of Europeans builds onto a history which is ever present. Europeans cannot escape their past, for each epoch must be built upon the very visible ruins of past epochs. Europeans have become so comfortable and familiar with their past that at times one generation will cannibalize the material remains of an earlier generation to construct its own monuments — as when ancient Roman structures were ransacked to provide building materials for medieval cathedrals. Moreover, historic artifacts often provide the focal point for a symbolic break with the past, as when iconoclasts of the French Revolution attacked the Bastille. But incidents of this sort are rarely possible in America, for Americans never built their material surroundings to last more than a single generation. In our rush to overrun and civilize a continent we threw up temporary dwellings so that we might always be prepared to abandon them and push deeper into the interior.

"Our past has not built monuments for us," writes Boorstin, "The democratic past of a mobile people uses up, improves, and replaces its artifacts."[2] Boorstin's argument becomes more believable when we remember that Pittsburgh's Three Rivers Stadium has replaced the historic and once vital Fort Duquesne as the major landmark at the confluence of the Monongahela and the Allegheny Rivers. Then, too, a scant three hundred and seventy years have elapsed since Europeans established their first, precarious settlements in North America. That hardly compares to the thousands of years of recorded history and civilization of which Europeans are heirs. While Europeans would find it impossible to destroy every remnant of the past, Americans look around and find that the material artifacts of their history have escaped them! What do Americans do to link themselves with their past? Americans, more perhaps than any other people, must re-

construct their past for use in the present — Colonial Williamsburg, New Salem, Illinois. We turn to local historical societies, the National Park Service, and private organizations
such as the National Trust for Historic Preservation to rebuild and reclaim our heritage. When we cannot reconstruct
our history we turn to monuments which represent the
essence of the past as we wish to remember it in the present
— the Lincoln Memorial, the Gateway Arch. We may collect
bits and pieces of our history for deposit in the great museums such as those of the Smithsonian Institution, the
"nation's attic." Local history is often preserved in the
small historical society museum. Properly preserved and presented, these relics become icons to be studied and adored.

Americans litter the landscape with icons to their history.
These icons of popular history form the basis of the American relationship with the past. It is a singularly peculiar relationship, for Americans are able to preserve, rebuild, and
order their past in the precise image they choose — perhaps
Americans simply rebuild their history in the image of the
present. Does the mighty Gateway Arch really symbolize the
winning of the west, or does it pay homage to the capacity of
American industry to conceive and construct monuments reflective of America's twentieth century technology? The
battlefield at Wounded Knee was relatively unknown until
Dee Brown buried his heart there and Russell Means and
the American Indian Movement decided it could be made a
focal point of Indian activism. Until the last few years the
battlefield at Little Big Horn more accurately symbolized
the place Americans accorded the Indian in history.

Many other historic sites and monuments have nothing to
do with the present. They really do look back. This category symbolizes the American tendency to nostalgia. We seek
in the past that which is missing in the present. Never really
the nation of yeoman farmers envisioned by Thomas Jefferson, we nevertheless preserve an inordinate number of rus-
tic homes and plantations which look backward toward a
past which might never have existed. We find pleasure in
viewing the quaint tools of our rural heritage — the apple
peeler, the original McCormick Reaper, the steam engine.
Too many Americans view Whitney's cotton gin and see only

the remarkable ingenuity of the machine. They do not see that this invention probably perpetuated the viability of the "peculiar institution" and its misery for a generation or more. Just as we watch "Happy Days" to recapture the imagined tranquility of the 1950s, so do we visit historic sites to experience the supposed simplicity of care-free eras from our past. A visit to Colonial Williamsburg is escapist. The memory of the Civil War and, more recently, the American Revolution becomes a pageant. At Gettysburg, Pennsylvania, the vicious clash between the largest armies ever assembled in North America becomes a pattern of flashing lights on a map; the tragedy of a young, civilian casualty becomes a "house with talking walls." In general, Americans do not wish to remember the unpleasant facets of their history in vivid detail.

For one reason or another, the Liberty Bell has become the preeminent historic icon of the American people. Miniature models — complete with crack — are marketed from Maine to California. I recently purchased a commemorative glass while in Washington, D.C. Emblazoned in gold upon the glass are the words, "WASHINGTON, D.C. SALUTES BICENTENNIAL UNITED STATES OF AMERICA — 1776-1976 — IN GOD WE TRUST." The lettering forms a circle, and within that circle is the image of the *Liberty Bell*! But the Liberty Bell belongs in Philadelphia, doesn't it? Why, with all the possible images and icons available in the Washington area, did the manufacturer of the glass select the Liberty Bell? There simply is no other historic icon which embodies God and Country so completely for Americans. The Liberty Bell belongs anywhere and everywhere throughout the land. It would be impossible for Americans to confine this symbol to Philadelphia, for all Americans have the sacred image of the Liberty Bell locked within their hearts.

But is the Liberty Bell really an icon? Just remember that it must be protected from visitors who file by in such multitudes that if each touched it the Bell would be worn down to nothing within a few decades. Only visitors of the stature of Queen Elizabeth II are permitted to touch the Bell. That Bell symbolizes for all Americans the spirit of the Founding Fathers and the Declaration of Independence like no other icon could. It serves the same purpose in our culture that Lenin's Tomb serves in the Soviet Union. The Liberty Bell is to Americans as St. Peter's Basilica is to Roman Catholics. Superimpose an image of the Liberty Bell upon an image of the moon (on a Bicentennial coin) and the American democratic ideal of 1776 is powerfully linked with the technological achievement of 1976.

What would happen if the Liberty Bell's crack did not have an attractive legend associated with it? Why, then we would reconstruct and restore the Bell to its original condition! In a slightly different context David Brinkley recently observed, "It is typically, if not uniquely, American to spend about as much money restoring as we do destroying."[3] As we look around us we find that Daniel Boorstin was correct. For the most part, the material remains of American history are still present because dedicated and energetic Americans have made an effort and committed dollars to preserve, restore, and collect their past. A pyramid lasts a millenium; a sod hut or log cabin lasts a few years. Even the larger, more permanent structures of our forebears were not intended to endure as historic monuments. With a few exceptions (Thomas Jefferson's Monticello, for example) our forefathers' homes, businesses, schools, and churches were not built of the stuff which lasts through the ages.

Washington's Mount Vernon is a case in point. The estate went into rapid decline shortly after the death of Martha Washington. Had the Mount Vernon Ladies' Association not stepped forward in 1858, the Washington Monument might stand as the most important of our icons dedicated to the "Father of Our Country." The efforts of this organization to preserve Mount Vernon have given Americans a truly magnificent icon of history. Williamsburg, Virginia, our nation's most significant monument to its colonial past, was allowed to disintegrate for a century and a half before John D. Rockefeller took interest. By the 1930s, when the reconstruction and preservation efforts began, it was necessary to expend millions of dollars to recapture this important link with the American past. The National Trust for Historic Preservation now owns a dozen historic homes. For the first time Americans are beginning to systematically plan and coordinate efforts to preserve the visible remnants of their history. An office of the National Park Service recently noted in a report to the National Conference of State Historic Preservation Officers that preservationists are in a "race against time in protecting an irreplaceable stock of vulnerable resources."[4] Perhaps the piecemeal approach to the preservation of historic icons will soon cease. Perhaps our icons will begin to explore the full range of American history instead of presenting the limited vision which is currently evident at so many historic sites and museums.

Americans are already beginning to preserve and reconstruct the most numerous class of historic homes and sites, those connected with the "everyman" of American history. The mud and wicker hovels of the first Jamestown settlers were reconstructed in the 1950s. New Salem, Illinois, is a far cry from Colonial Williamsburg. The National Park Service recently opened Turkey Run Farm near Washington, D.C. A working farm dating from the 1770's, this historic site may be a new beginning in the field of historic preservation. Here the daily life of the poor Virginia yeoman, forced to settle on cheap, worn out, former plantation lands, is depicted in all its Spartan simplicity. How this poor farmer and his wife scratched out a marginal existence on worn down land is illuminated by costumed Park Service workers whose sweat and soiled clothing bear witness to the character of the nation's early farmers. The world of hard work and grim determination depicted at Turkey Run Farm is a far cry from the world of mint juleps, formal balls, and leisure the visitor encounters at many preserved homes of the same period.

Turkey Run Farm is indeed a new type of historic icon. The goal of the farm is stated in the guide pamphlet:

> Turkey Run Farm demonstrates a type of small scale, low income homestead of the late colonial period. Agricultural and household activities seen on the farm today are ones which were of vital need to a poor family two centuries ago. . . . As either tenants or struggling free-holders, the family . . . had to depend on their own resourcefulness, good market conditions, plenty of hard work and considerable luck for any improvement in their own economic well-being . . . . Walking across Turkey Run . . . one can catch a glimpse into a world far removed from the present.[5]

In many ways Turkey Run Farm is the proper contrast to nearby Mount Vernon. Both sites should be studied to gain a more complete insight into the culture of Virginia in the formative years of the Republic. Turkey Run Farm is a missing link in the chain of historic icons linking modern Americans with their past.

Until very recently historic preservation in this country has had the tendency to "sanitize" and "beautify" our past. Robert M. Utley, a National Park Service official, recently spoke out in opposition to this "cosmetic syndrome" in historic preservation. According to Utley,

> The cosmetic syndrome . . . is found among people who see history not as it was but as they would like for it to have been. The results can be observed in lavishly furnished residences of notables who would have known such surroundings only in their private fantasies, in impeccably manicured grounds and gardens that in their heyday were quite unkempt if tended at all, in battlefields that look like the creations of amply funded and hyperactive landscape architects and in well-scrubbed, brightly painted historic communities that resemble sets of Hollywood musicals more than they do they dirty, smelly, often seedy aspects of historical reality.[6]

In all fairness, few Americans could stomach the full range of sights, sounds, and smells known to our ancestors. Yet something must be done to bring our historic icons more in line with the realities—including even the most unpleasant—of the past. As we eliminate the unpalatable from our past, we often deny the very real effects of the past upon the present.

Visit the slave quarters at Mount Vernon. Those which have been reconstructed are of fairly high quality, probably used only by house servants. They are of brick construction and contain an ample and functional fireplace, substantial and relatively comfortable beds (with *mattresses*), numerous solid chairs and a large table. Few field hands—including Washington's—had nearly so comfortable quarters. Indeed, the vast majority of American slaves had much worse housing. Then, too, the official Mount Vernon guide book tends to gloss over the institution of slavery—an institution which was most important to General Washington—by discretely referring to the slaves as "servants." A similar tendency to ignore this aspect of the American past is to be found in most reconstructed mansions, though efforts to reconstruct typical slave quarters are now underway at Northern Virginia's Gunston Hall. Slave quarters of any sort are conspicuously absent at Woodlawn, Carter's Grove, and many other famous

Southern homes. Yet the institution of slavery has perhaps had more impact on American history and culture than any other institution. We cannot eradicate this facet of our past without seriously damaging our perception of the present.

In spite of all the efforts of past preservationists to eliminate the painful from our historic icons, an astute and alert visitor to such sites may still glean some genuine understanding of the nature of slavery. In the museum at Mount Vernon, for example, are a pair of artifacts which, when taken together, tell modern Americans more about the nature of chattel slavery and its inherent caste structure than any other artifacts on the grounds. Side by side are two sets of dental tools, one used on George Washington and his family and one used on his slaves. The contrast is compelling: four poorly crafted, rough, simple iron implements next to a much larger set of finely polished, precision tools with ivory handles. The family's set closely resembles the implements in use in a modern dentist's office.[7] But too few visitors notice this contrast. Preservationists must make our history more accessible—all of it.

One preservationist recently wrote of his profession.

> We have learned that we have assumed the very presumptuous position of creators—interpreting the lives of those persons who faced the rugged past and who helped make our present possible. Preservationists assume an awesome responsibility.[8]

Indeed they do! For many Americans there is little contact with the past except at the historic sites, monuments, and museums. These icons of history shape not only the American understanding of the past but the image of the present. A recently elected Congressman, not unlike Jimmy Stewart's "Mr. Smith," visited Washington, D.C., for the first time shortly after his election on November 2, 1976. Flying into National Airport he noted that Washington is "breath-taking, with very impressive monuments." And, he continued, "Monuments are important to make people know the America they thought it was when they were younger."[9] We lean upon and use our historic monuments to understand our past and to plot our future.

As the United States moves into its third century we must reassess the manner in which Americans use and preserve their history. Many of our present problems and frustrations have grown out of past beliefs and attitudes which have been perpetuated and enhanced by historic icons. The antebellum American—North and South—attempted to deny the Afro-American his humanity. Do modern Americans perpetuate that attitude by eliminating the Afro-American presence from historic monuments and reconstructions of the period? Why are there so few Indian-related sites in the eastern regions of our nation? Have modern Americans sought to remove the Native American legacy from the east just as Andrew Jackson removed the Five Civilized Tribes? As we beautify and sanitize the past do we foster a numbing sense of nostalgia for "Good Old Days" which never existed? Since so many Americans gain their only understanding of the past from historic icons—monuments, reconstructions, museum artifacts—we must face such questions squarely. If it is important that we perpetuate the mythic dimensions of our past, then we might allow historic preservation to go on pretty much as it has. If fresh views of the past would strengthen our ability to understand and cope with the present, then we should rethink some of our approaches to American history and its icons.

NOTES

[1] Daniel J. Boorstin, "An American Style in Historical Monuments," Chapter Four in Boorstin's *America and the Image of Europe: Reflections on American Thought* (New York: Meridian Books, 1960), pp. 79-96. See Boorstin's thought-provoking discussion of the points raised in this paragraph.

[2] Ibid., p. 83.

[3] David Brinkley commenting on American conservation in the NBC special, "The Pursuit of Happiness," presented May 27, 1976.

[4] Quoted in Judith Kitchen, "How To Conduct An Architectural Survey," *Ohio Historical Society Echoes,* XV (4), April 1976, p. 10.

[5] A copy of this pamphlet may be obtained by writing to Superintendent, George Washington Memorial Parkway, Turkey Run Park, McLean, Virginia 22101. The site was established in 1971 under the "Legacy of Parks" program.

[6] Robert M. Utley, "A Preservation Ideal," *Historic Preservation,* XXVIII (2), April-June 1976, p. 44.

[7] I am indebted to Daniel Vellucci, my colleague and friend, for "discovering" these artifacts.

[8] Hal T. Spoden, "Pain and Pleasure—Heartache and Success: The Background for the Thrills of Preservation," *Echoes of History,* VI (1), January 1976, p. 14.

[9]Representative-elect Edward J. Markey (Dem. - Massachusetts) Quoted in *The Washington Post,* November 21, 1976, p. D1.

BIBLIOGRAPHICAL NOTE

There are many means of getting at the relationship of Americans to their icons of history. The following suggestions are only a rough guide and serve as a starting point. First, visits to the sites can be most productive, and pamphlets and guide books provide an important glimpse into the world of historic preservation. A word of warning: be on the lookout for the *missing* elements both in the sites and in the literature describing them. Most of the state historical societies publish newsletters which often contain valuable information related to historic sites, historic preservation, monuments, and museums. The publications of The Pioneer America Society, Inc., 626 S. Washington St., Falls Church, Virginia 22046, are noteworthy. Five other periodicals are especially useful: *Historic Preservation, Preservation News, History News, The History Teacher,* and *Museum News.* I have listed several recent articles and books below. As Americans begin the task of evaluating the Bicentennial activities more material should become available.

"Commission's Strict Guidelines Assure Quality Historic Sites," *History News,* XXXI (4), April 1976, pp. 84-85.

Describes efforts of the United Methodist Church Commission on Archives and History to elevate the quality of historic sites.

"Country Store Creates Mood of Earlier Times," *History News,* XXIX (2), February 1974, p. 47.

Gerlach, Larry R., "Viewpoint: Making the Past Come Alive," *History News,* XXX (9), September 1975, 222-223, 225.

Hartje, Robert G. *Bicentennial USA.* Nashville: The American Association for State and Local History, 1973.

Janiskee, Robert L., "City Trouble, the Pastoral Retreat, and Pioneer America: A Rationale for Rescuing the Middle Landscape," *Pioneer America,* VIII (1), January 1976, pp. 1-7.

Lowry, S. Todd, "An Economist's View of Preservation," *Pioneer America,* VIII (1), January 1976, pp. 28-35.

Lynch, Kevin. *What Time Is This Place?* Cambridge: M.I.T. Press, 1972.

Ortega, Richard I., "Unwanted: Historic District Designation," *Historic Preservation,* XXVIII (1), January-March 1976, pp. 41-43.

Yarrington, James, "The American Right of History," *Historic Preservation,* XXVIII (1), January-March 1976, pp. 4-9.

George Washington as Icon 1865-1900

Howard N. Rabinowitz

In the years before Watergate, Americans made icons out of their political leaders. George Washington is an outstanding example, and the late nineteenth century was a critical period in the evolution of his role as icon.

The Civil War greatly tried the nation's resolve and many Americans viewed its successful termination as vindicating the hopes of the Revolutionary generation. In the effort to begin anew after the long struggle, postwar Americans, both Northerners and Southerners, drew comfort from the faith of the Founding Fathers in the country's future.[1]

Americans found additional reasons to touch base with the founders. The late nineteenth century witnessed tremendous economic expansion, and the proponents of the new industrial civilization emphasized the nation's considerable progress since 1776.[2] Others, however, were less concerned with material gains than with the seeming decline in public morals. These critics looked nostalgically to the era when wise, public-spirited men governed free from the contamination of industrialization, immigration, and urbanization. They asked Americans to rededicate themselves to the ideals of their illustrious ancestors and to forsake their false gods. Speaking before both houses of Congress on the anniversary of Washington's inauguration, Melville W. Fuller, Chief Justice of the Supreme Court, emphasized the need to teach the life of Washington to the nation. "Whatever doubts or fears assail us in the turmoil of our impetuous national life, that story [of Washington] comes to console and to strengthen, like the shadow of a great rock in a weary land."[3]

Other factors such as the questioning of traditional religious beliefs and the growing involvement of the United States in world affairs further encouraged resorting to the wisdom of the Founding Fathers. In addition, the coincidence of chronology added its own considerable weight. National days of observance rekindled interest in the early years of the Republic, beginning with the hundredth anniversary of the Stamp Act, ending with the centennial of Washington's death, and including the special dates of 1876, 1887, and especially 1889. Local observances commemorated battles such as Saratoga and Trenton and the wintering of the troops at Valley Forge. It was the heyday of professional orators and a speech about Washington was always in order. The centennial fever finally brought about the completion of the Washington Monument in the nation's capital and led to the construction of smaller monuments in other cities.

In the face of a changing world, the admirers of Washington were not likely to picture him in any manner harmful to his reputation or to their own point of view. Holiday orators, authors of children's books, and other uncritical admirers approached him entirely with a didactic intent. Although a new generation of more objective writers attempted to picture Washington as he really was, even they shared a genuine admiration for the man and produced an account similar in many respects to that of the traditionalists.[4] The weight of the past and of the man himself proved too great, and their work further contributed to the iconization of Washington.

Everyone agreed that Washington possessed great physical strength. More attention, however, was given to his "strength of character," particularly his extraordinary self-control. Unlike pre-Civil War writers, later observers gave ample space to his violent emotions. Henry Cabot Lodge wrote of a "strong, vigorous man, in whose veins ran warm red blood, in whose heart were stormy passions, [who] had a dangerous temper, held under control." John Fiske referred to Washington's "prodigious nature [which] was habitually curbed by a will of iron."[5] The moral for young men was clear to a prominent New England Unitarian clergyman and Harvard professor: had Washington lacked this control, "he probably would have been nothing more than a hot-headed, reckless Virginia cavalier and slave driver."[6] His self-discipline or strength of purpose, was likened to a stock figure of late nineteenth-century American life and thought: the self-made man.[7]

And like the self-made men of the day, Washington had no ready place for "abstract reasoning" in his mind. When a problem was faced and solved, "it was a success from a practical rather than a theoretical point of view."[8] Expressing the views of many, John Fiske wrote that although Washington had "little book learning, . . . he possessed in the very highest degree the rare faculty of always discerning the essential facts in every case and interpreting them correctly."[9] No longer did admirers accept the image of the man as a perfect speller and grammarian as presented by Jared Sparks or as the model student that Weems and the other early biographers depicted. The author of one children's book retained the old view of Washington as an accomplished speller, but attributed this more to his diligence and industry than to any "uncommon aptitude at learning."[10] Paul Leicester Ford's biography contained none of this ambivalence. Although Washington may have studied hard, he was "a poor speller and worse grammarian though he improved over early training."[11] The public, however, was always reminded that Washington, like the nineteenth century's poorly educated philanthropists, regretted his lack of formal education and contributed generously to several colleges.[12]

Washington's educational experience brought him closer to the average American who had little schooling and enhanced his position as a democratic hero. So too did his activities during the years which otherwise might have been spent in school. His father had died when George was twelve and it was necessary for him to help support his family. He initially found work as a surveyor and then as a soldier in the service of the Crown. In both capacities he was frequently on the frontier. His wilderness exploits were of great interest to Americans who were witnessing the last of the Indian Wars and the passing of the West. Four years before Frederick Jackson Turner's famous paper, Lodge entitled a chapter in his biography "On the Frontier." In it, Washington seemed a refugee from Cooper's Leatherstocking Tales, "an adventurous pioneer, reckless frontier fighter and a soldier of great promise."[13] Authors delighted in recounting the scene in the House of Burgesses when the modest young man received that august assembly's plaudits for his able defense of the colony. Washington allegedly rose to acknowledge the thanks, but was so overcome that he could not utter a word.

The frontier was not merely a place to live dangerously and become a modest hero. Morrison Heady pointed out that it was during this part of his life that, like later pioneers, Washington learned the necessity of self-reliance. More importantly, according to William Trent, a professor at University of the South, the early frontier experience "gave him his true sympathy with democracy."[14] General Braddock's unsuccessful campaign allowed authors to contrast the practical, democratic behavior of Washington and his company of Virginia irregulars with that of the aristocratic, rigid, and status-conscious British troops.

But it was not forgotten that Washington was also an aristocrat. A heightened interest in genealogy resulted in the publication of numerous articles and at least two books dealing with Washington's ancestry. Several authorities were content to locate Washington's forebears in the time of William the Conqueror, but one intrepid genealogist produced a four hundred page tome tracing Washington's progenitors back to Odin, the legendary Scandinavian god.[15] Most serious biographers, however, focused on Washington's immediate aristocratic contacts. Washington was seen to have had the best of all possible worlds. Not only did he profit from the frontier experience, but through contact with his wealthy half-brother Lawrence and the Fairfax family (who played the roles of benefactors usually associated with a Dickens or Alger novel), he encountered the sophisticated life of eighteenth-century England.[16] Writers gave generous coverage to Washington's "aristocratic interest" in horses, fox hunting, and courtly balls, but the hero, while benefiting from the dignity bestowed on him by such treatment, was not allowed to wander too far from American ideals. As Woodrow Wilson wrote, "Washington was an aristocrat by taste, not by principle."[17]

Washington the gentleman received more attention than Washington the backwoods democrat. His uncompensated public service was deemed especially praiseworthy. The fact that he served as an unpaid volunteer under Braddock was given almost as much attention as his bravery under fire. Even more emphasis was placed on Washington's refusal of salary during his terms as Commander-in-Chief of the Continental Army and as president.[18] Furthermore, his career was free of corrupt behavior. The prominent Civil Service reformer Carl Schurz felt that Washington's conduct as president (especially his dedication to political morality) should serve as a model for future Chief Executives. The Reverend Andrew Peabody despaired that were Washington alive he could gain election in only a few Congressional districts and stood no chance of being nominated for the presidency for "he had none of the gifts by which in our day men grovel into power, obtain position by not deserving it and mount to higher places by intrigue and corruption."[19]

Washington was not only personally honorable, he demanded the same of others. Orators and biographers invariably commented on his hatred of wartime speculators, forestallers, extortionists, and suppliers who were making excessive profits. Few people who remembered the shabby profiteering of the Civil War could fail to be impressed by Washington's behavior.

Washington's reputation also owed a great deal to his image as a reluctant office seeker. Robert C. Winthrop, former Speaker of the House of Representatives and the most popular orator on Washington, declared that "from first to last, he never solicited, or sought an office, military or civil." Morrison Heady's view of Washington's election to the House of Burgesses in 1758 was typical: he had been chosen while on the last campaign of the French and Indian War "without, however, any particular desire or effort on his part."[20]

Washington's alleged attitude toward change in society was a further source of comfort to defenders of the status quo who had been frightened by the Haymarket Riot, the Homestead Strike, and protests couched in the language of Marxism and Populism. George R. Peck, one of the nation's foremost railroad attorneys, contrasted Washington with "the professional revolutionist, the agitator who has no real conception of what he is agitating."[21] To another prominent admirer, Washington "tolerated no extremity unless to curb the excesses of his enemy."[22]

Defenders of traditional religion, forced to contend with Darwinism, higher criticism, and the study of comparative religion, also praised Washington. To George Bancroft, whose *History of the United States* enjoyed a large audience, "belief in God and trust in His overruling power framed the essence of his [Washington's] character." Not surprisingly, clergymen including Andrew Peabody and B.F. DeCosta wrote of Washington's faithful attendance at Sunday services. The Episcopal minister and amateur historian Philip Slaughter in his celebrated pamphlet, *Christianity the Key to the Character and Career of George Washington,* maintained that Washington spent two hours per day reading the Bible and praying.[23] But Washington was not merely an example to be emulated; he was proof of God's continued intercession in man's affairs. To one writer he was "a chosen instrument in the hands of God"; to another it was clear that "Providence denied Washington children of his own that he might be Father of his country."[24]

As the century waned, less emphasis was placed on Washington's religious faith and more on his toleration. Lodge did not broach the subject of religion until the next to last page of volume two and then mainly to note that Washington, even though a member of the Protestant Episcopal Church, was not at all sectarian. Still, Lodge declared that Washington had deep religious beliefs and "knelt and prayed in the day of darkness or in the hour of triumph with a childlike confidence."[25]

For many people Washington the dutiful son, loyal husband, and tender stepfather provided an example worthy of emulation in a society threatened by the disintegration of family ties. Farm children were leaving home to make their fortunes in the burgeoning cities, lower-class women were finding employment in sweatshops and factories, and the new middle-class women were rejecting their traditional roles as wives and mothers to challenge the men in the colleges, professions, and settlement houses of America.

Since the time of Weems, Washington had been pictured as a truthful lad who obeyed his elders. His parents were regarded as excellent people who instilled in him religious principles, a respect for the truth, and a sense of responsibility. When his father died, George received guidance from his half-brother Lawrence who treated him like a son. After Lawrence's death, George assumed the responsibility of caring for his sister-in-law and her young daughter. Bound together by a series of mutual obligations, the Washingtons provided a worthy example for the youth and adults of nineteenth-century America.

Washington's mother Mary rang the most responsive cord in the hearts of Washington followers. A separate chapter on her even appeared in a book devoted to the lives of George Washington and the other signers of the Declaration of Independence.[26] Despite limited evidence, extravagant claims were made for her influence on her son's life. Caroline Carothers reported that "to his mother, Washington ascribed all that was good in him." This "discreet and affectionate mother" was pictured to have had a warm and personal relationship with her son throughout her life. Lodge observed that "even at the head of armies Washington would turn aside to visit [his mother] with the same respect and devotion as when he was a mere boy."[27]

If every hero must have a great mother, so too must he have the perfect wife. According to the common view, Washington had met the widow Custis at the house of a friend and it was love at first sight. A typical source described the young woman as "the sweetest little widow with dark eyes and a round little waist." Her whole life was seen to depend on him and when the great man died, Lodge tenderly reported that she said only, "All is over now. I shall soon follow him."[28]

Washington's personality, character, and private life were laudatory, but he was most appealing to the postwar generation in the guise of National Savior. For the generation that had recently seen the Union torn asunder by the tragedy of civil war, it was Washington the Nationalist and Washington the First American who was most worthy of praise.

Most observers were content to assign Washington a less than major role in the coming of the Revolution. Lodge was the most extravagant in his treatment of Washington's pre-Revolutionary activity, placing him among the earliest advocates of "violent separation from the mother country." Other writers, less motivated by Lodge's anti-British feelings, correctly presented Washington as coming more slowly to the idea of independence. British-born James Parton and the Anglophile Woodrow Wilson suggested that Washington was neither active nor conspicuous in the eleven year verbal dispute between the colonies and England.[29]

There was more agreement about the role Washington played after becoming head of the Continental Army. Most commentators heartily endorsed John Marshall's earlier assertion that "Washington was the Revolution" and viewed as preordained his appointment as Commander-in-Chief. Caroline Carothers declared typically that "there was only one answer to the question of who should command the armies." John Fiske claimed that because Washington had "a military reputation greater than any other American," John Adams strongly urged his appointment and the Continental Congress unanimously concurred. The real reason for Adams' action was overlooked until Worthington Chauncey Ford revealed that the appointment had been part of a "political deal between Massachusetts and Virginia."[30]

Once past the matter of appointment, the versions of Washington's role during the Revolution were remarkably similar. Assessments of his military capability varied, but the consensus was that he was the great thread that tied the colonies together, the indispensable man. John Fiske even compared him to Pericles.[31] That the success of the Revolution was ever in doubt could be ascribed to the many obstacles in Washington's path. When he lost a battle, it was due either to incorrect information or the incompetence of subordinate officers.[32] He had to overcome supply shortages, unruly troops, the Conway Cabal, and Benedict Arnold. The members of the Continental Congress were depicted as inefficient, incompetent, and often villainous. Worthington Chauncey Ford devoted several chapters to Washington's problems with Congress and the difficulties faced in organizing the army and keeping it in the field. Writers like Paul Leicester Ford and former Confederate General Bradley Johnson, who had reservations about Washington's generalship, saw his ability to keep the army intact as sufficient to support his claim to military greatness.[33]

With the revolution over, his staunchest nineteenth-century admirers viewed Washington as the strongest link among the colonies. He was, they wrote, continually urging "the formation of a more perfect union."[34] Many reasons, all of great concern to late nineteenth-century Americans, were suggested for Washington's advocacy of a stronger government—his fear of anarchy, his desire for a stable financial structure, the need to gain respect in the eyes of foreign powers—but what was stressed was his interest in the West and his perception of the necessity to tie that section to the older states.[35]

Washington was depicted as repeatedly clearing away difficulties which hindered the adoption of the Constitution. According to Fiske, initial interest in the Constitutional Convention had been minimal, but the choice of Washington as a delegate from Virginia resulted in "an outburst of joy throughout the land." After the delegates assembled, his "brief but immortal speech" inspired "the mood in which they worked." Washington squelched subsequent criticisms of the document by arguing that "the Constitution is the best that can be obtained at this time, and the nation must choose between the Constitution and disunion." In Lodge's picture, Washington, aided by Hamilton and Madison, played the major role in helping the nation choose between those alternatives.[36]

For those who had followed Washington through the Revolution and the events leading to the adoption of the Constitution, the presidency seemed the natural culmination to his efforts "to make one out of many." For some it seemed also anti-climactic, and the eight years he spent in office received a more cursory treatment than earlier periods of his life. This was especially true for children's books.[37] This de-emphasis could be expected since few youngsters cared about the development of political parties or administrative history. But Woodrow Wilson, a student of government, devoted less than half as many pages to the presidency as to the Revolution. Even Lodge, whose study was part of the "American Statesmen Series," spent fewer pages on his subject's years in office than on his role in the Revolution. At least four biographies focused on Washington the soldier, none on Washington the president.[38]

All of Washington's actions as president—especially the suppression of the Whiskey Rebellion, the avoidance of war with Britain and France, his Indian policy, and his economic program—were judged to be in the best interests of the nation. Washington's Farewell Address was accepted as ordained policy for the future of the Republic, to be read and adhered to for its comments on both domestic and foreign scenes.[39] The lesson drawn from these policies was clear: Washington was a nationalist. "From the moment when Washington drew his sword in defense of the liberties of his country men," wrote the popularizer Benson J. Lossing, "he labored to secure for them the blessings of Union and Nationality." General Bradley Johnson (who was greatly indebted to Lodge's biography) spoke of Washington's "deep faith . . . in the manifest destiny of the Union" and Chief Justice Melville Fuller declared that "[Washington] saw as if face to face that continental domain which glimmered to others as through a glass darkly."[40]

But Washington was a slaveholder and planter. Was not the continental empire he envisioned only an agency for the expansion of the slave power? Washington's position as the owner of slaves could have constituted a sharp setback for his popularity. Yet his proponents did not seek to hide this facet of his life. Pictured as bound to the institution by circumstances rather than by desire, his views on slavery became a source of strength rather than of weakness. In the introduction to an edition of Washington's papers relating to his role as *Importer and Employer of Labor*," Worthington Chauncey Ford noted that having slaves was natural in Virginia since they were needed for the health of the economy. Lodge added that "Washington accepted the system as he found it, as most men accept the social arrangements to which they are born."[41] But the hero did not merely accept slavery, he became the perfect master. The author of one children's book described him as "a just, humane and thoughtful master, considerate of their [his slaves,] comfort, welfare and happiness."[42] John Habberton, using the conversational idiom which marked his book, asserted that there was no record of Washington's having "licked his nigger." Instead, as Woodrow Wilson stated, he believed in "talking with them when he could and gaining a personal mastery over them." Wilson noted that Washington provided his body servant Bishop with a secure retirement, though the same sentence added that like provision was made for Washington's favorite horse. Bancroft reported that "no one of them was willing to leave him for another master. As it was his fixed rule never either to buy or sell a slave, they had the institution of marriage and secure relations of the family." Although Paul Leicester Ford proved that slaves were bought and sold, he agreed that Washington's kindness was reciprocated by a "real attachment" from his slaves.[43]

Despite this characterization of Washington as the model slave owner, one that has persisted to this day, all but a few commentators emphasized Washington's dislike of the institution and his hopes for gradual emancipation. Few, with the notable exception of the Southerner Wilson, failed to mention that he manumitted his slaves in his will and would have done so earlier but for the intermarriage between his slaves and those of his wife. One of the typical statements was made by Bancroft: "no one more desired universal emancipation" than Washington who strongly urged the Virginia legislature to endorse "gradual abolition."[44]

Northerners thus had no reason to hold Washington in disrepute for his ownership of slaves; Southerners, except for the most unreconstructed ones, could also be satisfied. Washington was the model slaveholder and reflected all that was good in the system. What could the ordinary slaveholder have done if even the great Washington remained a slave owner until his death? If Southerners could find a defense for their past, Northerners interested in the future of the country and tired of championing the Negroes' cause could find justification for reconciliation with the former slave states.

With the obstacle of slavery removed, Washington the Nationalist could become Washington the American. He represented the greatness of the American people, not only of the North and South, but of the West; not only of Southern planters, but of Yankee businessmen.[45] Woodrow Wilson, after discussing Washington's desire for a foreign policy independent of Europe, concluded that "truly this man was the first American, the men about him provincials merely, dependent still for their life and thought upon the breath of the Old World." This was critical for the nation's survival, argued Lodge, for "had he been merely a colonial Englishman, had he not risen at once to the conception of an American nation, the world would have looked at us with very different eyes."[46]

Today students read about the many foreigners who helped the rebellious colonists win their independence. In the late nineteenth century the foreign soldiers, with few exceptions, were not fondly remembered. To Habberton, most of the foreigners were simply adventurers seeking rank. Although Henry Cabot Lodge admitted that many of the European volunteers were excellent soldiers with noble motives, "many others were mere military adventurers, capable of being turned to good account, perhaps, but by no means entitled to what they claimed and in most cases received." Lodge emphasized that "Washington believed from the beginning and said over and over again in even stronger terms that this was an American war and must be fought by Americans."[47]

Washington's alleged anti-foreign bias was useful to the proponents of immigration restriction. At the New York Centenary Celebration of Washington's first inauguration, one of the speakers contrasted Washington's times when "though not all of us sprung from one nationality, we were practically all one people" to the present "steadily deteriorating situation" brought on by importation of "the lowest orders of people from abroad." Chief Justice Fuller who was greatly influenced by Lodge's biography told the Congress of the United States that Washington "discouraged immigration except of those who, . . . could themselves, or their descendants get associated to our customs, measures and laws; in a word soon become our people."[48]

Even if immigration could be restricted, what would be

done with the great number of immigrants already in the country? Here again Washington proved useful. The Chicago celebration of the first inauguration was aimed particularly at persons of foreign birth. The organizers of the commemoration told the leaders "of the foreign community" that they should go to their people and say "it is time for us to become Americans." Through a program of church sermons and addresses, exercises in the schools, mass meetings, and fireworks, the alien was exposed to the glories of Washington, the founder of his newly chosen nation. A suggestion to have foreign groups addressed in their own language in halls on the outlying portions of the city was voted down. The idea was to get the natives and foreigners to mingle at the great rallies held in the center of the city.[49]

Washington was clearly a popular subject with late nineteenth-century orators and writers. Many admirers, however, feared that Washington was losing his preeminence as the greatest American. Worried that he was being replaced by other figures in the hearts of their countrymen, they chafed at all criticism of their hero. Despite efforts to bring Washington closer to the people, William Trent was forced to acknowledge that "some of us, to our shame, have ceased to love him." Henry Cabot Lodge worried about "veiled attacks" on Washington, "all the more dangerous because they are insidious."[50]

To some extent these admirers were overreacting to the attempt by some scholars to view Washington in a more critical light. Yet as a result of the Civil War there were other symbols of Americanism to rival Washington. Ulysses S. Grant was one, but Abraham Lincoln presented the greatest threat to the Washington icon. Lincoln was the preserver of the Union, his assassination was fresh in the minds of many, and there was a belief that the postwar experience would have been better had he lived. Aside from his great accomplishments, Lincoln seemed more human; he had faults and suffered failure like everyone else. In contrast, Washington's life seemed unimpeded in its path to greatness. Somehow Lincoln seemed more American than the father of the country. Washington, with 97 votes (the maximum possible) led the balloting for American immortals admitted to "The Hall of Fame of Great Americans" at New York University in 1900; Lincoln with 96, was tied for second place.[51]

Washington's boosters sometimes directly attacked Lincoln's idolators, as when Lodge refuted James Russell Lowell's reference in his "Commemoration Ode" to Lincoln as "the first American." More often they chose to claim implicitly for Washington the same traits commonly attributed to Lincoln; this was one reason for the extensive association of Washington with the West.[52] An effort to describe Washington the man was largely due to the need to humanize him so that he could hold his own in the face of new competition. Under this impetus the goody-goody prig of Weems' story was systematically undermined by all but the most traditionally minded admirers.

Lodge was in the forefront of those who denied that Washington was dull and cold. He spent nine pages in his biography arguing that Washington had a lively sense of humor, characterized by the frequent use of sarcasm, off-color jokes, and urbane wit. James Parton and Paul Leicester Ford were more restrained; Parton claimed only that Washington had "a homely country humor." How could anyone accuse Washington of insensitivity, his defenders asked, when evidence was clearly otherwise? Was he not the man who was overcome with emotion at the farewell to his troops and who, according to Habberton, burst into tears upon seeing the fall of Fort Washington and the suffering of New Yorkers at the beginning of the war?[53] Any doubters of Washington's sensitivity merely had to look at his lifelong passion for women, a passion that began with the mysterious Lowland Beauty who first captured his heart.[54]

In place of the man who was "against duelling, drunkenness, swearing and gambling,"[55] we find a Washington who, if not exactly a libertine, was nonetheless a lover of the good life. We hear of his fondness for Madeira at dinner, his fashionable clothes, his penchant for gambling at cards or in lotteries, and his most frequent amusement, fox hunting. We learn that he loved the theater and that he enjoyed dancing so much that he often engaged in it during the harsh winter at Valley Forge.[56] Paul Leicester Ford devoted an entire chapter to the charge that Washington was without close associates. Failure to note Washington's friendships with men like George Mason, Alexander Hamilton, Henry Knox, and the Marquis de Lafayette demonstrated to Ford "how absolutely his private life has been neglected in the study of his public career."[57]

Washington as icon during the years 1865 to 1900 was, like the country itself, in the process of transformation. Searchers after the "real" George Washington, like Frank Carpenter, boldly asserted that "truly there is enough that is great and good in his character without attributing to him virtues and qualities which he never had."[58] Yet it proved easier to urge open-mindedness than to be open-minded. Washington's faults were usually suggested rather than singled out for examination. A leading member of the Pennsylvania Historical Society informed his readers: "We do not pretend to claim that the life of Washington was faultless; but it is not for us to attempt to point out his defects, when the civilized world, in all its criticism, has yet failed to point out a single incident in his life that would put a slur upon his far fame."[59] Even such a well-trained scholar as Henry Cabot Lodge discovered the perils of trying to separate what Marcus Cunliffe has called the Man and the Monument. "As I bring these volumes to a close," Lodge wrote, "I am conscious that they speak, . . . in a tone of almost unbroken praise of the great man they attempt to portray. If this be so, it is because I could come to no other conclusion."[60]

The difficulty involved in shaping a more balanced image of Washington was evident in the reception accorded Paul Leicester Ford's *The True George Washington,* termed by Allan Nevins in 1931 as probably having "done more to furnish the correct view of Washington than any other work."[61] Published in 1896, Ford's book aimed at "humanizing Washington and making him a man rather than a historical figure."[62] It did so by, among other things, pointing out Washington's lies, shady land deals, and election defeats. Two of its reviewers, B.A. Hinsdale, Professor of Education at the University of Michigan and former Superintendent of Cleveland public schools, and William Wirt Henry, the politician grandson of Patrick Henry and former President of the

American Historical Association, welcomed Ford's volume but with serious reservations. Each writer compared it with Woodrow Wilson's more iconographic approach and both preferred the latter. Henry was especially unhappy with Ford's unfavorable treatment of Washington's mother and his questioning of Washington's religious commitment. Hinsdale believed that "the great idealizations of history far from being sources of evil are sources of great good."[63] In the face of such sentiments and the need of many of the nation's leaders to produce a Washington who believed in the same things they did, it is noteworthy that a critical spirit could flourish.[64]

Whether Washington's image as icon was greatly changed among the people, however, cannot be known for certain. There was no Gallup or Harris to light our way.[65] It must be remembered that the Washington of juvenile books, holiday orations, and semi-fictional biographies still reached a far greater audience than the few works of factually oriented scholars. As Marcus Cunliffe has observed, the Washington of Weems' story had a strong hold on the minds of later generations.[66]

NOTES

This essay has been adapted from my article entitled "The Washington Legend 1865-1900; The Heroic Image in Flux," *American Studies*, XVII (Spring, 1976), 5-25). I wish to thank the editor of *American Studies* for permission to reprint parts of the original study.

[1]See, for example, Introduction by the Reverend William M. Thayer to [Morrison Heady] *The Farmer Boy and How He Became Commander-in-Chief*, by Uncle Juvinell (New York, 1863), 4-5; Franklin B. Hough, *Washingtoniana* (2 vols.; Roxbury, Mass., 1865), I, v; Benson J. Lossing, *Washington and the American Republic* (3 vols.; New York, 1870), I, v; John Greenleaf Whittier, "The Vow of Washington," *The Washington Centenary* (New York, 1889), 40. (Hereafter cited as *New York Centenary*).

[2]See *The Nation's Birthday: Chicago's Celebration of Washington's Inauguration April 30, 1889* (Chicago, 1890), *passim.* (Hereafter cited as *Chicago's Celebration*).

[3]Melville W. Fuller, *Address: Commemoration of the Inauguration of George Washington As First President of the United States Delivered Before the Two Houses of Congress, December 11, 1889* (New York, 1890), 708.

[4]See, for example, John Fiske, *The Critical Period of American History*

1783-1789 (Boston, 1888), 84; Frank Carpenter, "The Real George Washington," *The Cosmopolitan*, VI (April, 1889), 544-48; Woodrow Wilson, *George Washington* (New York, 1896); James Parton, "The Traditional and the Real Washington," *Magazine of American History*, III (August, 1879), 465-89; John Habberton, *George Washington* (New York, 1886); Henry Cabot Lodge, *George Washington* ("American Statesmen Series"; 2 vols.; Boston, 1889); Paul Leicester Ford, *The True George Washington* (Philadelphia, 1896); Worthington Chauncey Ford, *George Washington* (2 vols.; New York, 1900); *The Writings of George Washington* (14 vols.; New York, 1889-1893); Worthington Chauncey Ford's articles include: "How Washington Became Commander-in-Chief," *Nation*, XLVIII (June 13, 1889), 481-82; "Washington as an Employer of Labor," *Nation*, XLIX (September 19, 1889), 227-28; "The Forged Letters of Washington," *Nation*, XLIX (November 28, 1889), 427-28.

[5]Lodge, *George Washington*, I, 14, 107; John Fiske, *The American Revolution* (2 vols.; Boston, 1891), I, 135.

[6]Andrew Peabody, *Lessons for Our Times From the Life of Washington* (Boston, 1874), 9.

[7]George Bancroft, *History of the United States From the Discovery of the American Continent* (12 vols.; 11th rev. ed.; Boston, 1873), VII, 394. See also Lodge, *George Washington*, I, 51; Fiske, *American Revolution*, I, 135; Habberton, *George Washington*, i.

[8]W. Ford, *George Washington*, II, 139.

[9]Fiske, *American Revolution*, I, 134.

[10]Heady, *The Farmer Boy*, 39. See also Lodge, *George Washington*, I, 46, 59.

[11]P. Ford, *True George Washington*, 66.

[12]See, for example, Mrs. E. B. Phelps, *Memoir of Washington Written for Boys and Girls* (Cincinnati, 1874), 16. This highly moralistic account drew chiefly on the earlier works of Bancroft, Marshall, and Irving.

[13]Lodge, *George Washington*, I, 91.

[14]Heady, *The Farmer Boy*, 14; William Trent, *Southern Statesmen of the Old Regime* (New York, 1897), 26.

[15]Henry F. Waters, *An Examination of the English Ancestry of George Washington* (Boston, 1889); Albert Welles, *The Pedigree and History of the Washington Family Derived from Odin* (New York, 1879). See also *Nation*, XLVIII (June 27, 1889), 522; *ibid.*, XLIX (October 17, 1889), 306-307; *ibid.*, LV (November 17, 1892), 373-74; and practically any issue of the *Magazine of American History*, especially the letters to the editor.

[16]Lodge, *George Washington*, I, 54; Trent, *Southern Statesmen*, 26; Caroline Butler Powel Carothers, *Washington: The Most Distinctively American Character That Our Country Has Produced* (n.p., 1897), 3.

[17]Wilson, *George Washington*, 127.

[18]See, for example, Heady, *The Farmer Boy*, 161; Peabody, *Lessons for Our Times*, 11.

[19]*Chicago's Celebration*, 163; Peabody, *Lessons for Our Times*, 18-19. See also *ibid.*, 5, 17; *Nation*, LXIX (December 21, 1899), 460; Henry Adams, *Democracy* (New York, 1961), 72-82 (first published in 1880); W. Ford, *George Washington*, II, 16-17; Habberton, *George Washington*, 258.

[20]Robert C. Winthrop, *Oration on the Completion of the National Monument to Washington February 21, 1885* (Boston, 1885), 25; Heady, *The Farmer Boy*, 257.

[21]George R. Peck, "George Washington," *Address Delivered at the University of Chicago, February 22, 1898* (Chicago, 1898), 4.

[22]Address of Senator John W. Daniel, quoted Robert Haven Schauffler (ed.), *Washington's Birthday* (New York, 1925), 211. See also Fuller, *Address*, 725.

[23]Bancroft, *History of the United States*, VII, 398; Peabody, *Lessons for Our Times*, 16; B. F. De Costa, "The Traditional Washington Vindicated," *Magazine of American History*, V (August, 1880), 102; Philip Slaughter, *Christianity the Key to the Character and Career of Washington* (New York, 1886), 39. See also address of President William McKinley given February 22, 1898, quoted Schauffler, *Washington's Birthday*, 143-144; Fuller, *Address*, 720.

[24]Phelps, *Memoir of Washington*, 70; Slaughter, *Christianity the Key*, 8.

[25]Lodge, *George Washington*, II, 387. The biographies published by Woodrow Wilson and Worthington Chauncey Ford in 1896 and 1900 respectively made no mention of Washington's religious beliefs.

[26]James Tyson, *An Outline of the Political and Social Life of George Washington and Biographical Sketches of the Lives of the Fifty-Six Signers of the Declaration of Independence* (2 vols.; Oakland, 1895), 29.

[27]Carothers, *Washington*, 2; Lodge, *George Washington*, II, 365. During the dedication of a monument to her memory in Fredericksburg, Virginia, in 1894, Senator John Daniel called her "one who possessed only the homely virtues of her sex . . . unassuming wife and mother whose kingdom was her family, whose world was her home." Quoted Tyson, *An Outline of Washington's Life*, 164.

[28]Carothers, *Washington*, 7; Lodge, *George Washington*, II, 363.

[29]Lodge, *George Washington*, I, 118, 156; Parton, "Traditional and Real Washington," 482; Wilson, *George Washington*, 133-36.

[30]Carothers, *Washington*, 10; Fiske, *American Revolution*, I, 134; W. Ford, "How Washington Became Commander-in-Chief," 481.

[31]Fiske, *American Revolution*, II, 48. See also Parton, "Traditional and Real Washington," 482; Eugene Parsons, *George Washington: A Character Sketch* (Milwaukee, 1898), 41.

[32]See, for example, Lodge, *George Washington*, I, 150, 170, 192; Fiske, *American Revolution*, I, 210, 219-21, 312-17.

[33]P. Ford, *True George Washington*, 277, 286; Bradley T. Johnson, *General Washington* (New York, 1895), 211. See also Parton, "Traditional and Real Washington," 482; Habberton, *George Washington*, 103.

[34]Fiske, *Critical Period*, 54. See also Fuller, *Address*, 727; Lodge, *George Washington*, II, 19; Habberton, *George Washington*, 269.

[35]See, for example, Lodge, *George Washington*, II, Chapter 1, especially 7-16; W. Ford, *George Washington*, II, 88-92.

[36]Fiske, *Critical Period*, 221, 231-32, 329; Lodge, *George Washington*, II, 29.

[37]See, for example, the volumes already cited by Morrison Heady and Mrs. E. B. Phelps. A third, Josephine Pollard, *The Life of George Washington in Words of One Syllable* (New York, n.d.) devoted six of its 120 pages to Washington's presidency.

[38]Edward H. O'Neill, *A History of American Biography 1800-1935* (Philadel-

phia, 1935), 168 lists four such books; of these, I could find only two, General Bradley Johnson's book, already cited, and General Henry B. Carrington, *Washington the Soldier* (Boston, 1898). O'Neill does not account for this emphasis, but it was probably the result of interest in military affairs generated by the Civil War, Spanish-American War, and the numerous war scares in between.

[39]Authors agreed that the Farewell Address, though presenting Washington's ideas, owed much of its phrasing to Hamilton and Madison. See, for example, Habberton, *George Washington,* 311; W. Ford, *George Washington,* II, 266; Phelps, *Memoir of Washington,* 151.

[40]Lossing, *Washington,* I, v; Johnson, *General Washington,* 299; Fuller, *Address,* 715.

[41]Worthington Chauncey Ford (ed.), *Washington As An Importer and Employer of Labor* (Brooklyn, 1889), 5; Lodge, *George Washington,* I, 101.

[42]Phelps, *Memoir of Washington,* 169.

[43]Habberton, *George Washington,* 60; Wilson, *George Washington,* 240-41; George Bancroft, *History of the Formation of the Constitution of the United States of America* (New York, 1882), 179; P. Ford, *True George Washington,* 150-139-49.

[44]Bancroft, *History of the Constitution,* 179. See also the remarks of President McKinley, quoted Schauffler, *Washington's Birthday,* 160; Lodge, *George Washington,* I, 102.

[45]See, for example, Edward Everett Hale, *Chicago's Celebration,* 163; Trent, *Southern Statesmen,* 42; Heady, *The Farmer Boy,* 260; W. Ford, *George Washington,* II, 118-27; P. Ford's chapter on Washington as planter, *True George Washington.*

[46]Wilson, *George Washington,* 291-92; Lodge, *George Washington,* I, 245.

[47]Habberton, *George Washington,* 144; Lodge, *George Washington,* I, 185. See also W. Ford, *George Washington,* II, 233-34; Parsons (who relied heavily on Lodge), *George Washington,* 45. Washington's strictures against foreign entanglements were used to remind Americans of the need to pursue a limited role in world affairs. Fuller, *Address,* 721; *Nation,* LXIX (December 21, 1889), 460. Other writers found evidence linking Washington with the country's new, more aggressive foreign policy. Carrington, *Washington the Soldier,* 368-70; W. Ford, *George Washington,* II, 66; Bancroft, *History of the Constitution,* 182.

[48]Bishop Potter, *New York Centenary,* 36; Fuller, *Address,* 726.

[49]*Chicago's Celebration,* 7, 8-9.

[50]Trent, *Southern Statesmen,* 44; Lodge, *George Washington,* II, 301.

[51]Louis Albert Banks, *The Story of the Hall of Fame* (New York, 1902), 17. Tied with Lincoln was Daniel Webster who represented no threat to Washington's popularity.

[52]Lodge, *George Washington,* II (, 312-13. For a fuller discussion of the challenge of competing icons and the tactics of Washington's defenders, see Howard N. Rabinowitz, "The Washington Legend 1865-1900: The Heroic Image in Flux," *American Studies,* XVII (Spring, 1976), 17-19.

[53]Lodge, *George Washington,* II, 365-74; Parton, "Traditional and Real Washington," 480; P. Ford, *True George Washington,* 184; Habberton, *George Washington,* 104, 124.

[54]P. Ford, *True George Washington,* 84; Wilson, *George Washington,* 101.

[55]Phelps, *Memoir of Washington,* 164.

[56]Johnson, *General Washington,* 72; P. Ford's chapter on "Tastes and Amusements," *True George Washington;* Habberton, *George Washington,* 58-59; Parton, "Traditional and Real Washington," 480; Heady, *The Farmer Boy,* 261; Lodge, *George Washington,* I, 111-14; Wilson, *George Washington,* 109-11.

[57]P. Ford, *True George Washington,* 209.

[58]Carpenter, "The Real George Washington," 548.

[59]Tyson, *Outline of the Life of Washington,* 11.

[60]Lodge, *George Washington,* II, 387-88. See also *ibid.,* 284-85.

[61]Allan Nevins, "Paul Leicester Ford," *Dictionary of American Biography,* edited by Allen Johnson and Dumas Malone (20 vols.; New York, 1931), V, 518.

[62]P. Ford, *True George Washington,* 5.

[63]William Wirt Henry, "Review of Woodrow Wilson and Paul Ford Biographies," *American Historical Review,* II (April, 1897), 539-45; B. A. Hinsdale, "Two New Books on Washington," *The Dial,* XXII (March 16, 1897), 178-80. quote, 179. On the value of "hero-worship," see also the remarks of former United States Senator and Secretary of the Interior Carl Schurz, *Chicago's Celebration,* 162.

[64]For a closer examination of this new critical spirit and the central role of Paul Leicester Ford's landmark volume, see Rabinowitz, "The Washington Legend," *passim.*

[65]There was at least one crude attempt at opinion polling the Washington Image. After fifteen years of asking people their view of Washington, Kendall Otis Stuart, a prominent businessman, reported his findings in "The Popular Opinion of Washington," *The Independent,* LI (July 6, 1899), 1814-17. The responses indicated a great lack of knowledge and probably echoed the schoolbook accounts.

[66]Marcus Cunliffe, "Parson Weems and George Washington's Cherry Tree," *Bulletin of the John Rylands Library,* X (September, 1962), 58-96. See also *George Washington: Man and Monument* (New York, 1958).

The American Writer As Public Icon

David Madden

Writers look and act differently from the rest of us. That's the general public's attitude. Only a small percentage actually read fiction or poetry, or see plays. But somehow images of a few American writers have taken shape in the collective consciousness. I want you to read about ten writers who are basically serious and who have at some time produced quality work. I want to give an impression of the public image of each of them as I have sensed it over the years. I cannot hope to have chosen *the* most visible, but these ten are certainly *among* the most visible to the few who pay any attention at all to images of literary figures the mass media project. Some of these may be like the familiar faces of relatives we don't hear from much anymore but remember in frozen images. For each, I have chosen the features that are still or once were the most famous. Some of these writers have sought the limelight for greater visibility; others were thrust into the limelight. I'm not talking about popular writers, few of whom, oddly enough, are as visible as serious writers. Some writers are famous but we have no clear sense of their public personalities or their faces lack definition; for instance, secondary school textbooks have made John Steinbeck one of the most famous of American writers, but his name seldom conjures an image. Black writers remain relatively invisible. The black writer as mass media image is a recent phenomenon. Even many literary people have no clear image of the black writers we admire most: Richard Wright, Ralph Ellison, James Baldwin, Le Roi Jones. And the mass media that feed the public imagination has given few women writers monumental status. Emily Dickinson? Can you see her face? Joyce Carol Oates? Is she known well enough to the so-called general public, that segment that knows anything at all about writers? She is perhaps too recent for inclusion in this group. Kurt Vonnegut, too, has a rather fuzzy aura, as does J. D. Salinger. I might have with some confidence included Thomas Wolfe, Carl Sandburg, Henry Miller, Norman Mailer, and Allen Ginsberg. For each of us, there was a time when we could conjure up the pictures of certain writers; if we seldom see their pictures anymore, we retain an iconographic image in the mind. To test this thesis I have deliberately refrained from including photographs in this essay.

Edgar Allan Poe

"Dreaming dreams no mortal ever dared to dream before,"
Poe says to us, his voice, we imagine, soft, courtly, southern,
slightly sinister. "From childhood's hour I have not been
As others were." Poe's face: the popular image of the
haunted, neurotic literary genius. Like the Raven, "his eyes
have all the seeming of a demon's that is dreaming." I can
say Poe's name to anyone in the full expectation that she will
automatically recite the most famous line she was forced to
memorize in grammar school, "Quoth the Raven, 'Never-
more.' " The popular imagination has forged a Poe icon, the
Raven on his shoulder. In the background, we hear "the
moaning and the groaning of the bells." We remember his
vow to the dead girl he had married at 13.

> And neither the angels in heaven above,
>   Nor the demons down under the sea,
> Can ever dissever my soul from the soul
>   Of the beautiful *Annabel Lee.*

Poe is an "imp of the perverse." The demonic energy that
produced his poems and tales we feel full force when we read
them. Tales of "the grotesque and arabesque," tales of "mystery and imagination," of horror and the supernatural, of
decadence and dissipation, of madness and the macabre, of
suffocation and suicide, tales with titles like "The Masque of
the Red Death" and "The Tell-Tale Heart." Poe forces upon
us the question, "Is *all* that we see or seem   But a dream
within a dream?" Though Poe lived in New York and Philadelphia, we see him walking dark streets in Richmond, Virginia, his hometown, and dying in a gutter in Baltimore.
Though few of his tales are set in America, we picture "the
ghoul-haunted woodland of Weir" in the South. Heart-
chilling emanations from Poe's poems and tales mummify
his image: a drunken poet, beloved but feared, who died a
burnt out case at 40, an ancestral ghost, haunting America.

Walt Whitman

"One's self I sing, a simple separate person, Yet utter the word Democratic, the word En-Masse," says Whitman, his voice lyrical, extroverted. "I hear America singing, the varied carols I hear." The American public has fashioned a simple Whitman icon. We see him tramping along the open road, open-shirted, battered gray felt hat clapped cockily on his head, long gray hair and beard flapping in the breeze, carrying a stick, knap-sack full of his own books to sell, contemplating each leaf of grass, A-meri-ca growing up all around him, in the distance a locomotive, "free-throated beauty." "Strong and content I travel the open road." We hear him advocating a contemplative individualism, "I loafe and invite my soul." We see him giving generously of himself, "When I give I give myself." We hear him declare the euphoria of healthy egoism, "I celebrate myself and sing myself" and "I sound my barbaric yawp over the roofs of the world." That he is the father of American free verse seems crisply apt for one who walks our memory as the freest of American spirits. We see him recording details about common people, common objects, observing closely common feelings and thoughts. Whitman discovered within America a new continent—the human body, that Puritanism and Calvinism had rendered invisible. "If anything is sacred the human body is scared." Even if we don't read him, even if we only call his name, or chant it, as some do, Whitman makes us feel sex and spirit as a single natural force moving among mankind. "Divine am I inside and out, and I make holy whatever I touch." Whitman convinced the American of the "manly love of comrades," but the public icon goes out of focus when any allusion or reference is made to his homosexuality. Some people settle for a kind of androgynous image. That he published the first edition of *Leaves of Grass* (1855) himself, reviewing it anonymously as a masterpiece, strikes us as an example of Yankee enterprising spirit. We like the idea of his writing only one book, made up of many books, added to gradually over the decades. Whitman is the voice of the young Republic, of the Civil War, and of three decades after, on the verge of a new era, singing not only of the Jeffersonian farmer but of the worker in the Industrial Revolution. He shows us the natural man making a home in a new world of machines. Though the man who defended him against charges of obscenity called him the Good Gray Poet and we use that sobriquet with a sense of aptness, always over him hovers a child-like innocence. "What am I after all but a child!" yelling Yes into the winds of change.

Mark Twain

"We . . . judged that we was free and safe once more . . . . .
We said there warn't no home like a raft, after all, other
places do seem so cramped up and smothery, but a raft don't.
You feel mighty free and easy and comfortable on a raft."
The voice we hear is Huck Finn's, not whatever voice we
might imagine was Samuel Langhorn Clemens'. And over the
Mark Twain icon we have made, we superimpose two character images: Huck Finn and, less clearly, Tom Sawyer. We
see Twain as a whitehaired version of those two different
boys. Even for people who don't read them, Huck Finn is as
famous, in America, as Hamlet or Don Quixote. The picares-
que *Huck Finn* (1885) is a kind of epic, comparable to
Homer's in its rendering of the who, how, and where of a
people and in its effect on the young. *Tom Sawyer* is a children's book for children, but as the saying goes, *Huck Finn*
is a children's book for adults. *Tom Sawyer* is a fantasy of
childhood, a nostalgic idyll. The popular image of *Huck Finn*
is not much different. But readers are gradually coming to
see that it is a realistic critique of the civilization it so faith-
fully depicts. "All right, then, I'll *go* to hell!" declares Huck,
finally rejecting the code of a hypocritical, brutal, inhumane
society. Aunt Polly and Aunt Sally loom in the background
when we conjure images of Tom and Huck. "I reckon I got to
light out for the territory ahead of the rest, because Aunt
Sally she's going to adopt me and sivilize me and I can't
stand it. I been there before." What Aunt Sally failed to do
to Huck, generations of public school teachers have done to
the novel itself. Hemingway tried to rescue it: "All modern
American literature comes from one book by Mark Twain
called *Huckleberry Finn*." And so do all American boys,
including Holden Caulfield. As an icon, Huck Finn is so
lucid, we have to squint to see the creator himself. To see
him at the wheel of a steamboat going South. To see him as a
young journalist out west, gathering material. To see him
giving public lectures all over the world. Twain was our first
great American writer to become popular, to acquire fame
and fortune. He was one of the first to create his own legend,
his own icon, beginning with the colorful name, Mark Twain,
and the studied wearing of white suits while smoking black
cigars. We see him always on stage, entertaining us but also
instructing us. "Everybody talks about the weather, but nobody does anything about it." "Be good and you will be
lonesome." "When in doubt, tell the truth." "Man is the only
animal that blushes. Or needs to." Dressed in white, the
father of American black humor tells us, "Everything human
is pathetic. The secret source of Humor itself is not joy but
sorrow. There is no humor in heaven." We place Twain in
the mid-west, but there was in him always a strain of Southern Gothic horror. When we look at him, we get an end-of
-an-era feeling.

Robert Frost

> The woods are lovely, dark and deep,
> But I have promises to keep,
> And miles to go before I sleep,
> And miles to go before I sleep.

We have the gravelly voice on record, and many Americans have heard it in classrooms. We first *really* see him as an old man, that crusty, gnarled look, a glint in his eyes, his poetry always the wisdom of an old man. The poet as New England farmer—the icon declares. "My object in life is to unite My avocation and my vocation." "Love and need are one, And the work is play for mortal stakes." We see him on the same small farm in Vermont, writing (he had many other farms, in other states). We associate his poetry with people living on somber, cold, bleak New England landscapes, lonely, isolated. "I have been one acquainted with the night." We see him among the hills, through all seasons, especially fall, among woodpiles, fences, fields, apple trees, brooks. Sedentary, though he travelled. Always talking contraries. "Good fences make good neighbors." "Something there is that doesn't love a wall." The dialog of opposites overt in those lines is implied in most of his poems. Intellectually sly, emotionally reticent, epigrammatic, morally earnest, he makes us feel in his poetry the serenity of strength. "I bid you to a one-man revolution, / The only revolution that is coming." His wit and humor mask a serious mind at play. "I may as well confess myself the author / of several books against the world in general." His own epitaph conveys a full sense of who he is to us. "I had a lover's quarrel with the world." Frost wrote unknown for 20 years, then, like Whitman, published late in life. His first volume appeared to critical acclaim in England in 1913 when he was 39. With *North of Boston* (1914) he became famous in his own country, and honors, prizes, honorary degrees came in a steady stream up through the inauguration of President Kennedy. Americans cherish the image of him as the poet-farmer giving public readings, talking with students in New England colleges, telling them that poetry "begins in delight and ends in wisdom." That "Like a piece of ice on a hot stove the poem must ride on its own melting." The most praised of contemporary poets, he was a very public lone wolf. "I look at a poem as a performance," a poet as "a performer."

Gertrude Stein

"A rose is a rose is a rose," says Gertrude Stein, in a voice each reader must imagine for herself. That is the single most famous, often quoted phrase ever to come from an American writer. "When this you see remember me." she said. "It always bothered me that the American public were more interested in me than in my work." No other writer is so well known for only a few phrases, often quoted in a spirit of half-mockery. "Pigeons in the grass alas." Stein's works are less read than any other major American writer's. She is certainly the most famous avant garde or experimental writer in American literature. We know her as an innovator in style, and her icon conjures up the sounds of her odd syntax. People are inspired to describe her face, most commonly as that of a Roman Emperor. Because of her mannish appearance and her lesbian aura, the public icon conjures Alice B. Toklas in the shadows. Our image of her and of her work is set to the music of Virgil Thomson. Novelist Carl Van Vechten took some of the famous photographs, Stein wearing one of her many waistcoats in each. We see her pictured in her apartment in Paris among the paintings of early modern masters. Picasso's portrait of her is iconographic. And with words she constructed icons of painters themselves. "This one was one who was working," she said of Picasso. "This one was one being one having something being coming out of him. This one was one going on having something come out of him. This one was one going on working. This one was one whom some were following. This one was one who was working." She was more an international than an American figure. The public associates her with something bizarre called automatic or surreal writing. "Nearly all of it to be as a wife has a cow, a love story. All of it to be as a wife has a cow, all of it to be as a wife has a cow, a love story." Stein was not an American public figure until she lectured here in the Thirties. During the war she and Alice did relief work, visited soldiers, and in liberated Paris, G. I.'s flocked around her and spread legends about her back home. Despite *The Making of Americans,* we have little sense of her or her work among American places, but she caught the phrasing and rhythms of Negro speech in *Melanctha* as few other writers have. Her last words were characteristic of our image of her: "What is the answer?" Getting no answer, she asked, laughing, "In that case, what is the question?"

F. Scott Fitzgerald

"And as I sat there brooding on the old, unknown world,"
Fitzgerald's cultivated voice says to us, through Nick Carra-
way, "I thought of Gatsby's wonder when he first picked out
the green light at the end of Daisy's dock." Gatsby himself has
become an icon in the American mythic consciousness. Fitzgerald is for us now always a dashing, romantic, but dissi-
pated figure, a combination of Nick and Gatsby. In *The
Great Gatsby,* Fitzgerald's double nature, his double vision
were fused finally in a work of art. In a kind of twilight zone,
we see his classically romantic profile, reminiscent of Byron's,
of John Barrymore's. "The compensation of very early success is a conviction that life is a romantic matter." In the
background, we hear jazz and Charleston dance music. He is
the only one of the male icons whose wife is part of the picture. We see them in front of a huge Christmas tree, with
their daughter Scottie, doing a synchronized Charleston kick.
We see Fitzgerald and Zelda jumping into a fountain at the
Plaza hotel in Manhattan. "Mr. Fitzgerald is a novelist," said
Ring Lardner. "Mrs. Fitzgerald is a novelty." We see them in
high society, desperately fun-loving, envious of the rich.
"They are different from you and me." Hemingway quipped,
"Yeah, they have more money." We see Fitzgerald working,
smoking, drinking, hungry for fame and fortune, in love,
pursuing with Zelda a hedonistic life, at parties, in nightclubs,
on fashionable Mediterranean beaches. We see Fitzgerald
spanning America, from New York to Hollywood, out of a
Midwestern origin. We see him in Hollywood among Klieg
lights on a soundstage. " 'You can't repeat the past,' "
Nick says. " 'Can't repeat the past?' Gatsby cried incredu-
lously. 'Why of course you can!' " But Fitzgerald knew that
"there are no second acts in American lives." At Fitzgerald's
funeral, Dorothy Parker summed him up, echoing a minor
character at Gatsby's grave, "The poor son-of-a-bitch!"

Ernest Hemingway

"It is awfully easy to be hard-boiled about everything in the daytime, but at night it is another thing," says Jake Barnes, emasculated tough guy, afraid of the dark. We may imagine a barrel-chested bass, but we have little sense of Hemingway's voice, except in his work. We hear his prose more clearly than we see his characters. "What is moral is what you feel good after and what is immoral is what you feel bad after." But we also hear him saying through Wilson, the hunter, speaking to Macomber, "Doesn't do to talk too much about all this. Talk the whole thing away." In *A Farewell to Arms,* as in all his work, Hemingway as writer went to war against empty talk. "There were many words you could not stand to hear and finally only the names of places had dignity . . . . Abstract words such as glory, honor, courage, or hallow were obscene beside the concrete names of villages, the numbers of roads, the names of rivers . . . and the dates." A credo for the underwritten style that made him famous. "The most essential gift for a good writer is a built-in, shock-proof shit detector." Such statements add to his public visibility. We see him at work, as in the jacket photo for *For Whom the Bell Tolls,* his first bestseller. A perfectionist. "I always try to write on the principle of the iceberg. There is seven eighths of it underwater for every part that shows." The rhythm of his prose is like the rhythm of his life. In both he achieved, in moderation, a sophistication of the primitive. The simplicity of Hemingway's prose is inseparable in the public mind from the simplicity of his interests: war, sports, hunting, drinking. For Hemingway, play was serious, a matter of life and death. The icon portrays him as a wounded warrior who became an *aficionado* of bull fights and boxing matches. His life was the expression of Spanish machismo. There is more a sense of Spain than of America in his work. A man's man—that was his self-image. And Gary Cooper, star of *A Farewell to Arms* and of *For Whom the Bell Tolls,* Hemingway's hunting partner, helped get that image in focus. But we sometimes see Hemingway as a middle-aged man desperately trying not to grow old, going where young men fear to tread, as the correspondent of several wars, the man of many injuries. After a plane crash, he said, "Reports of my death are greatly exaggerated," quoting Twain. We see him being photographed doing these things, his famous grin, his hairy chest bared to the glare of the lime-light. We see him writing, growing old in the Florida Keys. He left us images of himself as an old man. We see that old man, a character icon: in nature, at sea, and up in the mountains, and superimposed the old man in his fishing boat at sea combating the shark. The suicide in Idaho hovers over our memory.

William Faulkner

"I decline to accept the end of man," we hear Faulkner's distinctively southern voice telling the world in his Nobel Prize acceptance speech. "I believe that man will not merely endure: he will prevail." Faulkner's is the voice of a teller of tales, macabre, bizarre, folksy, humorous tales, depicting a microcosm symbolic of the world, expressing universal emotions and values. We see him listening to old men at the courthouse and on front porches of mansions and shacks. None of his characters are icons as Huck Finn and Gatsby are. We see family tableaux: the Sartorises, the Compsons, the Snopses. We hear him say of the blacks, "They Endured." Of these public icons, Faulkner is most intimately and securely seen in relation to a place, an exotic landscape, the pillars of a white mansion and the posts of a shack, cotton fields and swamp, poor blacks and poor whites in the shadow of decaying aristocracy. We feel a sense of the past in that place, the present haunted by the past in an agony of recall. In the heat and silence, we feel a sense of violence on the verge of eruption. We see that place in evening shadows, dogs barking in the distance. We learn through Faulkner about a way of life, we hear the authentic speech of the people. We know Faulkner's own omniscient style that, in its tortured syntax, is like the South's own tangled past, a past of secrets, shame, pride, violence, mystery, folly, and idealism confounded by guilt over slavery. We get from Faulkner a sense of sin, the sins of the fathers visited upon the sons. In *Absalom, Absalom!*, Quentin Compson's Canadian roommate at Harvard asks him why he hates the South. "I don't hate it, Quentin said . . . . *I dont hate it* he thought, panting in the cold air, the iron New England dark; *I dont. I dont! I dont hate it! I dont hate it!*" Faulkner was the only one of these icons to settle in his own home town, to live there throughout most of his literary career. But in 1955, he was thrust center stage, saying from Rome, in response to the killing of Emmett Till, "If we in America have reached that point in our desperate culture when we must murder children, no matter for what reason or what color, we don't deserve to survive, and probably won't." In 1956, a rash, rare public statement was imputed to him: "I . . . between the United States and Mississippi . . . would choose Mississippi . . . even (at the price or it meant) shooting down Negroes in the street." He repudiated that statement often. Shy and reclusive by nature, he was the least public of these writers, saying, "I myself am too busy to care about the public." Good writers "don't have time to bother with success or getting rich." But in the Thirties, he was lured to Hollywood. Part of his legend is the story that he told the studio he couldn't write in an office on the lot, that he was going home to work on the script, and permission was granted, but his bosses were shocked to discover that "home" meant Oxford, Mississippi. In his old age, in his declining productivity, he was lured to universities, not as a reader of his work, but as a celebrity willing to talk. To give advice to young writers. The best place for a young writer to work and live, he said, was a brothel.

Tennessee Willians

"Yes, I have the tricks in my pocket, I have things up my sleeve. But I am the opposite of a stage magician. He gives you illusion that has the appearance of truth. I give you truth in the pleasant disguise of illusion." We know his soft, lyrical but humorous southern voice. We see him always as a sensitive young man of the South, never as a gray-headed, venerable old man (he's now 64). We see him on TV often, and his garrulousness and his laugh are familiar. We sense he's high on something. We recall him always in context of the world of the theater, those celebrated sets at his back, as in the *Life* photograph showing him sitting on the famous staircase of the set for *A Streetcar Named Desire*. Brando screaming for Stella is one of the public icon's motifs. We see no actor as Tom, the autobiographical character, but young Williams himself, speaking to us in front of a scrim about his family, always Laura, his crippled sister, and her glass menagerie in the background. His father "was a telephone man who fell in love with long distances." Even before the playwright spoke publicly of his homosexuality, we sometimes saw, superimposed over the Tennessee Williams icon, the image of Blanche, as if she were Williams himself, saying to the poker players, "Please don't get up. I'm only passing through," the asylum attendant comforting her, Blanche saying, "I've always depended on the kindness of strangers." When we think of his plays, we hear echoes of poetic speech, laced with colloquialisms, clichés, slang. Around the icon there is an aura of the exotic, the Gothic, a mood, an atmosphere, where bizarre, truly imagined characters act out stark emotions, sexual perversities, religious obsessions, a range of pyschological torments, the sensitive Toms and Blanches pitted against the brutal Stanley Kowalskis and Big Daddys. For decades, we have pictured Williams living in Key West, New Orleans, Rome. We respond to the glamour of the flamboyant nickname he gave himself: "Tennessee." Who more than Tennessee Williams fits our public romantic image of the playwright? With *Glass Menagerie* (1944), "I was snatched out of virtual oblivion and thrust into sudden prominence . . . success has often come that abruptly into the lives of Americans." We have watched him strive desperately (a contrast to our image of Arthur Miller) to maintain his status with a long, compulsive parade of plays, most of them inferior to standards his best plays set. "The public Somebody you are when you 'have a name' is a fiction created with mirrors." We have watched him live his public and theatrical life as if he were always only too keenly aware that "at ` ? m. your disgrace will be in print."

Truman Capote

"I'm a completely horizontal author. I can't think unless I'm lying down." We hear his high ultra-effeminate voice clearly in our living rooms on talk shows. The most famous contribution to the Truman Capote icon is the first, on the jacket of *Other Voices, Other Rooms* (1948). The author was 24. That sensational first novel was an "attempt to exorcise demons." In the final line, Joel Knox, an adolescent male version of Gothic romance heroines, "stopped and looked back . . . at the boy he had left behind." But the public won't let Capote leave that boy behind. We persist in seeing that reclining precocious author. "I was stage-struck for years and more than anything I wanted to be a tap-dancer." We can believe that the boy in the picture would never relinquish that camp ambition. At 51, he's acting in a Neil Simon movie comedy, *Murder by Death*. Behind Capote, we see the iconographic image of the grass harp, the young man, like Huck Finn, and the two old women (reversals of Aunt Polly and Aunt Sally?), escaping civilization by living in a tree. "It was a grass harp, gathering, telling, a harp of voices remembering a story. We listened." The public impression is that Capote's work is autobiographical, personal, subjective; but very little of it finally is. *In Cold Blood* was an effort, he told us, to establish a serious new literary form, the non-fiction novel. "Ha!" said the critics. "Let's see," said millions of paying customers. Our image of Capote is expressed in his own ambition: "I want to try something else, a kind of controlled extravagance." We have a sense of him as the fat, aging child prodigy. Each time we see him, and that's frequently, on TV, exhibited as a major exponent of the new journalism, as a dabbler in theater, movies, television drama, and documentaries, he reminds us of the unfulfilled promise of *Other Voices, Other Rooms*. In the jet set society, he plays to the hilt the role of the rich and famous writer, hinting in his condescending tone with others a kind of self-contempt. He is a sort of Oscar Wilde-Dorian Gray figure, exuding an aura of decadence, of hedonism. "I intend to have footloose escapades as long as frontiers stay open." We watch the celebrity "make a spectacle of himself," saying, with that sudden, sunny smile, "witty," outrageous things. "Actors are stupid." Many writers are just "sweaty typists." What will he do or say next? He is currently the most quoted, photographed, watched American writer, though with diminutive reputation abroad. And we are a little weary of his weary sophistication. Still, as he said of Holly Golightly in *Breakfast at Tiffany's*, "She may be a phony, but she's a real phony."

Jack Kerouac

Dean Moriarty's " 'criminality' was not something that sulked and sneered; it was a wild yea-saying outburst of American joy; it was Western, the west wind, an ode from the Plains, something new, long prophesied, long a-coming (he only stole cars for joy rides)." A hip voice, blowing hot. We saw few pictures of Jack Kerouac when his fame was soaring. We see fewer today, but even those who never saw a picture would probably imagine him as he looks here, the spittin' image of the beat prototype. He was not of the lost generation. "You know," he said, "this is really a beat generation." Also called "beatniks," "bums," "disaffiliates," "Holy Barbarians," who were not the same breed as the Greenwich Village bohemians. In whom Dada was reborn, out of whom would come the hippies. We see Kerouac coming toward us from having made touchdowns in Lowell, Massachusetts, from work on the railroad, voyages in the merchant marines, duty in a forest fire tower. We see him living a sleazy proletarian life, the romance of poverty—no money, no great thirst for fame and fortune, living for the present moment only, no past, no future. We see him in the 50's among neon lights on skid rows all over America, see him in highway truck stop diners, imagine yellow white shirts, stinking armpits, dirty white socks, toe-jam. Always on the move, on the road, never settled into one place, moving from friend to friend, with Whitmanesque cameraderie, lover to lover (some know he lived long and often-times with his mother). "Live your lives out? Naw, *love* your lives out." In the public imagination, that meant free love orgies. Kerouac meant more. Exuberant, he pursued kicks and karma, with wine and hallucinogenic drugs, Zen Buddhism on mountain tops. In the background of the public icon, the influence of French post war existentialism, Charlie "Bird" Parker's jazz, Jackson Pollock's abstract expressionist paintings. The false image sensationalized by mass media was of the beats as amoral, immoral, the poet as juvenile delinquent, if not criminal. They were called humorless, but they were in fact quite zany, their models, the Three Stooges, the Marx Brothers, and, unconsciously perhaps, the commedia dell' arte. They called attention to popular culture as a serious influence in our lives— The Shadow and other radio, comics, and pulp heroes, movies, pop music, pop fiction. "Beat comes out, actually," said Kerouac, "of old American whoopee." We see Kerouac reading his poetry and prose to jazz in coffee houses. His image of himself writing in a "semi-trance," "swimming in a language sea," is our image of him. His favorite word was, too obtrusively, "sad," and that gave his semi-tough image a sentimental aura. The beat movement was destroyed by Madison Avenue and the mass media, through over-exposure, assimilation, and ridicule. "Woe unto those who spit on the Beat Generation," Kerouac told us, "the wind'll blow it back."

Shirley Temple: Super Child

Phyllis Zatlin Boring

The bicentennial cover of New Jersey Bell's telephone book salutes 32 guests of honor. This select group of "American heroes, myths and common people" includes obvious historic and symbolic figures—George Washington, Benjamin Franklin, Thomas Jefferson, Uncle Sam, the American Indian, the Statue of Liberty. And there on the front cover, smiling at us, between Abraham Lincoln and John Davison Rockefeller is the mighty moppet herself—Shirley Temple. That the dimpled curly-top should have been chosen to appear in such august company comes as no surprise, but whether the artist chose her as "hero" or as "myth" remains open to question.

One of the most remarkable aspects of Shirley Temple's life is that she has succeeded in living beyond her image as a child star. In June, 1976, following two years of service as the U.S. envoy to Ghana, she became the first woman Chief of Protocol of the Department of State and was named to the rank of Ambassador. She is one of only two women to appear in the current organizational chart of the Diplomatic Missions and Delegations to International Organizations of the Department of State. Her appointment to a high-ranking office in the diplomatic service came after several years of distinguished public service. But the picture on the telephone book is not of the adult woman, but rather of the curly-headed child.

When the real Shirley Temple Black entered the political scene in 1967, she began her campaign by proclaiming, "Little Shirley Temple is not running." But Shana Alexander astutely observed at the time that Black had long since lost control of "little Shirley Temple." "The moppet belongs to the ages," Alexander explained. "The fact that Mrs. Black survives in northern California is merely an accident of history." Shirley Temple, she added, was "Myth-on-the-hoof, real living legend."[1]

Certainly the legend is a fascinating one. Little Shirley Temple became the youngest person ever listed in *Who's Who in America*.[2] In 1935, 1936, 1937 and 1938 she was the number one box office attraction in America, pushing aside such rivals as Clark Gable, Joan Crawford and Bing Crosby.[3] Between 1934 and 1938, she had fourteen straight smash hits.[4] Entire industries sprang up because of her popularity, manufacturing and selling Shirley Temple dresses, dolls, toys, gadgets, underwear, coats, hats, shoes, books, soap, hair ribbons, tableware, merchandise of every shape and kind (Zierold, p. 72). In spite of the economic situation in the 1930s, or perhaps because of it, the famous polka dot dresses sold by the millions at high prices.[5]

The New Jersey Bell artist, in explaining his choice of Shirley Temple for the bicentennial cover, remarks that "bleak thoughts of the Great Depression were left at the box office as America watched her sing and dance."[6] In so saying, he echoes the observation of President Franklin Delano Roosevelt: "When the spirit of the people is lower than at any other time, during this depression, it is a splendid thing that for just fifteen cents an American can go to a movie and look at the smiling face of a baby and forget his troubles" (Zierold p. 69).

One may well explain Shirley Temple's meteoric rise to fame at least in part by the backdrop of economic crisis and impending war against which she played her greatest scenes. There is no doubt that her movies were escapist: modernized fairy tales presented always in that mythic realm where poor orphan girls may turn into little princesses, where dead fathers may turn out to be alive after all, where queens and presidents will intervene to help children, and where a strong child may in her wisdom lead them all to the inevitable happy end.

The escapist aspect of the Shirley Temple movies is often enhanced by the choice of historic or exotic settings—the Civil War, Victorian England, Kipling's India or Heidi's Switzerland—and just as frequently emphasized by developing a world of fantasy within the movieland of make-believe: the recently-adopted child in *Curly Top* (1935) acts out several roles in a benefit performance on behalf of the children remaining in the orphanage; the newly-orphaned Sara in *The Little Princess* (1939) dreams of being royalty; Shirley Temple is both *Heidi* (1937) and the little Dutch girl in the book Heidi's grandfather is reading to her. In a dazzling display of Chinese boxes, there may even be a level of fantasy within the fantasy within the movie. While Sara dreams of being a princess, the princess discovers that one of the dancers performing for her is "very familiar"—Shirley herself. The little Dutch girl in Heidi's book, because of her magic shoes, is whisked away to an elegant fancy-dress ball. All is not sweetness and light in these movies, however; little Shirley is almost always faced with the gravest problems in life, and, in fact, the very problems faced by the nation and the world in the 1930s: poverty and war. That she is able to overcome them may well be the escapist message of hope in the films.

The sociological background of the period cannot, however, completely explain Shirley's enormous popularity. Rodney G. Minott, in his not unbiased account of Black's loss to McCloskey in the California primary of 1967, may not be in error when he states that "showings of Shirley Temple films of 30 years ago elicit responses not always respectful,"[7] but he might with equal truth have stated that reruns are earning her new fans all the time and even her less successful films still have audience appeal. One of the Christmas television specials of 1975 was *The Blue Bird*, a technicolor adaptation of Maurice Maeterlinck's play which in 1940 had the dubious distinction of being the first Shirley Temple picture to lose money (Zierold, p. 68). A New York channel annually presents a "Shirley Temple Theater" on Saturday afternoons during the winter months. Similar series are aired across the country and are not necessarily aimed solely at children. In St. Petersburg, Florida, for example, one day last fall Channel 44 showed *Wee Willie Winkie* (1937) at 1 p.m. and *The Little*

Princess at 9 p.m. The local paper labeled the former movie "entertaining" and the latter, "excellent."

I was born too late to see the original Shirley Temple movies and did not have access to a television set when the reruns began in the 1950s. But her smiling face is part of my experience nevertheless. In the scrapbooks my mother made in the 1930s for my older sister, cutting out magazine pictures of those things that would appeal to a child, there was Shirley on page after page, along with puppy dogs, Santa Claus, the Dionne Quintuplets and the Campbell Soup kids. As Alexander says, "She has become part of the common subliminal experience of Americans . . . knotted tight into our national collective unconscious" (*loc. cit.*). For me, she rose to the conscious level only last winter when my eleven-year-old son discovered her and began to spend his Saturdays admiring the moppet and "the way she could always con people into doing something." Obviously, Shirley Temple fans come in both sexes and all ages and one does not have to search far to find them. With very little effort I have uncovered three women who "looked" and dressed like Shirley Temple as little girls—one contemporaneous with Shirley and the others a generation later—a woman who saw all the early films in Germany as a child before the movie house was closed down for showing American films, and a male college student who not only considers Shirley Temple's *Heidi* to be the definitive film version but also deeply regrets having had to miss one of the Saturdays in this year's rerun of the "Shirley Temple Theater."

The continuing appeal of the movies can certainly not be attributed to their plots, which tend to be repetitive despite changes in setting or time. Nor can it be explained by the caliber of Shirley's co-stars, although that group included some of the finest talents in Hollywood: Lionel Barrymore, Bill Robinson, Adolphe Menjou, Gary Cooper, Carole Lombard, Arthur Treacher, Jean Hersholt. No matter what the plot or the cast, the center of attraction was always Shirley herself. As one critic noted in 1936, to appear in a film with Shirley was to become anonymous.[8] Reviewers may have "felt a constant need to apologize for the fact that they had thoroughly enjoyed her sentimental dramas" (Zierold, p. 79), but they did not hesitate to praise the super child herself. For them, she was a "delightful child," a "miracle of spontaneity," an "astonishingly delightful infant," "the most improbable child in the world," "the wonder child," "the mighty moppet," "Public Cherub Number One."[9] One of the critics ultimately decided that the films needed neither titles nor plots, that, in the fashion of certain children's books, they should just be named after their star: Shirley Temple in the Country, Shirley Temple in the City, etc.[10] My eight-year-old daughter has apparently reached similar conclusions, for she has asked not only why Shirley is called Sara one week and Heidi the next but whether or not there ever was a Shirley Temple. My daughter understands, of course, that what happens in a given movie is just pretend, but she cannot quite believe in the real existence of a little girl like the one she sees on the screen.

To what may we attribute the Shirley Temple magic? Was it her appearance, her intelligence, her personality, her talent? That was one question I asked of a small group of people I had identified as remembering having seen at least 3 to 5 Shirley Temple movies. I asked those surveyed to rank these four characteristics in order of their importance. All but three put personality in first place. Appearance was rated first or second by more than half of the respondents, while talent and intelligence came in third and fourth, in that order. Although references in the news media to little Shirley Temple or to the adult Shirley Temple Black tend to emphasize the child star's appearance—dimples and curls—and her talent—tapping toes and "Good Ship Lollipop"—it is possible that neither of these traits was the outstanding one in her popular image.[11]

The greatest difficulty in establishing that popular image, however, arises from the virtual impossibility of separating the fictional Shirley of the movies from the real child, whose public image may in itself have been a somewhat inaccurate reflection of reality. While most of my respondents correctly perceived that the fictional Shirley could be a "stubborn," "disobedient," "mischievous" and even "naughty" child, for some my question on the characteristics of Shirley's typical role elicited a response that more nearly coincides with the media picture of the real child: "a perfectly sweet, loving, obedient child," a "sweet girl who fulfilled the needs of the adults portrayed; those needs were primarily of having a physically attractive child dependent and affectionate." It must be noted that the latter two descriptions would give us a pretty wishy-washy and uninteresting character, the same kind of lifeless Jane of the "Dick and Jane" books who passively stands by, looking feminine and helpless, waiting for someone to rescue her. The fictional Shirley never waited for help; in fact, it was generally she who saved the day.

An analysis of the Shirley Temple roles shows that she was a charmer, but that her charms did not affect everyone. While she could swiftly unbend the world's most formal butler by merely beckoning with her finger (*Curly Top*) and the matter of winning over a crotchety grandfather was child's play indeed (*The Little Colonel*, 1935; *Heidi, Wee Willie Winkie*), the really bad characters were never converted. The woman who runs the orphanage in *Curly Top* labels Shirley "incorrigible." The woman who runs the girls' school in *The Little Princess* relegates her to a life of hard labor in the kitchen when she finds that the child's father has died in battle and left her penniless. Later she tries to have the little girl arrested. The dreadful Fräulein Rottenmeier of *Heidi* even tries to sell her to the gypsies. Dimples and smiles are to no avail with the truly hard-hearted. And with those people Shirley uses other methods. She may be able to win over Abraham Lincoln (*The Littlest Rebel*,1935) and Queen Victoria (*The Little Princess*) with good manners and reasoned pleading, but with villains she resorts to kicking, screaming, cunning and stealth, although always within the context of her infallible sense of morality. Her screams of "Cap! Cap! Cap! I don't want to go! I don't want to!" when she is being dragged off by a truant officer in *Captain January* (1936) became, according to Norman J. Zierold, a classic plea, repeated with variations in most of her films (p. 66). Nor is she ready to forgive and forget. When her aunt has unceremoniously left her with her inhospitable grandfather, *Heidi*'s prayer is that her aunt stay away a long, long time. While good always triumphs over evil in the end, in the Shirley Temple movies the bad guys do not reform, they merely fade away.

In the fairy-tale realm of the Shirley Temple movies, she is typically cast in a quasi-Cinderella role: the orphan or alleged orphan left in poverty who ultimately finds love and happiness. But the fictional Shirley Temple differs from Cinderella in two essential ways. The Cinderella-Prince Charming romantic love may be present, but always subordinate to the child's role and often the results of her efforts. It is Shirley who helps along the romance of her older sister and their foster father in *Curly Top,* sees that the village pastor marries the right young woman in *Heidi,* helps the young lovers in *The Little Princess,* brings her parents back together again in *Our Little Girl* (1935), and serves once again as matchmaker in *Little Miss Broadway* (1938). While she is always properly grateful and appreciative of any assistance that she receives from a Fairy Godmother figure, unlike Cinderella, Shirley does not stand around and wait for help to come but rather goes out actively seeking it. Queen Victoria may give the child permission to search for her father among the wounded men in the hospital, but it is only because she has slipped away from the evil schoolmistress and eluded the police that Shirley is there at all (*The Little Princess*). Abraham Lincoln may pardon the child's father (*The Littlest Rebel*), but he is only able to do so because she has managed to slip through the enemy lines to seek his help. Grandfather may rescue her sick father from the clutches of the two bad men (*The Little Colonel*), but that happy event only takes place because little Shirley has bravely run through the dark, scary woods and then bullied the stubborn old Southern gentleman into stepping foot in his Yankee son-in-law's house. To single-handedly end a rebellion in India (*Wee Willie Winkie*) or quell a Blackfoot Indian uprising in Canada (*Susannah of the Mounties,*1939), calls for bravery, persistence, intelligence, diplomacy and an unbreakable spirit. Without Dick, Jane would never have made it—but Shirley is a heroine who can tackle life's problems on her own. Far from being sweet and helpless, it is she who takes her little brother's trembling hand in *The Blue Bird* and leads him through the gloomy cemetery to the Land of the Past.

The roles that Shirley Temple played were thus far removed from the "perfect little lady" image that many people tend to have of them. It is true, however, that she wore a red and white polka dot dress in *Stand Up and Cheer* (1934) and that in many of her films, particularly those with a historical setting or a fantasy sequence, she dressed very elegantly indeed. Besides the elaborate gown in the ballroom fantasy of *Heidi,* her grandfather decks her out in elegant ante-bellum style in *The Little Colonel,* she acts the role of a bride in *Curly Top,* and she dresses up in a beautiful, blue, floor-length gown when visiting the Land of Luxury in *The Blue Bird.* On the basis of these episodes it is no wonder that mothers thought that their daughters had to be neat, clean and frilly to look like Shirley Temple. One of my respondents recalls that she owned all the Shirley Temple dresses, took dancing lessons, and sat through nightly settings of her hair, all to look and act like Shirley, but that finally her own life style got in the way: "I lived out the fantasy until my grandmother tried to get me to give up my bike (my scraped knees didn't go well) with the dresses and my place on the track team (after all, Shirley wasn't a tomboy and running messed up my curls) so I had to make a choice." But was Shirley really that dainty and perfect?

A closer look at the roles and a glimpse at the public image of the real child both reveal that often she was not. Outside the fantasy sequences in the movies, she was frequently dismayed with clothes that got in the way. When her grandfather first sees her in *The Little Colonel,* she is dirty from head to toe from making mudpies. When we first see her in the opening minutes of *Heidi,* she is standing in a village square taking off her Sunday best, until her aunt forces her to put the restrictive clothes back on. She may not be on a track team, but she certainly can run when she has to, as she proves in *The Little Colonel* and *The Little Princess.* In the latter film she takes riding lessons, in *Curly Top* she has her own pony, and in *Susannah of the Mounties* she not only learns to ride but also wears a cowboy outfit at times. In *Wee Willie Winkie* Kipling's boy character was adapted for Shirley, who wants to be a soldier just like the grown men. At the end of *Curly Top* she makes a good try at ending sex-role stereotyped toys by thanking her foster father for a gift of pearls but hinting that she would have preferred roller skates. In *Susannah* she is decidedly upset when Little Chief insists upon treating her like a subservient squaw. In real life, she may well have had all the earmarks of a so-called tomboy. In one magazine interview at age 10, she said that she liked to sew but that she also played with guns, liked to play with boys, and enjoyed *Gangbusters*.[12] Also high on her list were *The Lone Ranger* and *Tarzan* (Zierold, p. 81), skipping rope, watching marching bands, and playing army (*ibid.,* p. 78). In her last letter to Santa Claus she asked for a pair of blue dungarees, a blue and red checked cowboy shirt, and a pair of six-shooters.[13] But legends are not necessarily based on reality, and it is unlikely that the image of the immaculate and ultra-feminine Shirley Temple will soon change.

For the newest generation of mighty moppet fans, there is only one Shirley Temple—the one they see on the screen. For adults, however, there is always the ambiguity between th child legend and the real person. Such ambiguity for me was typified by the comment of a librarian when I came in one day to pick up some Shirley Temple material. "Ah," she said, "you must be a conservative Republican." For many people there are now overlaying images of Shirley Temple— the child star, the ambassador to Ghana, the wife and mother, the unsuccessful political candidate, the has-been at 15, the brave mastectomy victim. The images so tend to superimpose themselves on one another that for some people it is now difficult to separate the child actress from the adult politician-diplomat or to judge the adult on her own merits and not on that of the "Lollipop." The complexity of this identity problem is further compounded for many blacks who feel, undoubtedly with considerable justification, that movies from the 30's project a negative image of minority people and should not be recommended for young viewers today.[14]

It is not the purpose of the present paper to analyze these various aspects of the historic Shirley Temple Black or to review the sociological background of her films from the perspective of the present. A glance in those directions, however, reveals possibilities for interesting research. If the popular image of the child Shirley Temple was that she was the "feminine ideal," that type of sex-role stereotyping also carried over into her subsequent life. In some respects her experience follows the trajectory of the role of women in American society through the 40's, 50's, 60's, and 70's. As a teenager in the 40's, she accepted the idea that to be a success as a woman she had to catch a man. She recalls, "My own early marriage was based partly on the competitive spirit among the seniors in the girls' school I went to: Who would be the first to get a ring, be engaged, get married, have a baby? I wanted to win the race."[15] Louise Tanner correctly notes that Shirley's courtship and youthful marriage to John Agar "followed a pattern all too frequent during the war years" (p. 189). Their subsequent divorce apparently crushed Shirley's fans. When her second marriage to Charles Black proved to be a stable one, popular magazines in the 1950's heaved a sigh of relief and tended to portray her as the contented wife and mother, unwilling to leave her happy home for a moment.[16] When she later went back to work as the hostess on a children's television series, an article in *Coronet* dutifully reported that she only did so because her husband "let her" and because the job only took her away from home and family one day a week.[17] By the 1960's, when the current women's movement was beginning to surface, Shirley Temple no longer felt that she had to apologize for wanting a career. In fact she opened her Congressional campaign by noting that California had no Congresswomen and "that it wouldn't hurt to have a woman's viewpoint expressed in that delegation of men" (Minott, p. 6). It is possible that her failure in that primary was due not only to her politics but also to her sex and, of course, to her continuing public image as a "Lollipop."[18] It is perhaps a sign of the times that in the 1970's, when she is featured in magazine articles, it is in her role as "Madam Ambassador."[19]

In her heyday as a child star, Shirley Temple was known as "America's Greatest Unofficial Ambassador." But I suspect that if someone had told her then that when she grew up she would really be an ambassador, she would have clapped her hand to her face and said, "Oh, my goodness!" in that special way that only the mighty moppet could.[20]

[1] " 'Little Shirley Temple' Lives," *Life,* November 3, 1967, p. 17.

[2] *Newsweek,* May 25, 1942, p. 62.

[3] Norman J. Zierold. "What Was Shirley Temple Really Like?" In *The Child Stars* (New York: Coward-McCann, 1965), p. 65.

[4] Louise Tanner, "The Good Ship Lollipop: Shirley Temple" in *Here Today. . .* (New York: Thomas Y. Crowell, 1959), p. 180.

[5] As part of the research for the present paper, I elicited written questionnaires from a diversified group of 15 people ranging from two eleven-year-old boys to an eighty-year-old woman. One of those surveyed noted in her response that the dresses cost between $14 and $18, "an outrageous sum to pay for a kid's dress" at that time.

[6] Inside back cover, New Jersey Bell Telephone Directory, November, 1975.

[7] *The Sinking of the Lollipop: Shirley Temple vs. Pete McCloskey* (San Francisco: Diablo Press, 1968) p. 19.

[8] Frank S. Nugent, *The New York Times Film Reviews,* June 26, 1936.

[9] Quotations are from various critics and come, respectively, from *The New York Times Film Reviews* of April 20, 1934; June 30, 1934; December 21, 1934; December 20, 1935; June 26, 1936; November 6, 1937.

[10] Nugent, *The New York Times Film Reviews,* October 10, 1936.

[11] Having personally heard so many references to Shirley's singing and dancing, I was surprised to learn that the majority of her films were not musicals. Typically the song and dance routine was worked into each film only once either in a fantasy sequence or at some more or less logical point relative to the plot: Bill Robinson trying to help her overcome her apprehension at going upstairs in grandfather's big house in *The Little Colonel,* Shirley trying to hastily teach Randolph Scott to waltz before he goes off to a dance in *Susannah of the Mounties,* Shirley singing to the dying Sergeant MacDuff in *Wee Willie Winkie.*

[12] *Parents,* October, 1938, pp. 22-23.

[13] Martin Levin, ed. *Hollywood and the Great Fan Magazines* (New York: Castle Books, 1970), p. 46.

[14] I am not yet convinced that the image of blacks in the Shirley Temple movies is as negative as either the black respondents to my questionnaire or the authors of a letter to the editor of the *Women's Studies Newsletter* (3iii&iv:28) believe it to be, but I have not had the opportunity to see all of the films and therefore cannot reach any conclusion. One woman observed that it was degrading for Bill Robinson, a grown man, to be depicted playing with a little girl, but certainly grown white men were also frequently cast in that role. Moreover, Robinson at least is given credit for being her hero and mentor (*Time,* April 27, p. 39) —it is he who teaches her to dance in *The Little Colonel*—while Randolph Scott has to crouch down in a most undignified position while she teaches him to dance (*Susannah of the Mounties*).

[15] *Good Housekeeping,* November, 1957, p. 131, quoted in Tanner, p. 190. This attitude might, of course, explain why "One-Take Temple," the child of high I.Q. and extraordinary memory did not excel in her studies.

[16] See *Colliers,* October 11, 1952, pp. 60-61.

[17] *Coronet,* March 1961, pp. 69-82.

[18] Minott's book is illuminating in this regard because his own bias against

Black is so strong on all three counts.

[19]Linda Susan Black, "Shirley Temple Black in Africa," *Ladies' Home Journal,* October, 1975, pp. 72ff.

[20]I would like to express my thanks to Dr. Kay F. Reinartz who read my brief note on Shirley Temple in the *Women's Studies Newsletter* 3ii(1975):11 and encouraged me to explore the subject further. Without her interest the present paper would not have been written.

Iconic Modes: The Beatles

Ralph Brauer

"Yeah, well, if there is a God, we're all it."
John Lennon

"God," noted Pogo from his vantage point in the comics, "is unemployed." Words have been discarded, retooled, or vulgarized accordingly. "Idol" now pertains to anyone or anything to the group doing the idolizing. For example, a high school sports hero can be an idol to a grade school sand-lot jock while his older sisters "just idolize Paul Newman's eyes." Charisma is no longer a word applied only to religious figures who have received a special grace from God; instead a political hero like John Kennedy can be said to have "that special grace" and a TV newscaster like Walter Cronkite is spoken of as having charisma. Icon has come to be a word used by cultural analysis to describe images which in Marshall Fishwick's words "are admired artifacts, external expressions of internal convictions, everyday things that make everyday meaningful."[1]

It is a pointed comment on our world today that some like Fishwick believe icons can only be objects. Although the religious figures of the medieval icons were materially dead, they were still spiritually alive and their presence was felt as surely by their devotees as if they had been living. Death and life did not have the same meaning then as they do now. To see our contemporary icons as being only objects is to too literally interpret the medieval icon and in turn cut off from our understanding the study of the cultural significance of people who have affected our experience in iconographic ways. To say for instance that a poster of James Dean is an icon, that perhaps his role in *Rebel Without a Cause* could be, but that the living individual could not is to draw an all too literal line between life and death, person and object, thing and no thing, which circumscribes rather than enlarges our understanding. If we are to use the concept of icons to gain an understanding of the deep visions and values of our culture we must examine those individuals as well as those objects which we endow with our beliefs in their sacredness. As Fishwick put it, "what is central to the concept of icon is touching a center near man's essence."[2]

In contemporary America perhaps nothing touches the center of certain people as much as our popular music stars. American teenagers, especially girls, place on their walls pictures or posters of their favorite pop idols and surround them with other objects of devotion—concert tickets, record jackets, and perhaps, if they are lucky enough and impertinent enough, a lock of hair, a cufflink, a ripped piece of clothing. Like pieces of the True Cross or vials of the Holy Blood, these objects from the person of the pop star are deeply venerated. They may well be kept in specially designed reliquaries. Unlike their religious counterparts, though, these pop icons are only temporal. Their devotees grow up or find new objects of veneration. Even the most devoted admirer of Donny Osmond ultimately knows that some day the picture, tickets and other objects will end up in the trash can.

During most of the sixties there were probably no pop stars as high on the iconographic scale as the Beatles. Their devotees came from every class and age group. Many of them willingly had their hair clipped in imitation of their idols (whose haircuts resembled those worn by monks in many a Hollywood movie—perhaps that's why their imitators were called Monkees) or invested five to ten bucks in a similarly styled wig. Others bought collarless jackets and a type of leather boot which came to be called, appropriately enough, "Beatle boots." Original posters from their concerts sold in galleries for astronomical prices. Yellow submarines appeared on the sides of brick buildings. Thousands of children were named after them as were stores, free schools, amusement parks and a host of products. Above all, though, we bought their records—and in greater volume than we have ever bought records from a single group or individual. We made millionaires of four plain lads from Liverpool along with a multitude of managers, merchandizers and assorted hangers-on and rip-off artists. We made those records so popular that today they are still used to draw in customers when sold at a discount. Revivals on radio are so frequent one wonders whether they ever really "left" us.

Like true devotees we spent hours discussing and memorizing the verses of these recorded "texts." Decyphering them became a world-wide pastime. Even the photographs on the album covers were analyzed. When rumor spread that cypher experts had determined that certain messages spoke of Paul's death, even the real Paul had trouble denying it.

Then there were the rites at which the Beatles themselves presided: those live concerts where all one could hear were literally thousands of screaming, shrieking, hysterical people. Only at brief moments could you catch slices of the music, but since you had heard it before, your mind filled in the blank spots. What was important above all else at these rites was to show your devotion, to show how *they* moved you, how much you felt about *them,* what it did to you. Ushers spoke in awe of the wet seats left by teenage girls. As John Lennon tells it in *Lennon Remembers* many of these female devotees went a great deal further in satisfying their sexual stirrings. According to Lennon the Beatles on tour resembled something from Fellini's *Satyricon:* "We had four bedrooms separate from . . . tried to keep them out of our room. And Derek's and Neil's rooms were always full of fuck knows what."[3]

For all Lennon's efforts to set the record straight, though, most of the Beatles' fan preferred to keep their sexual stirrings in the realm of fantasy. This fantasizing about the private lives of pop icons, of course, has a long history. Its most prominent exponents have always been the gossip columnists and the Hollywood fanzines. For rock fans the biggest fanzine of all was and still is *Rolling Stone,* which comes in tabloid form like the *National Enquirer* and at its best is an articulate alternative to the regular press, while at its worst it is nothing but a gossip sheet and trend spotter.

It was in *Rolling Stone* that Lennon finally, as he put it in the language of these times, "let it all hang out." In his remarks about the Beatles one senses a strong self-destructive tendency—about which I'll say more later—which in its attempt at realism rings not unlike the criticisms of the Beatles that were issued throughout their reign as pop icons.

No icon is without its iconoclasts—you cannot have one without the other. They are the negative image of the icon and their attacks on the icon help to define it, many times help to fuel its power, and probably tell us as much about the icon as those who are its devotees. During the sixties these iconoclasts (who would, no doubt, become quite heated at being so labelled) were by and large represented by what was then known as the Establishment. These Establishment/iconoclasts decried the early Beatles in unison, viewing them as shallow popular artists bent on making money or as long-haired corrupters of youth. Then as the Beatles' music grew more complex, the Establishment splintered. Liberal intellectuals suddenly began embracing the Beatles, proclaiming their profundity in such journals as *The Partisan Review*. College campuses were full of professors lecturing about the musical and cultural significance of the latest Beatles album. Looking back on it one can see that this splintering of the Establishment presaged the deeper split which was to break out openly in 1968. Suddenly the Blue Meanies became real— Blue Meanies being the name given the the Chicago cops by protestors at the Democratic Convention.

The Blue Meanies becoming real marked the beginning of the end for the Beatles. In the heated conflicts of the late sixties and early seventies their music became middle-of-the-road. The *White Album* is a good example of the Beatles' inability to cope with the new times. It never presents a consistent unified whole as *Pepper* did. Jann Wenner reviewing the album at the time prophetically remarked that the album seemed the work of four individuals rather than a group. So like the rest of us in those times, the Beatles fragmented.

Ironically it was the love of the intellectuals which helped to kill the Beatles. Even though they were embraced by only part of the Establishment, that embrace was a slow strangle-hold which eventually would kill them. Hearing their professors lecture about the Beatles, the students, who had been the largest group of devotees of the pop idols, began to wonder about the quartet. This is because there is perhaps no surer kiss of death in the pop music business than for a performer to be embraced by the Establishment—to be analyzed, lectured on and written about. I can remember my own sickness on seeing Poirier's article "Learning from the Beatles"—if the Beatles could be learned from like a book, if professors could write papers about them, then their music had no power.

In pop music above all, power, especially a power that had the magic of the Beatles, was not something that could or should be discussed logically. Like the devotees of medieval religious icons, devotees of contemporary pop icons relate to the power and the magic of their idols. The ultimate paradox of the pop idol is that in this business of packaging and selling music as if it were a car or deodorant, the pop idol must have that indefinable something that cannot be lectured about.

There must be what Erich Neumann in *Art and the Creative Unconscious* called a numinous quality in the pop icon. Neumann speaks of this quality throughout his book as being that transcendent, other-worldly element that all great art and artists possess.

> The need of his times works inside the artist without his wanting it, seeing it, or understanding its true significance. In this sense he is closer to the seer, the prophet, the mystic. And it is precisely when he does not represent the existing canon but transforms and overturns it that his function rises to the level of the sacral, for he then gives utterance to the authentic and direct revelation of the numinosum.[4]

Neumann borrowed the term numinous from the theologian Rudolf Otto who coined it to describe the essence of the religious experience. Otto's book, *The Idea of the Holy* is a lengthy attempt to outline the elements of the numinous experience, yet from the beginning he knew he was trying to articulate the inarticulatable. It was for him an attempt to describe a deep emotional and intellectual experience which went beyond our individual consciousnesses.[5]

This numinous quality which Neumann found in great art and Otto found in religion, Franz Neumann found in the charismatic leader.6 The quality possessed by the pop icons is certainly quite similar to that possessed by charismatic religious and political—leaders figures as opposite and yet the same as Christ and Hitler—and by Erich Neumann's great artist figure of Leonardo Da Vinci.

That pop icons possess this numinous quality can be seen in looking at a figure like James Dean. As David Dalton describes Dean in his book *James Dean: The Mutant King,* Dean "like Gatsby . . . 'sprang from his Platonic conception of himself' and in this form carried his incorruptible dream through the movies and into our lives, . . . What happened to Jimmy became a record of what was happening to America."7 Dean was a mutant and "the mutant must arise to make transition from the old organism to the new, . . . Mutant derives its meaning from the same root as myth and James Dean became a myth through his mutations, a mystery we will never completely comprehend."8

It is interesting that Dean—a pop idol—should possess qualities that have been associated with charismatic leaders because Max Weber's original use of charisma—and Weber was the one who gave the term its contemporary context— was to describe leaders whose power went beyond bureaucratic structures in an irrational way. As Weber saw him the charismatic leader was one who was opposed to the rational rules and normal routines of a bureaucratic society. "In contrast to any kind of bureaucratic organization of offices the charismatic structure knows nothing of a form or of an ordered procedure of appointment or dismissal. . . . The charismatic leader gains and maintains authority solely by proving his strength in life."9

Like Weber's political charismatic leader who functions against and beyond bureaucratic society, so our popular icons function against and beyond popular norms. Like James Dean, the Beatles were as much a revolutionary force as any charismatic leader and their effect was a profound one which changed our cultural as well as our musical perceptions. Despite the efforts of people like Otto, Weber and the two Neumanns, we still only dimly understand the phenomenon of charismatic individuals like Dean and know even less about the numinous quality they possess. In the realm of popular culture it is this numinous quality which above all separates the great popular artist—the pop icon—from the run-of-the-mill. Elvis Presley had it. Bessie Smith had it. Certainly Louis Armstrong had it. The Beatles had it. While some people believe we can describe much of popular art as formula—taking the lead from John Cawelti's brilliant essays and his book *The Six-Gun Mystique*—it is the numinous quality in these popular artists which resists formulation and makes popular art so interesting. For Cawelti, "formula stories . . . are structures of narrative conventions which carry out a variety of cultural functions in a unified way. We can best define these formulas as principles for the selection of certain plots, characters, and settings which possess in addition to their basic narrative structure the dimensions of ritual, game, and dream that have been synthesized into the particular patterns of plot, character and setting which have become associated with the formula."[10] Understanding the formula will to some extent help us understand those who go beyond formula. The concept does not, however, help us understand the numinous quality of our pop idols. Formula tells us not what a popular artist's power is but what it is not. If all popular music, for instance, were mere formula then the record companies could predictably package one string of hits after another. They do this often enough, that's for sure; but every once in awhile someone comes along who creates that special magic. Then we enter the realm of the numinous and they enter the Valhalla of pop iconography.

In that realm of the numinous, performer and audience do not need words to describe their mutual sharing of magic—as the behavior of the Beatles' concert goers shows so well. The attraction shared is not unlike that which one finds in charismatic leaders and their movements and mass rallies. The numinous performer and the charismatic leader have more in common than most of us care to admit. Yet if we could understand more of the nature of this quality in pop idols we might also come to a greater understanding of the power of a Hitler.

Looking back on the Beatles' reign as pop heroes, I believe

that a great deal of their magic came from their talent as comedians. In fact they may well have been the greatest comedians since Chaplin. (In light of my previous comments about the numinous qualities of pop stars and charismatic leaders there is that curious relationship between Chaplin and Hitler—Hitler looked like Chaplin, Chaplin parodied Hitler in *The Great Dictator*.) Like Chaplin they were masters of timing and mimicry. There is even a parallel in their work —the early shorts, Chaplin's film *The Circus* and *Sgt. Pepper*, the *White Album* and *Modern Times*. (I have always thought of the *White Album* as a time capsule—a collection of observations about the world at that time). Like Chaplin, the Beatles had a vision behind their work—an affirmation of the humanity of us all, a belief in freedom in its fullest sense and above all a spirit of fun. Like Chaplin's, the Beatles' vision sometimes slipped into sentimentality—in fact the same kind of winning sentimentality that Chaplin had. The audiences who left *Yellow Submarine* singing "All You Need Is Love" were not unlike the audiences who left *Modern Times* humming "Smile".

In the tradition of Chaplin and other truly great popular artists the Beatles were powerful because they were at once so different and yet so much like all of us. (Historians have speculated that this was also Hitler's great appeal.) Just as we all could see something of ourselves in Chaplin's little tramp, so the collective individuality of the Beatles fits those pop stereotypes that are deeply ingrained in all of us: Ringo, the folksy "good ole boy", Paul, the teenage heart throb; John, the irreverent whippersnapper; George, the quiet intellectual who as some put it must be "deep". Each of them said things people wanted to say but couldn't. They put down all the pretensions of modern life. Chaplin's famous kick in the pants—the thing we all wanted to do to some pompous personage—was as much as the basis of the Beatles' humor as it was Chaplin's. When their own pretensions were getting a bit thick, the Beatles were not above poking fun at themselves just as Chaplin could do so well.

Coupled with their collective identities, the Beatles brought with them a great sense of timing. As with Chaplin the essence of their timing was the use of the unexpected. Certainly one of the most remarkable things about the Beatles' icon was how it varied.

The phrase that so many people uttered back then—"growing up with the Beatles"—was not an idle phrase, for perhaps unique among pop icons the Beatles ranged across all facets of twentieth-century music and created for us an amazing stew full of heady ingredients. They were constantly surprising us with their inventiveness. If Cawelti is right about the essence of popular art being convention and given in extreme cases the rote repeating of the same patterns, then the Beatles were superb—in the sense of being above—popular art, for they took the conventions, mixed them in that fabulous stew of theirs and produced works that turned the conventions back on themselves or went beyond them. Space, time, language, musical styles were mixed so freely they became irrelevant. Andre Bazin once said the essence of Chaplin's comedy lay in his irreverent use of objects—remember the immortal scene of Chaplin eating his shoe in *The Gold Rush*? So the essence of the Beatles' music was their irreverent use of the conventions of popular music. Chaplin eating his shoe left one laughing and crying at the same time, the same feeling one gets from songs like "Happiness is a Warm Gun" or "Maxwell's Silver Hammer." "Maxwell's Silver Hammer" is the food-feeding machine gone mad in *Modern Times* or in the same film the crazy Charlie tightening the buttons on a woman's dress with his wrenches.

As Chaplin helped us get through the twenties and thirties so the Beatles helped us get through the sixties. The sixties—two decades compressed into one—first the wild free times then the times of social upheaval. In the end both were superseded by evil not even their comedy could exorcise, (Spencer Bennett in an article "Christ, Icons and Mass Media" pointed to the Beatles' role of exorcism: "They have been molded as exorcisers of society by media just as Jesus was given stature by the Church as healer in iconographic form."[11]). Chaplin submerged by Hitler and the American McCarthyite fascists, the Beatles by Nixon, their song "Revolution" seeming a tame message after the deaths at Kent State. Black comedy became the style. Whimpy Mick Jagger singing "Street Fighting Man" seems a bit silly now but it was all the rage then as thousands of middle-class white college students who had never been closer to the streets or a fight than the nearest TV set donned fatique jackets and Chairman Mao caps and exclusive dress shops sold cartridge belts to debutantes all bent on bringing about revolution. Such earnest figures, whether they be pseudo-revolutionaries, the ad men and lawyers who surrounded Nixon, or the stormtroopers and assorted deviants who surrounded Hitler are beyond comedy. (My father who escaped from Germany in the thirties said he thought *The Great Dictator* wasn't really that funny at the time, because Hitler couldn't be parodied.) You can laugh at cartoon Blue Meanies but the real ones are more deadly and not so humorous.

In considering the demise of the Beatles it is pertinent to remember that icons are above all objects. They can be plain and everyday or beautiful and unusual in their own right, but still they are only objects. These plain everyday objects do not become icons until we endow them with those other-worldly qualities that we ourselves find necessary to give them. The qualities we choose and the reasons we choose them are as varied as all the vagaries of human nature.

So it was with four plain lads from Liverpool, each—as John Lennon put it—an individual in his rite. Collectively they became the Beatles and we made a cultural icon of them. For awhile they threatened to outshine even the most sacred of the old icons—remember when it was said the Beatles are bigger than Christ? The Beatles made the remark themselves at a press conference. To some it was blasphemous while to others it was a part of a press conference put-on, which stars like Dylan cultivated and whose precursors were the conferences given by idols like James Dean and Chaplin. The remark, though, was a bit more complex and profound than that. It illuminated the secular, popular nature of our society in a sudden dramatic way which hundreds of scholarly and not-so-scholarly articles could scarcely duplicate. In another way it eluded to the numinous quality the Beatles radiated for they did seem to possess something given to them by contact with what Rudolf Otto called "mysterium tremendum." This relationship with the other worldly is something many would dismiss as sheer crap, but David

Dalton was perhaps closer to the truth than he realized when he spoke of James Dean as a modern Osiris: "It is through our eyes that we have taken Jimmy into ourselves, and he remains there magically present like Osiris, god of regeneration."[12]

Perhaps if we are to search for formula and conventions in figures like Dean and the Beatles we would do well to look at religious and charismatic archetypes. Dalton's brilliant insight could open the door to a whole area of cultural investigation which would serve to begin to illuminate the numinous side of our psyches: a revival of Otto's attempt on a secular level. As a beginning of such an attempt maybe we should differentiate between popular, political and religious charisma. It also might be more useful to refer to all these figures as charismatic icons to differentiate them from Fishwick's objective icons. Unlike those medieval icons which were paintings and objects, the Beatles were four living human beings. Ultimately they could not live as a collective idea and once again became mere mortals. Unlike Jimi Hendrix, Jim Morrison, Janis Joplin, and a host of burned out blues musicians, they at least were able to live with their humanity. That they are now less than perfect is not without its satisfaction.

In this light I wonder why so many of our charismatic icons die such untimely deaths. Even Hemingway—at once the strongest and the most vulnerable—succumbed. Those that do not die untimely deaths become sickening parodies of themselves like Elvis had become or like Mick Jagger is well on his way to becoming. The easy answer is that they could not live up to their own hype. No doubt there is a great deal of truth to that but it is still too simple. The fate of the human beings we choose to elevate to the status of charismatic icons reminds me more of the archetypal ritual Sir James Frazier described in his study *The Golden Bough*. In Frazier's story there was a ritual slaying of the old king by a newer and younger one. Reading Frazier's story one's mind conjures visions of two men in jaguar skins, bedecked with jewelry and gold fighting to the death under the ritual tree. Cultures like to create their charismatic icons, endow them with magic and mystery (perhaps send them on tour), and then find they must slay them because they're so heavy. The Beatles realized this as much as anyone when they wrote "Sexy Sadie" or "When I'm Sixty-Four"—and still they were caught in the trap. Luckily today's pop idols are not destroyed in ritual fights to the death, although the game and the results can be as deadly. All charismatic idols—like Frazier's old king—know their time is limited. The determination of that time is based on popular mood and on the appearance of a new challenger. When the inevitable happens their popular identity will be destroyed. If they become too wrapped up in that popular identity then death can become quite literal. So they burn the candle at both ends with sometimes fatal consequences. Jim Morrison's "Light My Fire" with that awful line "and our love becomes a funeral pyre" summarized the relationship between the pop star/icon and the audience.

NOTES

[1] Marshall Fiswick and Ray Browne eds., *Icons of Popular Culture*, (Bowling Green, Popular Press, 1970), p. 1.

[2] *Ibid.*, p. 4.

[3] Jann Wenner, *Lennon Remembers*, N.Y., 1971, p. 84.

[4] Erich Neumann, *Art and the Creative Unconscious* (N.Y.; 1966), p. 97.

[5] Rudolf Otto, *The Idea of the Holy* (N.Y.: 1958).

[6] Franz Neumann, *Behemoth: The Structure and Practice of National Socialism*, (N.Y.: 1966).

[7] David Dalton, *James Dean: The Mutant King*, (N.Y.: 1975) p. 375.

[8] *Ibid.*, pp. 377 & 379.

[9] Max Weber, *On Charisma and Institution Building*, Chicago 1968, S.N. Eisenstadt ed., pp. 19-20, 22.

[10] John Cawelti, "The Concept of Formula in the Study of Popular Culture," *Journal of Popular Culture* III:3, Winter, 1969, p. 390.

[11] *Icons of Popular Culture*, p. 10.

[12] Dalton, p. 373. A lengthy comparison of Dean and Osiris appears on pp. 370-373. Dalton's book is full of intuitive insights of this sort and is highly recommended to anyone studying the power of popular charisma.

Serpent Handling as Sacrament

Mary Lee Daugherty

"A serpent did beguile me."
Eve

Serpents have always beguiled us—not only since, but probably even before Eve.[1] In some parts of America (my research centers on West Virginia) they have become, in the true sense of the word, iconic. Serpent handlers know that Mark himself wrote, "They shall take up serpents"; and take them up they do. For thousands of contemporary Americans, it is considered the ultimate act of faith to reach out and take up the serpent when one is filled with the Holy Ghost. Thus the serpent has become an Old Testament icon, terrible in its wrath but somehow purifying in the sacrament. Old timers here in the mountains, before the days of modern medicine, could only explain that those who were tested and lived were somehow chosen by God's special mercy and favor.

Today serpent-handlers are experiencing, as are other West Virginians, great economic improvement. Many now live in expensive mobile homes that dot the mountain country side. They purchase and own brand new cars and modern appliances. Many of the men now earn from twelve to eighteen thousand dollars a year, working in the revitalized mining industry. Most of the young people are now going to and graduating from high school. I know of one young man with two years of college who is very active in his church. He handles serpents and is looked upon as the one who will take over the pastor's position sometime in the future. What the effect of middle-class prosperity and higher education will be among serpent-handlers remains to be seen. It may be another generation before the effects can be adequately determined.

I

Knowing serpent-handlers to be biblical literalists, one might surmise that they, like other sects, have picked a certain passage of Scripture and built a whole ritual around a few cryptic verses. While this is true, I am persuaded, after years of observation, that serpent-handling holds for them

the significance of a sacrament. It is like an icon representing life and death. They do not worship the serpent but it is filled with deep meaning.

Tapestry paintings of the Lord's Supper hang in most of their churches. Leonardo da Vinci's *Last Supper* is one picture I have seen over and over again in their churches and in their homes. But in West Virginia, the serpent-handlers whom I know personally do not celebrate the Lord's Supper in their worship services. It is my observation and hypothesis that the ritual of serpent-handling is their way of celebrating life, death, and resurrection. Time and again they prove to themselves that Jesus has the power to deliver them from death here and now.

Another clue to the sacramental nature of lifting up the serpents as the symbol of victory is to be observed at their funerals. At the request of the family of one who has died of snake bite, serpents may be handled at a funeral. Even as a Catholic priest may lift up the host at a mass for the dead, indicating belief that in the life and death of Jesus there is victory over death, so the serpent-handlers, I believe, lift up the serpent. Of course, none of this is formalized, for all is very spontaneous. But I am convinced that they celebrate their belief that "in the name of Jesus" there is power over death, and this is what the serpent-handling ritual has proved to them over and over again. This is why I believe they will not give up this ritual because it is at the center of their Christian faith, and in West Virgina, unlike all the other States, it is not illegal.

Many handlers have been bitten numerous times, but, contrary to popular belief, few have died. Their continued life, and their sometimes deformed hands, bear witness to the fact that Jesus still has power over illness and death. Even those who have not been bitten know many who have, and the living witness is ever present in the lives of their friends. If one of the members should die, it is believed that God allowed it to happen to remind the living that the risk they take is totally real. Never have I heard any one of them say that a brother or sister who died lacked faith.

The cultural isolation of these people is still very real. Few have traveled more than a few miles from home. Little more than the Bible is ever read. Television is frowned upon; movies are seldom attended. The Bible is communicated primarily through oral tradition in the church or read at home. There is little awareness of other world religions. Even contacts with Roman Catholics and Jews are rare. Most of their lives revolve around the local church where they gather for meetings two or three times a week.

When one sees the people handling serpents in their services, the Garden of Eden story immediately comes to mind. In the Genesis story, the serpent represents evil that tempts Adam and Eve and must be conquered by their descendants. But the serpent means something far different to West Virginia mountain people; it means life over death. There is never any attempt to kill the snake in Appalachian serpent-handling services. Practitioners seldom kill snakes even in the out of doors. They let them go at the end of the summer months so that they may return to their natural environment to hibernate for the winter. They catch different snakes each spring to use in their worship services. When you ask them why, they tell you quite simply that they do not want to make any of God's creatures suffer. The serpent is always handled with both love and fear in their services, but it is never harmed or killed. Handlers may be killed from bites, but they will not kill the snake. Neither do they force the handling of serpents on any who do not wish to do so.

The snake is seldom handled in private, but usually in the community of believers during a church service. Members may encourage each other to take the risk, symbolically taking on life and testing faith. Their willingness to die for their beliefs gives to their lives a vitality of faith. Handlers usually refuse medicine or hospital treatment for snake bite. But they do go to the hospital for other illness or if surgery is needed. In the past, they usually refused welfare. They revere and care for their elderly who have usually survived numerous snake bites. Each time they handle the serpents they struggle with life once more and survive again the forces that traditionally oppressed mountain people. The poverty, the unemployment, the yawning strip mines, death in the deep mines have all been harsh, uncontrollable forces for simple people. The handling of serpents is their way of confronting and coping with their very real fears about life and the harshness of reality as experienced in the mountains in years gone by and, for many, even today.

Yet in the face of all this, they seek to live in harmony with nature, not to destroy it or any of its creatures, even the deadly serpent. It is only with the Holy Ghost, however, that they find the sustenance to survive. They live close to the earth, surrounded by woods, streams, and sky. Most live in communities of only a few hundred people or less.

II

The deep longing for holiness of these Appalachian people stands out in bold relief in the serpent-handling ritual of worship. The search for holiness is dramatized in their willingness to suffer terrible pain from snake bite, or even death itself, to get the feeling of God in their lives. The support of their fellow Christians is still with them. In their experience, God may not come if you don't really pray or ask only once. The person in the group who has been bitten most often and who has suffered the most pain or sickness is usually the leader. While it is the Holy Ghost who gives the power, those who have survived snake bite do get recognition and praise for their courage and their faith from the group. They have learned to cope with their anxieties by calling upon the name of Jesus and the power which he freely offers. Support is given to each member through the laying on of hands in healing ceremonies, through group prayers, and through verbal affirmations, such as: 'Help her Jesus,'' "Bless him, Lord,'' "That's right, Lord.'' Through group support, anxiety about life is relieved. They feel ennobled as God becomes manifest in their midst.

The person of the Holy Ghost (they prefer this to Holy Spirit), enables them not only to pick up serpents, but to speak in tongues, to preach, to testify, to cure diseases, to cast out demons, and even to drink strychnine and lye, or to use fire on their skin when the snakes are in hibernation during the winter months. In these dramatic ways, the mountain folk pursue holiness above all else. They find through their faith both meaning and encouragement. Psychological tests indicate that in many ways they are more emotionally healthy than members of mainline Protestant churches.

Having internalized my own feelings of insecurity and worthlessness for many years because I was "no 'count" having been born from poor white trash on one side of my family, I have in my own being a deep appreciation and understanding of the need of these people to ask God for miracles accompanied with spectacular demonstrations. Thus they are assured of their own worth, even if only to God. They have never gotten this message from the outside world. They know they have been, and many still are, the undesirable poor, the uneducated mountain folk, locked into their little pockets of poverty in a rough, hostile land. So the Holy Ghost is the great equalizer in the church meeting. One's age, sex, years of schooling are all of less value. Being filled with the Holy Ghost is the only credential one needs in this unique society.

III

The Holy Ghost creates a mood of openness and spontaneity in the serpent-handling service that is beautiful to behold. Even though there is not much freedom in the personal lives of these people, there is a sense of power in their church lives. Their religion does seem to heal them inwardly of aches and pains and in many instances even of major illnesses. One often sees expressions of dependence as men and women fall down before the picture of Jesus, calling aloud over and over again, "Jesus . . . Jesus . . . Jesus . . ." The simple carpenter of Nazareth is obviously a person with whom mountain people can identify. Jesus worked with his hands, and so do they; Jesus was essentially, by our standards, uneducated, and so are they; Jesus came from a small place, he lived much of his life out of doors, he went fishing, he suffered and was finally done in by the "power structure," and so have they been in the past and often are today.

As I think about the mountain women as they fall down before the picture of Jesus, I wonder what he means to them. Here is a simple man who treated women with great love and tenderness. In this sense, he is unlike some of the men they must live with. Jesus healed the bodies of women, taught them the Bible, never told jokes about their bodies, and even forgave them their sexual sins. In the mountains, adultery is usually punished with beatings. Maybe it should not surprise us that in a State where the strip miners have raped the earth that the rape of the people has also taken place, and the rape of women is often deeply felt and experienced. Things are now changing, and for this we can be grateful.

IV

In the serpent-handlers' churches, the Bible usually remained closed on the pulpit. Since most older members cannot read very well and have usually felt shy about their meager education, they did not read the Bible aloud in public, especially if some more educated people were present. They obviously read the Bible at home, but most remember it from stories they have heard. The Bible is the final authority for everything, even the picking up of serpents and the drinking of poison. It is all literally true, but the New Testament is read more often than the Old Testament.

In former years, their churches have given these poor and powerless people the arena in which they could act out their frustrations and powerless feelings. For a short time, while in church, they could experience being powerful when filled with the Holy Ghost. Frustrated by all the things in the outside world that they could not change, frustrated by the way the powerful people of the world were running things, they could nevertheless run their own show in their own churches. So they gathered three or four times a week, in their modest church buildings, and they stayed for three to five hours for each service. On these occasions, they can feel important, loved, and powerful. They can experience God directly.

I am always struck by the healing love that emerges at the end of each service when they all seem to love each other, embrace each other, and give each other the holy kiss. They are free from restrictions and conventions to love everyone. Sometimes I have the feeling that I get a glimmer of what the Kingdom of God will be like as we kiss each other, old and young, with or without teeth, rich and poor, educated and uneducated, male and female. So I have learned much and have been loved in turn by the serpent-handlers of West Virginia. As they leave the church and go back to their daily work, all the frustrations of the real world return, but they know they can meet again tomorrow night or in a few days. So they have faith, hope, and love, but the greatest message they have given to me is their love.

V

There are thousands of small Holiness churches in the rural areas of West Virginia. While four-fifths of all Protestants are members of mainstream denominations, no one knows just how many attend Holiness churches. Membership records are not considered important to these people, and although I personally know of about twenty-five serpent-handling churches, there may be others, for those in one church often do not know those in another. They laugh and make jokes about churches that give you a piece of paper as you enter the door, telling you when to pray and what to sing. They find it difficult to believe that you can "order around" the worship of the Holy Ghost on a piece of paper.

Those who make up the membership of the serpent-handling churches are often former members of other Holiness churches or are former Baptists or Methodists. In the Holiness churches, the attainment of personal holiness and being filled with the Spirit is the purpose and goal of life. Members view the secular world as evil and beyond hope. Hence they do not take part in any community activities or social programs.

Fifty-four percent of all persons in the state of West Virginia still live in communities of 1,000 people or less. Freedom of worship is the heritage of the Scotch-Irish, who settled these mountains 200 years ago. In more recent times, among Holiness groups there were no trained ministers. So oral tradition, spontaneous worship, and shared leadership are important.

Holiness church members live by a very strict personal code of morality. A large sign in the church at Jolo, W. Va., indicates that dresses must be worn below the knees, arms must be covered, no lipstick or jewelry is to be worn. No smoking, drinking, or other worldly pleasures are to be indulged in by "true believers." Some women do not cut their hair, others do not even buy chewing gum or soft drinks. For years, in the mountains, people have practiced divine healing, since medical facilities are scarce. Four counties in West Virginia still do not have a doctor, nurse, clinic, dentist, or ambulance service.

In a typical serpent-handling church service, the "true believers" usually sit on the platform of the church together. They are the members who have demonstrated that they have received the Holy Ghost. This is known to them and to others because they have manifested certain physical signs in their own bodies. If they have been bitten by snakes, as many have, and have not died, they have proved that they have the Holy Ghost. And those who have been bitten many times, and survived, are the "real saints." The "true believers" also demonstrate that they have the Holy Ghost by speaking in tongues, by the jerking of their bodies, and by their various trance-like states. They may dance for long periods of time or fall on the floor without being hurt. They may drink the "salvation cocktail," a mixture of strychnine or lye and water. They may also speak in tongues or in ecstatic utterances. Usually this is an utterance between themselves and God. But sometimes members seek to interpret the language of tongues. They lay their hands upon each other to heal hurts or even serious illnesses such as cancer. They sometimes pass their hands through fire. I have witnessed this activity and no burn effects are visible, even though a hand may remain in the flame for some time. A few years ago, they picked up hot coals from the pot bellied stoves and yet were not burned. They apparently can block out pain totally, when in a trance or deep into the Spirit of God.

One woman who attended church at Scrabble Creek, W. Va., experienced, on two occasions, the stigmata as blood came out of her hands, feet, side and forehead. This was witnessed by all present in the church. When asked about this startling experience, she said that she had prayed that God would allow people to see through her body how much Jesus had suffered for them by his death and resurrection.

A local church in the rural areas may be known as "Brother So and So's" or "Sister So and So's" church to those who live nearby, but the sign over the door will usually indicate that the church belongs to Jesus. Such names as "The Jesus Church," "The Jesus Only Church," "The Jesus Saves Church," and "The Lord Jesus Christ's Church" are all common names. The churches do not belong to any denomination, and they have no written doctrines or creeds. The order of the service is spontaneous and different every night. Everyone is welcome and people travel around to each

other's churches, bringing with them their musical instruments, snakes, fire equipment, poison mixtures, and other gifts.

Often the service begins with singing which may last thirty to forty-five minutes. Next, they may all pray out loud to-

gether for the Holy Ghost to fall upon them during the service. Singing, testifying, and preaching by anyone who feels

God's spirit may follow. Serpents then will be handled while others are singing. It is possible that serpents will be handled two or three times in one service, but usually it is only once. Serpents are only handled when they feel God's spirit within them. After dancing ecstatically, a brother or sister will open the box and pull out a serpent. Others will follow if there are other snakes available. If only one or two serpents are present, then they may be passed around from believer to believer. Sometimes a circle may be made and the snakes passed. I have only once seen them throw snakes to each other. Children are kept far away.

There is much calling on the name of Jesus while the serpents are being handled, and once the icon has been handled, there is a great prayer of rejoicing and often a dance of thanksgiving that no one was hurt. If someone is bitten, there is prayer for his or her healing and great care is taken. If the person becomes too ill to stay in the church, he or she may be taken home and believers will pray for the person for days, if necessary. Even if the person does not die, and usually he or she doesn't, the person is usually very sick. Vomiting of blood and swelling are very painful. Some persons in the churches have lost the use of a finger or suffered some other deformity. But in many years of serpent-handling, I believe there are only about twenty recorded deaths.

VII

The iconic symbolism of the serpent is found in almost all cultures and religions, everywhere, and in all ages. It suggests the ambiguity of good and evil, sickness and health, life and death, mortality and immortality, chaos and wisdom. Because the serpent lives in the ground but is often found in trees, it conveys the notion of transcendence, a creature that lives between earth and heaven. And because it sheds its skin, it seems to know the secret of eternal life.

In the Bible, the serpent is most obviously associated with the Adam and Eve temptation (Gen. 3:1-13), but we also read of the sticks that Moses and Aaron turned into snakes (Ex. 7:8-10), and of Moses' bronze serpent standard (Num. 21:6-9). The two entwined snakes in the ancient figure of the caduceus, symbolizing sickness and health, has been widely adopted as the emblem of the medical profession. And sometimes in early Christian art, the crucifixion is represented with a serpent wound around the cross or lying at the foot of the cross (cf. Joh 3:14). Here again good and evil, life over death, are symbolized.

In early liturgical art, John the Evangelist was often identified with a chalice from which a serpent was departing, a reference to the legend that when he was forced to drink poison, it was drained away in the snake. Among the early Gnostics, there was a group known as Ophites who were said to worship the serpent because it brought "knowledge" to Adam and Eve and so to all humanity. They were said to free a serpent from a box and that it then entwined itself around the bread and wine of the Eucharist.

But, of course, this ancient history and symbolic lore are unknown to the mountain serpent-handlers of West Virginia, and even if they were told, they probably would not be in-

terested. Their own tradition is rooted in their literal acceptance of what they regard as Jesus' commandment at the conclusion of Mark's Gospel. The problems of biblical textual criticism, relating to the fact that these verses on which they depend are not found in the best manuscript evidence, does not bother them. Their Bible is the English King James Version, and they know through their own experience that their faith in the healing and saving power of Jesus has been tested and proven without question. In any case, their ritual is unique in church history.

What the future holds for the serpent-handlers, no one can tell. Although the young people have tended to stay in their local communities, the temptation in the past to move out and away to find work has been very great. Now many of the young people are returning home as the mining industry offers new, high-paying jobs. And a new era of relative economic prosperity is emerging as the energy problem makes coal-mining important for the whole Appalachian area. In the meantime, serpent-handling for many mountian people remains a Jesus-commanded act whereby physical signs communicate spiritual reality.

NOTES

*This article appeared, in a somewhat different form, in THEOLOGY TODAY, XXXIII, no. 3, October 1976. Reprinted by permission.
[1]*Theology Today* Vol. XXXIII Oct. 1976, Princeton N.J.

The Little Red Schoolhouse

Fred E. H. Schroeder

Through icons, we see beyond material reality. Therefore, whenever someone reports seeing more than what is "really there," we may reasonably search for an icon. To illustrate this statement, let us step back in time to May 7, 1945, "VE Day." The radios thrilled with the news of the surrender of Germany to the Allies, and even the normally reserved and precise New York *Times* broke into large type to tell of the Nazi capitulation at "the little red schoolhouse that is the headquarters of General Dwight D. Eisenhower." It wasn't actually a little red schoolhouse, not by any definition. The building in which the surrender documents were signed was the technical college of Rheims, France—built of red brick, it is true, but three stories high, with extensive wings that made for a building about half a city block in length. The icon value to Americans in reporting this to be a "little red school-house" was clear, and might be characterized in these terms: the Nazi warlords—professionals and aristocrats—had been humbled on American grounds, brought to heel within a symbol of equality, the simple one-room schoolhouse where people are not graded and isolated from one another, but where one simple teacher, neither professor nor college graduate, inculcates young Americans in homegrown values of independence, self-reliance, democracy and simple rural virtues.

This illustration of the power of an icon from VE Day is only a more emphatic, more public characterization of the typical popular attitude about the little red schoolhouse. As with all icons, however, the mythic significance of the physical thing is a blending of fact and fancy. In the case of the schoolhouse, the blending applies to the thing itself, for, as a matter of fact, relatively few American schoolhouses were red. Thus, in an affectionate memoir entitled *Country Schoolhouse,* Elsye Davey Larson wrote in 1958 of her school in southern Minnesota: "This was a typical country schoolhouse of that era [1892], not the little red schoolhouse. They may have existed in the minds of poets. The nearest to the poetical building I have ever seen was one of reddish yellow brick along the highway up in central Minnesota. I first saw it more than forty years ago and at that time, the windows were boarded up just as it stands today." Even when Frank Lloyd Wright (who once had written that every Wisconsin farmer should be required by law to paint his barn red) designed a rural schoolhouse in 1957 for his neighboring valley, he replaced the old white one-room school with a two-room building of gray concrete blocks. Where then, did the popular image of the red schoolhouse begin?

It began in reality, we can presume. There *were* red schoolhouses. But the color probably became fixed in the popular mind in poets' and artists' renderings. As to poetry, one example is a folk song that I learned from Georgia schoolfriends in 1945:

(Sing) In the little red schoolhouse, with my book and slate;
    In the little red schoolhouse, where I was often late.
        Could hardly wait for the four o'clock bell,
        And when it rang we ran like . . .
            O, gee,
            Just to be,
      In the little red schoolhouse.
(Spoken) Johnny hit the teacher with an awful smack.
        She turned around, said, "Who did that?"
        Pretty little Percy in the very first row
        Held up his hand, said, "Teacher, I know."
(Repeat *ad infinitum*)

Undoubtedly other folklore examples can be found, but literary instances do not surface in any of the standard reference sources. *Granger's Index to Poetry* lists an anonymous "Little *Brown* Schoolhouse," and although one suspects that such popular poets of nostalgia as Eugene Field, James Whitcomb Riley, and Edgar Guest would all have celebrated the little red schoolhouse, this appears not to have been the case, at least in their well-known poems. The best known schoolhouse poem is John Greenleaf Whittier's "In School Days." Despite the judgment of Matthew Arnold that it is "one of the most perfect poems that must live," it has an almost carnival history of mishap and misquotation. Most frequently the first stanza is rendered as we find it in Whittier's 1869 manuscript:

> Still sits the school-house by the road,
> A ragged beggar sunning;
> Around it still the sumachs grow,
> And blackberry-vines are running . . .

but in many editions it appears:

> Still sits the school-house by the road,
> A ragged beggar sleeping;
> Around it still the sumachs grow,
> And blackberry-vines are creeping . . .

while Robert Penn Warren, in 1971, shows the third line as:

> And it still the sumachs grow . . . .

The actual school building of which Whittier was writing had a similar history. Abandoned in 1815 in anticipation of a new building, it was allowed to fall into disrepair. Almost sixty years later a new school was at last erected, and somewhat later the now famous old schoolhouse was to be moved to another site. Unfortunately, one of the wheels on which it was being transported broke, and so once more the ragged beggar was abandoned, this time in the middle of the road—until some schoolboys burned it down. Whether or not it had ever been painted red is not recorded; certainly Whittier's word would have to be regarded as suspect, because he was colorblind. But the overall pattern of nostalgia and neglect in the Whittier chronicle is appropriate to the ambivalent attitude Americans have shown toward this popular icon.

It is more likely that a place of origin for the popular image is to be found in paintings of little schoolhouses by Winslow Homer. These provide a good center point for the visual and architectural history of the little red schoolhouse. Two of Winslow Homer's best-loved paintings depict one-room

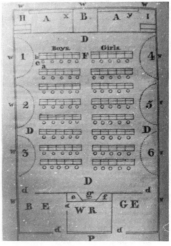

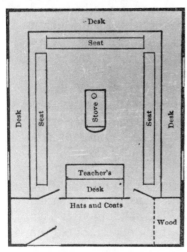

Upper left; Winslow Homer's *Snap the Whip;* upper right, James Johonnot's dilapidated school-house are nearly identical buildings from the same year. Middle left, Homer's *School-house* from about 1870 has the very outdated furniture arrangement shown below. The 1850 fieldstone "Stone Jug" school near Sheboygan, Wisconsin is square and doubtless had the same type of interior arrangement. Lower right, William D. Alcott's 1831 design.

Architect designed buildings. Upper left a Greek Revival Connecticut school by Henry Barnard; upper right; Gothic revival by Charles P. Dwyer; middle row, 1910 Minnesota state plan for a Palladian style is perfectly executed near Sleepy Eye. Lower left, typical 1936 WPA schoolhouse; lower right, Frank Lloyd Wright's rural schoolhouse, 1957.

country schools. One of these paintings, *Snap The Whip,* shows schoolchildren at recess play with a red frame schoolhouse in the background. The other, *The Country School,* is an interior scene showing a young teacher and her dozen pupils during classtime. The atmosphere in both paintings is clear, sunny and warm; the children playing snap the whip at recess are thoroughly happy in their play, while the children inside the schoolroom are fully attentive to their studies. The expression on the face of the attractive young teacher is neutral; she is waiting without impatience while one of the two older boys untangles a problem in the book from which he is reciting.

The two paintings were executed in 1871 and 1872 when Homer's work was still largely rural in topic, serene in mood and warm and sure in technique; yet there is nothing to suggest that the artist had any particularly strong feeling of nostalgia regarding these rural schools. Indeed, the schools that are pictured are probably not part of the artist's life. Very likely the country school was no more than an interesting subject for painting to Winslow Homer, and he probably found it during summer wanderings in western New England or in the Catskills, up-river from his Manhattan studio.

This artistic objectivity of Homer's affords us a useful and rare view into a schoolbuilding design that was out-dated even in 1870, although some of its outmoded architectural characteristics have persisted to this moment. The single room is almost obsolete, but it was commonplace nationwide throughout the 1950s. What is most outmoded in Homer's paintings are the seating and window arrangements which should have shown changes as a result of architectural reforms dating from as early as 1832.

Public concern about the physical design shortcomings of schoolbuildings was widespread in the third decade of the nineteenth century. A prize of twenty dollars was offered for the best essay on school construction in 1831, and with the awarding of the prize to William A. Alcott, we may say that public school architecture and schoolroom design begins. The reforms that Alcott had worked in his own school had been modest enough, starting with the humane placing of backs on the school benches, but his prizewinning *Essay on the Con-*

struction of School-Houses is more comprehensive. The *Essay* is primarily a plea for order and for space. Better order was to be achieved mostly by means of setting desks in neat rows in the middle of the room, but in addition, disorderly distractions were to be eliminated by means of raising window-sills above the eye-level of the pupils. Space provisions included the space under the now elevated windows for "paintings, prints, engravings, maps and charts," space behind the master's desks for books, scientific paraphernalia and a museum, space for each pupil (at least nineteen square feet of floor-space), space between the desks for storing books and slates (though not "the shells of nuts and the cores and stones of fruits . . . accumulated . . . by indolent or vicious pupils"), and, finally, space was provided around the school-building for fresh air, light and recess activities.

The significance of these simple reforms will not escape an elementary-school teacher: they are all designed to make easier the maintenance of comfort, of discipline, of efficient learning. But neither will the significance of these reforms escape modern critics of American education. The reforms are authoritarian in effect, sacrificing individuality for orderliness and convenience. Still, there is no need to romanticize Homer's school and classroom and to deplore the nineteenth-century reforms. *Snap The Whip* and *The Country School* depict the *ideal* of the old, vernacular one-room school. The *norm* was far more likely to reflect the penny-pinching policies of rural school boards. The placement of Homer's red schoolhouse in a lush meadow, for instance, was uncharacteristic. Both Henry Barnard, a mid-nineteenth century educator, and Ellwood P. Cubberly, an early twentieth century authority on rural education attested to that. Schools were usually located on useless land, on hills or in hollows, or close to the concentrations of population. Either way, they were ordinarily placed on small plots hemmed in by roads, tilled fields, swamps, and farmyards. A country school in Vermont, for example, served as one wall to a putrid swine pen, where unwanted calves were thrown to be torn and devoured by the hogs; this gruesome spectacle all in full view of the schoolchildren. Generally the adjoining open fields were used to answer the calls of nature. In 1844, a survey of over 9000 schools in New York State revealed that more than 6000 of them had no privy whatsoever for the pupils or for the teacher. In the classroom, seating was on backless benches, and if desks were provided, they were likely to be no more than unplaned wood counters stretched across the width of the room, making movement around the classroom nearly impossible.

Overcrowding was the pattern, ventilation almost nonexistent. In wintertime, the heating was inadequate or totally absent. There were no cloakrooms to hang and dry wet clothing. Floors were caked with mud and manure. It was common practice to crowd as many as sixty pupils into rooms of the size that Winslow Homer depicts. Overall, the usual district school was a dirty, crowded, fetid carton where school was held because the law required it.

In brief, then, American popular education was at best a disorderly process, and any reforms that might reduce the disorder were to be regarded as desirable. The strongest force of order in the American educational establishment was not even mentioned by Alcott, though it was expressed as a utopian goal in an appendix to Alcott's pamphlet (by William C. Woodbridge). Here it was suggested that in villages and populous neighborhoods children be "classed in a *series of schools, according to their attainments.*" Over the years, this classification into grades has been achieved, and, consequently, over the years, less and less attention has been given to one-room or two-room schools among educators, designers and architects.

There are two design strains in American rural school houses. The one, the vernacular, is typified inside and out by Winslow Homer's paintings of schools. Like the old New England meeting house, these schools were basically square or rectangular frame houses with small-paned windows, and usually with an added bell-tower. Occasionally built of brick, sometimes painted red or left to thriftier natural weathering, the vernacular schoolhouses were most often built like New England churches of white-painted clapboard. In opposition to the vernacular design are the many architecturally designed buildings, which, from Alcott's 1831 Doric facade to Frank Lloyd Wright's 1957 two-room school in the Wyoming Valley of Wisconsin, attempted to bring the rural schoolhouse into the mainstream of whatever was the current style. First came Greek revival, then Gothic revival, then Queen Anne-Romanesque, then Renaissance, then colonial, finally Bauhaus-International. Despite these patterns, the architect-designed plans generally failed in rural schools. One way or another, the vernacular asserted itself. Exemplary schools might be built in the cities of New England, but invariably the scaling down of size along with the necessary paring down of appropriations simplified and obscured the mainstream styles, and, like irrepressible mongrels, the rural school houses continued to assert and reassert their homely design genesis as a house for holding school. The final product was a native American architectural style. This style is functional to a degree, partly as a result of planning and design, but mostly it proved to be functional because of the resiliency of the people within— the jack-of-all-trades teacher and the children, all gristle, not yet bone—who together managed to accommodate their processes and personalities to any schoolroom. A brief look at some important design manuals from Alcott's day to post-World War II can help us to understand the interplay of the vernacular and the "architectural" school building.

William Alcott was a schoolmaster, not an architect, and he drew only floor plans for his schools. However, the second of his two plans indicates a portico with Doric columns, and thus, quite properly for 1831, he envisions a Greek Revival schoolhouse. Another Yankee educator, Henry Barnard, was an architect; that is to say, he designed several school buildings, one possibly while he was a member of the Connecticut state legislature, pressing for educational improvements. This is an attractive little temple, with two columns in the front and two separate entries from the vestibule for the forty girls and boys.

Barnard's *School Architecture* (1838-1848) also includes plans in the very latest style, the carpenter Gothic Revival urged by A. J. Davis and Ithiel Town. Octagonal buildings of all kinds were to become a fad of the 1850s, although earlier octagonal schoolhouses had existed in southeastern counties of Pennsylvania in the second decade of the nineteenth-century, apparently deriving from Dutch church designs. But Davis and Town's design for Barnard's book is cleverly

planned to solve the everpresent problem of ventilation. The
stovepipe rises through the center cupola, but the tower itself has an outer sleeve that can be raised to admit fresh air.
Surrounding this, the cupola is an eight-sided skylight that
admits diffused light at the same time that it thwarts the
children's penchant for staring out of the windows.

In 1856, a handbook of school (and church and parsonage)
designs was published by Charles P. Dwyer, a professional
architect from Buffalo. Dwyer's life is a mystery but he
ought to be remembered for his highly practical *Emigrant
Builder* (1878), which took architecture at its most rudimen-
tary and vernacular, urging log, plank, sod, fieldstone and
rammed earth construction—whatever material was at hand.
But in this earlier book Dwyer had been caught up in the
Gothic enthusiasm of the day. His school design No. 1, a
two-room school, completely divided "with distinct sitting
places for the males and females; and with separate en-
trances", also, has Gothic peaks and spikes, but, Dwyer adds,
"it could, in a thickly timbered locality, be constructed of
hewn logs, and yet, with very little extra cost, be made to
look well."

Unlike Alcott and Barnard, Dwyer was not a schoolmaster,
and his floor plans are typical of many school architects in
their naive impracticality. His two-room design, planned for
"limited localities," would require two teachers, and it has
seats arranged like pews with no possible circulation. His
version of the "octagonal"—a diamond-shape—has the teacher
situated in the center, a disturbingly vulnerable position, as
any middle-school teacher could point out. Two of Dwyer's
plans call for two-story buildings of which the second story
is intended "to have the master (if a married man) live above
the school. It is very obvious that many advantages would
arise from this arrangement," Dwyer argues, "as rent being
saved to the teachers, it would induce competent married
couples to undertake the conduction of male and female de-
partments; and being constantly on the premises, more vigil-
ance and care would, of course be exercised."

All these trends and issues relating to rural school design
are incorporated into the two design books of James Johonnot of New York. Johonnot appears not to have been a

draughtsman, for his design renderings are done by one S. E. Hewes, but neither does he appear to have been a teacher by calling, for he does not write at length about classroom methods. Nonetheless, his books are well-informed. The first, *Country School Houses,* was published in 1859; the second, *School-Houses,* came out a dozen years later, in 1871, the same year that Homer first painted a vernacular school. But in those dozen years between editions, urbanization had made it necessary for Johonnot to add a lengthy appendix on *graded schools.* In addition, public schooling had become a big business. The later edition, *School-Houses,* was published by J. W. Schermerhorn, a dealer in school furnishings and co-owner of the patents to Allen's folding seats, and so Johonnot's book was now bound with Schermerhorn's furniture catalog.

On the matter of vernacular versus revival architecture, Johonnot's words are vigorous but ambigous. America has shown great advances in building design, Johnnot allows, but "the last to feel this progressive impulse were school-houses . . . They are the most unsightly buildings in the district . . . exposed to the depredations of stray cattle and unruly boys. Its style is nondescript, being too small for a barn; too deficient in the elements of just proportion for a dwelling, too lonely and too much neglected for the outbuilding of a farm, and in short, too repulsive in all respects, and exhibiting too many marks of the most parsiminous economy to be anything but a schoolhouse." In the 1871 version an illustration is added to this description. The "repulsive structure" is the same as Winslow Homer's idyllic schoolbuilding!

In the fourth chapter, Johonnot carefully explains the characteristics of the popular Greek and Gothic designs, but he points out that either style must undergo great bastardization to become scaled down to schoolhouse size. The wasteful pretensions of the Greek portico and colonnade are absurd: "Their introduction into schoolhouse architecture was unfortunate, and we trust the time is not far distant when they will fall into disuse." The Gothic style fares little better in Johnnot's words. The decorative variety so necessary to true Gothic is "utterly impracticable."

Notwithstanding the words, S. E. Hewe's accompanying

designs tend toward the Gothic. The cheapest school (Design no. 1) in the 1859 edition has some scroll gingerbread
along the eaves, false hoods over the windows and it is built
with the vertical board-and-batten sheathing so dear to the
hearts of Gothic enthusiasts such as Downing, Dwyer, and
Davis. Stripped of these minimal decorations, we can see that
underneath it is really the "repulsive" vernacular building—
more symmetrical, it is true, and with a greater feeling of
substance deriving from the deeper eaves—but it is the vernacular district schoolhouse nonetheless.

Two things in Johonnot's 1871 *School-Houses* foreshadow
the next period in school design. First, there is an increase in
window-glass area in every building, and second, one of the
largest building designs (No. 11) is in a Renaissance revival
style, with an emphasis on horizontal string courses, and with
symmetrically placed doors and windows with round arches.
Such a "pure" design is rare in schools, and a Renaissance
style is ten to twenty years in advance of the time. This
period in American architecture was more notably marked
by a waning of the Gothic perpendicular and the advent of
rather complicated "aesthetic," Romanesque and "Queen
Anne" styles, with heavy stonework, many gables and a
general massiveness, but without special emphasis on symmetry or balance. These massive structures were to be the
national urban patterns up to World War I, and many
Americans who were born before 1945 have attended school
in one of these buildings.

But all this is idle prattle if we are to speak of rural schools.
How are we to achieve a one-room Romanesque, or a Floren-
tine Palazzo in a cow-pasture, or a Palladian classic with
school windows? The answer is that it can be done, and it
has been done, but in all cases, the stylish motifs are reduced
and simplified by the vernacular axioms. Of these, the rock-
bottom axiom is the human dimension dictated by the range
of the teacher's voice. By 1919, Edward C. Earl, a Washington, D. C. architect, advised on the basis of educators' research that "a teacher should have not more than thirty
pupils . . . the ultimate or emergency limit should be forty."
Further, "a classroom 25 by 32 feet has been found to be
about the practical limit of voice and vision for teacher and

pupils." This size is very close to that prescribed by all of the earlier architects.

The one-room schoolhouse, therefore, developed along a rectangular or nearly square pattern. Attempts to increase the size of the student body, along with the size of the single room eventually produced a high school pattern that persisted from about 1840 into the early 1920s, and of which nothing remains but "study halls." The architecture of village and city high schools, and of teachers colleges built up to about 1930 reflects this attempt to increase classroom size. Dominating each floor is a central assembly room, seating several hundred pupils of different levels of achievement, and surrounding the assembly are satellite recitation rooms of manageable dimensions, to which homogeneous groups are summoned from the assembly for instruction. By the early twentieth-century, more progressive schools had reversed the direction; the assembly became the place where the pupils were sent when they weren't "in class." Hence, the study hall.

The point of this is that any modern school is in its design of class-room space an agglomeration of one-room units, each with a floor area about equal to that of a one-room school, whose size and shape are functions of human limitations. Outward shape of the large school is not determined by the basic unit, however, but the arrangement of those units, which may be a pile, a sprawl, a geometric conceit, or part of the landscaping, all of which make possible architectural style in larger schools.

In one-room schools, however, almost any "styling" will be added expense without functional value. The Greek colonnade, the Gothic gingerbread, the Queen Anne gable, the colonial portico, even the octagonal floor plan do nothing to improve instruction, other than the moral improvement urged by Johonnot, by Barnard, and by Alcott, whose opening thesis spoke for all: "the general arrangement and appearance of even inanimate things around us have an extensive influence in forming our character." Aside from the additions of cloakrooms, and (rarely) indoor toilets, and (much later) kitchens, additional space in a rural school was practically self-defeating, since it made necessary additional teachers and a graded school system. Thus, "Queen Anne" in a one-room school is marked by the addition of one or more windowed dormers, these enclosing useless attic space, and by the characteristic Queen Anne use of small panes in the upper portion of a window with a single pane in the lower portion. With the possible addition of a bell-tower, we have one of the most common turn-of-the-century designs. One architectural plan-book of 1910, *New School Buildings. Plans of One-Room and Two-Room School Buildings in Minnesota* has typical designs of this sort, along with Renaissance and Georgian colonial stylings, which are largely marked by Palladian porticoes, low hip-roof lines, and oftentimes, by the suppression of the tell-tale large school windows in the facade. This had been made possible by the development of statutes requiring larger window areas but with natural lighting only from the left side — a practice that yielded three unfenestrated walls in each class-room, achieved at the apparently negligible cost of eyestrain for left-handed pupils. Two-room schools lent themselves especially well to this Palladian balance; one-room schools had little more than a portico and a hip roof.

Some particularly apt designs of this sort are found in a pamphlet that recalls some earlier themes. Charles Dwyer, it will be remembered, had suggested a second-floor apartment for the master and his wife. This idea was reborn about 1910 as the "teacherage" concept. By that time, the advances in urbanization, suburbanization and teacher training had left the district school far behind, without pelf or champion. Few architects would waste time on commissions for $1500 one-room schools when towns and cities were building graded elementary schools and large high schools with gymnasiums, shops and domestic science rooms. No well-educated young teacher would choose lonely isolation in a rural district when she could be a highly-paid specialist in a city.

In 1916, N. A. Young, editor of the *Rural School Bulletin*, admitted to all the fiscal and physical shortcomings of country schools, but added that "it is highly probable that a greater contributor to the failure of our rural school system is to be found in the corps of employees who are actively engaged in work of teaching." The problem, Young maintained, was recruitment, and the underlying difficulty was housing.

"Have you ever tried to secure a boarding place in the country in a given locality?" he asked. "If you have, you probably know, especially if you told people you were a rural school teacher, that the best homes are usually not open to you; the less desirable homes frequently are not; the ones which you are able to secure are many times at a long distance from the place where you work and often so bad that you cannot stay in them; and it frequently happens that no place at all can be obtained."

During the nineteenth century, "teachers' homes" had become commonplace in the remoter areas of England, Switzerland and Scandanavia, but the American teacherage developed spontaneously, and in a singularly American fashion, in Walla Walla County, Washington, where, in 1904, a young woman teacher lost her boarding place in mid-year. With the help of the county superintendent of schools, she was able to move a ranch chuckwagon from the property across the road to the schoolyard, and there she and her twelve-year-old brother lived for the balance of the school term. The following year a two-room cottage was built for her. Some ten years later, there were more than a hundred teachers' homes in the state of Washington. By 1909, teacherages had been added onto two one-room schools near Embarrass, Minnesota. Within seven years, E.P. Shurick, an architect in nearby Duluth, had become a specialist in these constructions and published in 1916 a "Phamplet" on the subject, with school designs ranging from the palladian to the bleakly vernacular. The teacherage arrived too late, of course; the very pamphlet that promoted it acknowledged the advantages born of better roads, telephone service, rural free delivery and the more common use of the automobile. All of these factors served to promote consolidation, which had been urged seventy-five years earlier by Henry Barnard.

Rural schools are still being built, though rarely of the one- or two-room type. For those, the last cresting (save one) came in a booklet published in 1949 by The Teachers College of Columbia University. This booklet, *Planning Rural Community School Buildings,* was written by Henry H. Linn and Frank W. Cyr, "the man who made school buses yellow," and who, after retirement from the Columbia University faculty, became the enthusiastically imaginative administrator of a resource center for the small, isolated schools of the Catskills, where mountains and sparse rural population still make extensive schoolbusing impractical. Dr. Cyr's center provided radio contact, closed circuit television, audiovisual equipment, maps, art works, museum "suitcase" exhibits and a wealth of other resource materials that are made available by means of a daily truck circuit. These Catskill schools are now consolidated graded schools, but in 1949, when the book of plans was published, it was still appropriate to design one-room schools.

Cyr and Linn's schools (there are several architects represented) are similar to earlier architectural designs in that they, too, reflect domestic architecture of the day. They are generally in the "International Style," although in Frank Gilson's design for a one-teacher school, the vernacular core is disguised by an L-shape, by shake siding, by small-paned colonial windows, and by a residential-style porch. This domestic coziness underscores the fact that after World War II schools had lost their monumentality and it would be safe to say that this one-teacher school-*house* stands virtually alone in the sterile landscape of post-war functionalism. Only Frank Lloyd Wright's 1957 two-teacher school avoids the boxy mainstream of design antecedents for school buildings.

Wright's Wyoming Valley Grammar School was designed free of charge, with the architect himself supervising construction on land he had donated. "His only rural [public] schoolhouse," Robert C. Twombly states, "consisted of two classrooms separated from a gymnasium-cafeteria-assembly hall combination by a skylit central corridor under a forest of crossed beams. Its roof line almost exactly reproduced the contours of the hill behind it, and in its bucolic setting it was a quaint and simple expression of organic architecture." Built of concrete block and redwood, with a shingled roof, with 60 and 120 degree angles providing a geometric unity, and with a fireplace in each classroom, this Wisconsin schoolhouse was yet not too startling a departure from Davis and Town's octagonal sky-lighted Gothic board-and batten designs. But it was a genuine departure from both the now moribound vernacular and from the prevailing International "functional" style. Nevertheless, Frank Lloyd Wright's quixotic gesture appears to have rung down the curtain on the architectural history of rural district schools.

So ends the architectural history. What of the icon? The little red schoolhouse, we have seen, was rarely red. Greek revival architecture always preferred white, the Gothic revival tended toward earth and forest tones, and, while the Queen Anne and American Georgian colonial did utilize red brick, the buildings in the former style were generally monumental urban structures, while the Georgian brick style was most prevalent in the WPA buildings of the 1930s, too late in time to contribute toward the nostalgic icon. Further, in the frame and stucco renderings of all of these styles, the builders certainly must have eschewed barn paint. Indeed, in a comprehensive survey of rural school designs nationwide, S. A. Challman assumed in 1917 that "pure ground white lead" was the paint to be used for a new schoolhouse. And we must not be too easily convinced by historical societies' restored examples of rural schools which are often painted in fire engine red enamel rather than barn paint. Moreover, these may be unwitting renditions of the popular icon rather than the historical fact.

The nostalgic feeling about the school apparently dates back a century or so to the time that Whittier was writing his poem, Homer painting his pictures, and, ironically, when Johonnot was revising his modern attack on these repulsive, ragged beggars. There, in about 1870, the icon originated, and became fixed in the popular mind notwithstanding the changes being wrought all around. The succession is typically represented by the Wisconsin one-room school in which I did my student teaching in 1952. This, the "Sunny Crest" school of Manitowoc County, was first housed in a log cabin, to be replaced in 1879 by a red frame building, which in turn was sold to a farmer and once again replaced, in 1894, by a white frame building. In the 1930s this structure was at last provided with electricity, but it has only recently had plumbing installed, because it has been remodeled almost beyond recognition into a private residence. This succession is typical, but the variations are probably as myriad as the district schools that have survived, in one form or another. How many this may be, no one knows, but during World War II there were estimated to be about 121,000 one-teacher schools in operation in the United States, and that 7000 other schools had closed during the first two years of war, due to lack of teachers.

These figures were drawn from a pamphlet entitled *Still Sits the Schoolhouse by the Road,* prepared in 1943 by the Committee on Rural Education. It is a factual publication, but it may provide a key to an understanding of the popularity of the icon of the rural school. The icon is very likely a product of urbanization, of the movement from farm to city that has accelerated throughout this century. While there does not seem to be any deepseated feeling of guilt associated with the icon, it does bespeak of regrets and wistful longings to return to "a simple life." Evidence of this feeling of regret is condensed into two "pictographs" in the pamphlet. In the one labelled "Now," we see alienated twentieth-century man, standing alone and immobilized before a threatening, inanimate city, while behind him are boxy, frenetic school buildings, and no path to follow between the two. The opposite "Once" pictogram of "A Simple Life" is infinitely more appealing. Yet the committee urged the "Complex Life" of consolidation, redistricting, larger schools and bussing. Why? Because the schoolhouse icon of the simple life is a mask behind which lurked inefficiency, incompetence, malnourishment, poor sanitation and cultural provincialism, all of these being founded upon a lack of commitment to quality education on the part of the rural school board. A representative case is that of the Hillside school in Manitowoc Rapids township. Built in 1873, the schoolhouse did not have a basement until 1933, when federal funds paid for it and for the remodeling of the windows to make their arrangement consistent with the designs that had been introduced to some schools when the Hillside school first had been constructed; "The list of teachers is incomplete," the teacher-historian at the Hillside school apologized in a 1948 county history. "Teachers usually stayed only one year, evidently because the salary paid was below that of surrounding districts." In the same volume, the County Superintendent reported that in 1948, only thirty of the ninety rural districts maintained

THE LITTLE RED SCHOOLHOUSE 157

schools with indoor toilets, running water and adequate electric service. All this was in a county in Wisconsin rich both in dairy agriculture and in diversified urban industries that had dramatically augmented farm incomes during war years.

Clearly, the little red schoolhouse is valid as a positive icon only in retrospect, in minds such as that of Edward Kennedy, the New York *Times* correspondent who wrote of the surrender at Rheims. The real value placed upon this artifact by its constituency is exemplified by the only extant little red schoolhouse that I have yet seen, in Allamakee County, Iowa. Known only as "the Red School" by old timers, it was not abandoned until the early 1970s, and now stands neglected, a beggar not yet ragged, the barn paint weathering off the schoolhouse and its attendant outside privies; textbooks and globe bleaching in the sunlight that streams through the still intact windows; nothing missing but the schoolbell from the steeple—which probably fetched a nice sum at a local auction.

Nevertheless, there is much to be learned from the ideal achievements of the small rural school. At its best, the rural school has never been out of the intellectual mainstream: the scientific, geographical, mathematical and artistic paraphernalia called for by Barnard and Alcott would have made any rural school equal to the best academies of the day; while more recently Dr. Frank Cyr's Catskills resource center has demonstrated that the only limit to enrichment of the small school experience is the limit of imagination in the use of modern technology.

Imagination is a human limit, however, and in the one-teacher school it was all or nothing for the pupils who could not balance an unimaginative, ill-trained teacher for one subject against a brilliant teacher in the next class. They could not even look forward to a better teacher in the next grade. But it still was unlikely that they were doomed to suffering through eight years of one teacher. Career teaching in district schools was always the exception, and teachers never lasted very long. In the nineteenth century, bright young women teachers were waiting for a marriage proposal; bright young men were teaching only temporarily while they sought escape into law, higher education, or, as in the case of William Alcott, into medicine. In this century, rural school teaching for young men and women has been a stepping-stone career until completing of a baccalaureate degree would give access to a city school system.

But in the hands of the bright temporary teacher or of the seasoned career teacher, the one-room school could become an educational experience second to none. An eighth-grader learned contemporaneously with all the earlier grades of his educational career. Lessons were brief, but reinforced by repetition over the years. No knowledge was isolated. Nearly all the children served as teachers of the younger pupils, and all were imaginatively resourceful for recreation on sunny and stormy days alike. Botany, zoology, ecology, and agriculture were taught in the school yard. Maintenance of building and grounds was divided among pupils and the teacher. And the walk to and from school provided variety, adventure, and leisure for flights of imagination and for youthful conspiracy.

There are yet more transcendant ideals embodied in the district school in its proper place. One of these ideals is expressed in Winslow Homer's paintings and in Frank Lloyd Wright's school: this is the ideal of organic harmony of building, people and environment, and this is why Homer's rural-school paintings continue to appeal to us. In them, by means of the artist's unifying medium of sunlight, we see a rare sight: An institution serving people as individuals, within a non-compartmentalized community, and as sympathetic parts of an accessible natural environment.

LIST OF SOURCES USED

Alcott, William A., *Essay on the Construction of School-houses, was awarded the prize offered by the America-Institute of Instruction, August 1831.* (Boston: Hilliard, Gray, Little and Wilkinson, and Richardson, Lord and Holbrook, 1832.)

Barnard, Henry, *School Architecture: or Contributions to The Improvement of School-Houses in the United States, Second Edition.* New York: Barnes, 1848. (Classics in Education No. 42, edited by Jean and Robert McClintock, New York: Teachers College Press, 1970).

Challman, S. A., *The Rural School Plant for Rural Teachers and School Boards, Normal Schools, Teachers' Training Classes, Rural Extension Bureaus.* (Milwaukee: Bruce Publishing Company, 1917.)

Committee on Rural Education, The, *Still Sits the Schoolhouse By the Road.* (Chicago: The Committee on Rural Education, 1943.)

Cubberley, Ellwood P., *Rural Life and Education. A Study of the Rural-School Problem as a Phase of the Rural-Life Problem*. (Boston: Houghton Mifflin, 1914.)

Cyr, Frank W., and Henry H. Linn, *Planning Rural Community School Buildings*. (New York: Teachers College Press, 1949.)

Dabb, A.N., *Practical Plans for District School Houses*. (Philadelphia: J.A. Bancroft, c. 1874.)

Davidson, Marshall B., *Life in America*, vol. 2. (Boston: Houghton Mifflin, 1951.)

Dresslar, Fletcher B., *Rural Schoolhouses and Grounds*, U.S. Office of Education *Bulletin*, 1914, No. 12. (Washington: Government Printing Office, 1914.)

Dresslar, Fletcher B., and Haskell Pruett, *Rural Schoolhouses School Grounds, and their Equipment*, U.S. Office of Education *Bulletin*, 1930, No. 21. (Washington: Government Printing Office, 1930.)

Dwyer, Charles P., *The Economy of Church. Parsonage and School Architecture Adapted to Small Societies and Rural Districts*. Buffalo: Phinney Company, 1856.)

Earl, Edward C., *The Schoolhouse*. (Washington, D.C., 1919.)

Eells, Harry L., Hugh C. Moeller, and Carl C. Swain, *Rural School Management*. (New York: Charles Scribner's Sons, 1924.)

Eveleth, Samuel F., *School House Architecture*. (New York: Geo. E. Woodward, c. 1870.)

Farnum, Paul E., "The Rhodes School," *Old Time New England*: 27 (October 1936), 73-76.

Finkelstein, Barbara J., "The Moral Dimensions of Pedagogy; Teaching Behavior in Popular Primary Schools in Nineteenth-Century America," *American Studies*: 15 (Fall, 1974), 78-89.

Flexner, James Thomas, *The World of Winslow Homer 1836-1910*. (New York: Time Incorporated, 1966.)

[Halden, F.E.,] *New School Buildings. Plans for One-Room and Two-Room School Buildings in Minnesota* [St. Paul], 1910.

Johonnot, James, *Country School Houses*, (New York: Invision and Phinney, 1859.)

Johonnot, James, *School-Houses*, (New York: J.W. Schermerhorn, 1871.)

Kallier, Otto, *Grandma Moses*, (New York: Harry Abrams, 1973.)

Larson, Elsye Davey, *Country Schoolhouse*. (New York: Comet Press, 1958.)

MacCallum, Ian C., "Little Red SchoolHouse," *Architectural Forum*: 103 (July, 1955), 131.

New York *Times*, May 8, 1945, p. 1.

[Peterson, Charles E.], "Eight-Sided Schoolhouses, 1800-1840," *Society of Architectural Historians Journal*: 12 (March, 1953), 21-22.

Pickard, Samuel T., *Life and Letters of John Greenleaf Whittier*. (Boston: Houghton Mifflin, 1907.)

Poetical Works of John Greenleaf Whittier, Vol. II. (Boston: Houghton Mifflin, 1892.)

Pollard, John A., *John Greenleaf Whittier, Friend of Man*. (Boston: Houghton Mifflin, 1949.)

Rappel, Joseph H., *A Centennial History of the Manitowoc County School Districts and its Public School System*. (Manitowoc: County Superintendant of Schools, 1948.)

"Rural School-Houses," *The Architecutral Review and American Builders' Journal* (January, 1869), 435-437.

Shurick, Edward Palmes, *The Teacherage: A Phamplet (sic) of Valuable Imformation [sic] on Rural School House Construction,* (Duluth: Shurick & Hansen Company, 1916.)

Storrer, William Allen, *The Architecture of Frank Lloyd Wright* (Cambridge,: The MIT Press, 1974.)

Twombly, Robert C., *Frank Lloyd Wright: An Interpretive Biography.*

United States National Capitol Sesquicentennial Committee, *American Processional 1492-1900.* (Washington, D.C.: Corcoran Gallery, 1950.)

Warren, Robert Penn, *John Greenleaf Whittier's Poetry; An Appraisal and a Selection.* (Minneapolis: University of Minnesota Press, 1971.)

Wheelwright, Edmund March. *School Architecture. A General Treatise for the Use of Architects and Others.* (Boston: Rogers & Manson, 1901.)

Wright, Frank Lloyd, "Why I Love Wisconsin," *Frank Lloyd Wright on Architecture.* (New York: Grosset and Dunlap, Universal Library, 1971.)

Wriston, Barbara, "The Use of Architectural Handbooks in The Design of Schoolhouses from 1840 to 1860," *Society of Architectural Historians Journal:* 22 (October, 1963), 155-160.

CB Radio As Icon

Jim Pollman

Driving on any thoroughfare these days is much like being asea in the days of the tall masted schooners. One spies a proliferation of new masts, neither wooden nor for motive power, some of which seem to reach as high as former main skysail; all are white or silver wonders of fiberglass and steel. One seems to beget another till the vehicle is overridden with them, creating the impression of carrying too much "canvas" in this CB storm. These modern masts are not designed to ferry the vehicle on; they are partially to aid in the vehicle's movement, especially through dangerous straits on superhighways, and particularly to serve ends in themselves. They have become icons of the individual who wants relative freedom of movement in his vehicle and complete freedom of uninhibited talk and chatter. These masts are products of American space-shot technology—Citizens' Band Radio antennae.

It is out in the airwaves, the ether, that these icons come alive with the rhetoric of their owners. Once the proscenium and the theatre walls marked the limits of the stage voice;

now, the only limits are terrain obstructions and restricted transmitter wattage. To the uninitiated, all the air "out there" may seem empty. But one look at the jaunty 108" whip antenna tells the CBer that the "mast" is not there to carry clipper ship sail but is ubiquitously punching out a steady tide of prattle and discourse, none of which is ever in plain English: "Pick'em up truck, you git an eyeball on that Kojack with the Kodak up at the one-seven, ten what?"* Just as the masts of the schooners were utilitarian things of beauty and worship, so the whipping CB antennae have become the democratic icons of the individual communications media and membership badges in the last true American community—the fellowship of the road, the fraternity of mobility.

The idea of Citizens' Band Radio Service, CB, came about when FCC Commissioner E.K. Jett foresaw a revolution in communications technology springing from WW II. By 1947 CB was established reality as the FCC recognized the public's need for a spectrum of the airwaves for business, personal, and emergency purposes. The public was allocated a 10MHz spread (460-470MHz) but it was not until 1958, when the CB band was changed to its present 27MHz band that CB began to grow. This spectrum, while allowing for equipment at a more reasonable cost ($200 vs. $800-900), is conterminous with such interference sources as some industrial equipment and certain medical devices, principally diathermy machines, making this AM band not the most attractive available.

CB foundered along for 16 years, treated like the bastard brother of Ham radio before taking root across the country like some mutant weed gone berserk. While there were no Morse code or electronic exams necessary for licensing and use as a Ham radio, there were some obstacles in the early days: few people were aware of CB's existence; the license form was a horror akin to IRS forms, required notorization, plus a $20 fee; and, the sets were still relatively expensive, in

---

*Calling the pickup truck. Did you see that radar patrolman at the 17 mile marker, do you understand.

addition to being prone to tube failure and tremendous drains on automobile batteries and generators. A typical mobile/base (car or fixed) transceiver (*trans*mits and re*ceives*) of the early 60's weighed just under 13 pounds and measured 6 x 8 x 8". Contrast that to the more sophisticated "little black box" of the 70's which is about the size of a cigar box. The analogy of 40's AM portables compared to the tiny Japanese transistors is parallel in technological terms, popularity and price.

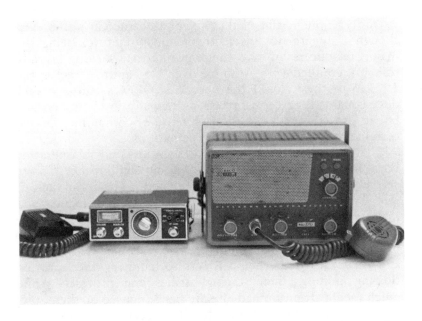

After the 1958 frequency change, it took CB 16 years for the number of licenses to reach the 1 million plateau. After that base the numbers moved logarithmically: 8 months to hit the 2 million mark; 3 months for 3 million; and, today, the number of licensed operators stands somewhere near 5 million and is growing explosively. There is great disparity between the number of licensed operators and sets in use; FCC regulations allow a licensee to operate multiple sets and many people never bother to obtain a license. The figures on the number of sets varies according to sources; some estimate 15 million, others 17 million. However, the swaying sea of masts on the highways and the flood of license applications mark CB's popularity. In April 1976, the latest date for which statistics are available, the FCC was swamped with over 560,000 applications. Faced with a literal mountain of paper bursting its offices, the FCC devised a system whereby set purchasers are issued interim licenses at the point of sale. Now buyers "get on the air" immediately and the FCC has time to sort out its paperwork. In the face of all these numbers and the airwaves jangling like screech owls, one wonders what started it all.

Oddly enough, the Arabs precipitated the CB boom even though they are not in electronics manufacture. Being the major producers of the fuel our modern society literally rolls on, coupled with Arab ire over U.S. aid to Israel in the 1973 War, they closed the petcocks. OPEC's embargo produced many long term effects, principally in energy policy, but it also created a cohesion or sense of community among certain groups, if not indeed whole nations.

The embargo created gas shortages and long exasperating lines for the higher priced fuel. Long haul truckers were severely hit, not only in the pocket book, but in the tank itself. Truckers needed full tanks to keep their schedules and make a profit; to them *time is money,* "down time" or delays mean losses. Shortages, dry pumps, delays, higher prices, empty tanks, and unkept schedules incensed truckers and they turned to their CB sets to band together locating flowing pumps, then staging strikes and protests. While much media attention had already been focused on them, picturing them as folk heroes, the "Last American Cowboys," the gas shortage redirected the spotlight of publicity on them once more in a far more serious matter which concerned everyone who had to endure long waits on frosty morning for a tank of gas. These "last cowboys" packed a different weapon than the old Colt .44's, they had Cobra Cb's—the electronic magnum. As they banded together on the road in camaraderie and protest, they broadcast a message which moved through the ether faster than any restrictive "double nickel" (55mph) speed limit.

It was a divided message highlighting their complaints and lifestyle, reifying the cult status of this "new fangled" radio and its cosmos. Exposed to this, Americans began buying CBs, listening in to these "ghosts of the rolling nights," investigating their mystique and orbit, learning that a diverse populace can, with a communications tool, create a community.

As the truckers learned, so the public began to understand that they could travel the roads and chat with one another and the big-wheeling folk heroes; they no longer had to sit silent, passively confined to their steel boxes on wheels; they could communicate with their fellow travelers, help each other in emergencies, find gas, obtain directions, seek good food, or simply pass the time on long boring trips with the equivalent of gossiping on the telephone. People in passenger cars soon began to adopt the colorful southern twang and expressive language of the truckers and the whole phenomenon was on.

CB takes in all stratums of society, from the elite in expensive cars to the rather marginal in clunkers. Even the most articulate Brahmin will affect the twang for the fun of it, trying to create the impression he is an "eighteen wheeler," a trucker. The stage was set for the actors to emerge, an invisible stage, for in CB most "actors" never "eyeball" or see one another, enabling them to take on any evocative role, title, or name he/she wishes. One does rename one's self in CB with a moniker, "handle," which reflects whatever Walter Mitty vision one wishes to convey. Meek Al becomes "Big Al," "Magnum Force," "The Gunfighter," or whatever conjured dream lies in the mind. In this faceless communications medium, the dramaturgical model plays a large role. And it is not the passive medium we know from exposure to commercial radio or television; people using CB can talk back, project themselves through the air, create and carry on in a two-way process. The colorful speech and equally inventive "handles" are as plentiful as are CB sets and imaginations.

Since this is a faceless communication, with an aural world of its own, perhaps it is best to deal with the iconic external, the visible aspect of the medium. That outwardly visible icon, the antenna, the rising mast of electronic expression, is rich in history and connotative associations.

Just as contemporary archeologists unearth other, older cultures' signs and symbols, their icons, so may future civilizations snort like truffle hunting hogs discovering our vehicles in some hardened ooze, caught in some catastrophic second like that of Pompeii. What would they make of our cars adorned with those spines like so many species of rockfish? Without a knowledge of CB, perhaps they might make a similar assessment as did the Indian returning from a visit to Britian reporting that the English worshiped animals, unaware the eagles, lions, and oxen he had seen painted in old churches represented the Evangelists seen in a vision of Ezekiel. To future excavators, and indeed to many of us, the antennae may have meaning only as immanent in the object, not as symbol, but as the technological given, an artifact electronically tuned to receive and radiate a certain frequency efficiently. Yet, this is an icon of our culture, with its roots deep in the past, possessing inherent connotations beyond its use in ordinary daily life. Like the eagles, lions, and oxen the Indian mistook at face value, the antenna is symbolic and analogous.

It seems all cultures produce artifacts of iconic value indigenous to their millennium which reflect the culture's warp and woof. Note Greek architecture, Egyptian stele, heraldry, and the whole impossible range of badges, insignia, logotypes, signs of office, power, nationality, tribe, regiment, and so forth. It seems, too, that as these external signs of internal convictions and identity take on greater representative and mutually recognized values, they become invested with a mythology greater than the sign itself. The characters or ideas embodied become "fixed" within the culture and are transformed into part of the culture's overall identifying heritage. While some signs and symbols may be unique to a certain culture, there are those embracing and reflecting general human thought and vision. That is, there are those more basic and universal signs that involve general needs and perceptions—the universal thread of commonality.

A most illustrative example is found in the masculine martial tradition. Uniforms, insignia, the whole amalgamation of accouterments—all these vary and change; yet such basics as warrior customs, pomp, flags, the stance of show and dash remain predictable and universal. This martial tradition has its hierarchical structure with subordinate roles, yet everyone is usually subservient to the symbol simultaneously representing both the subgroup and the larger totality—state, nation, leaders, etc.

In this tradition the flag symbolically represents the community and its leaders. Flaglike objects, protovexilloids, have been found in ancient organized societies in the Near and Far East far back in history. Generally they were poles to which carved figures or animal skins were attached, bearing some symbolic meaning, and carried into battle. They range from Assyria to China, and we can speculate our American Indians brought with them some protovexilloid relatives of the feathered lances displayed by Plains Indians. The early Romans marched behind a *signum,* a pole with various carved images, and later they fought under a more "modern" flaglike arrangement, the *vexillum,* on which a square of cloth hung from a crossbar atop the pole. Around A.D. 300 Emperor Constantine introduced the first Christian flag adorned with the Greek letters for "Christos." During the Crusades, the men followed a divers group of flags inspired by visions, saints, and whatnot. Perhaps with a sense of historical continuity and a bit of prophetic vision, some Crusaders displayed their flags thusly, "Some were flown from tall iron sheathed masts mounted on four wheeled frames . . . ."[1]

The staff, mast, standard, or pole on which the flag is flown has been termed a male identification symbol—phallic certainly, but much more. The *signum,* almost a bare sapling in our view, was still the rallying point for the men, the repository of the community or nation's honor and traditions, and most of all, the leading, never bending object which implied thusly "standing up for one's beliefs," the "collective spine" of the men, the "West Point Backbone," the chine running through the people and nation as a whole. People, Americans especially, tend to identify with the underdogs, those brave, heroic, daring and dauntless leaders who march forth against intolerable odds, but have a conviction of unassailable victory. The symbols then become defined as "good" over "evil." On our part, militarily, the Revolution was pure madness, idiocy, doomed to failure, yet it succeeded and we came away with a foundation on which to build a weight of tradition.

In American Revolutionary lore we notice the iconic quality akin to the "backbone" motif in the painting "Washington Crossing The Delaware;" taller in stature than the flag, dominant, upright, personifying all the latter-day ideals and popular conceptions of the U.S. He is the standard on which "hangs" the "ideological flag." Another American icon, the "Spirit of '76," is one of indestructible statues, human though interchangeable with the flag that follows, all transcendental symbols. In song we have the allegorical persona of Yankee Doodle sticking a feather—cockade, flag, ideals, the spine—in his hat transforming himself literally and figuratively into the staff and flag. During a more recent revolutionary period we had a president who obsessively pinned a flag to his lapel, becoming the iconic repository of the nation's ideals and its symbolic standard bearer, to much irony as it later turned out. Any movie goer is familiar with the guidon (French, *guide-home,* 'a guide to the men') bearer leading the cavalry to the rescue of a beleaguered wagon train. The guidon, cresting the hill, and the men behind, were one and the same—a mark of immediate symbolism to the people besieged. While CB antennae do not usually carry flags, though some people do attach small ones, they serve the same functions as guidons, their flaglike identity apparent even though lacking cloth. Above one can see the human form as interchangeable with inanimate symbolism—flag, guidon, pole, antenna. Man and the transcendant meanings are equivalants; as are fully rigged masts, bare standards or poles, and naked antennae. They are all invested with cultural infusions of meaning. CB antennae may have a linear history through ages, yet they have a more recent origin which can be traced through several avenues: products of societal realities and cultural conditioning; recent history; design and advertising; and, the whole confluent melange we call the "collective unconsciousness."

First, in military life, the once exclusive male provence, men readjust their values and shift identities to an "altered self," the unit. An outfit's history is told in the cluster of streamers hanging from the unit's colors, plus unique insignia and patches they design which not only depict their public image, but show their smartness and panoply. This is primarily a function of the group as a whole. In World War II we find, conversly, more personal expressions of internal convictions together with the usual soldierly manifestations of bravado, derring-do, braggadocio, and esprit de corps. While the WW II GI's were caught in a constraining military system, the individual nonetheless brought with him a civilian egalitarian sensibility, as he knew he was only there for the "duration." Perhaps this spirit was best manifested in the semi-independent, self-reliant group formed around a machine nucleus—the tank. Being small, the crew could create its own personal identity about this sphere. The tank became an extension of the group's collective personality as they flourished it with names and slogans, as well as tagging on a pennant to the end of their radio antenna. This identification with and expression through the vehicle came from their civilian life where another machine, the car, was a status symbol, a projection of the self, and a mark of mobility and freedom. The pennant atop the antenna was the flaunt, the wavering neon ad presenting the daring, hell-bent-for-leather image the men wanted. From Patton's pistols to their antennae, these signs conveyed the romantic, rough 'n ready character they wished themselves to be. They became the collective personnae, a meld of man and machine as the central ego focus in a battle envoling millions of men, all dressed in the same mufti.

Due to the exigencies of tank design, the antenna was mounted on the stubby rear overhang, counterweighted to balance the cannon's thrusting mass. Just as the small overhang balanced the cannon physically, the radio antenna balanced the tank symmetrically, and also sharpened the tank's sense of kinetic motion, adding to and relieving its ponderous bulk with the antenna's offsetting delicate reaction to the huge machine's lumbering wallow and bucketing. As the "spine" of the machine, standing tall for all to see, the mast of this antenna led the men while being a symbol of the power underneath. As a guidon it was no different than the

iron clad machine of the Crusader's time.

Post World War II America was the antithesis of what it had been upon entry to the war—now a prodigy of productivity, the churning craw of mass mechanization. The Great Depression was over, society was hopeful, a new technological age was emerging and technology brings expanded dreams. The wealth allowed for more than eeking out a living, a period of sinecure and meeting the basic needs of a nation with leisure. The production line and its standardization produced sameness; a mass uniformity in a mass society where the populous strives for diversity, an originality, an ideal of individualism. It forced man to put his stamp on goods, as he'd done with the Gov't. issue tanks. Simple Detroit Iron was not enough, it had to be customized, molded and plugged into an identity, given a name, be a panegyric of the owner. Utility was a stage society had long passed. No longer did objects have to meet the basic standards, they had to serve other functions as well. In 1953 the Chevrolet Corvette was introduced, the first American sports car, not a means of transportation per se, but a toy, a plaything. Certainly it had many design innovations that separated it from domestic models, and one was the rear deck placement of the radio antenna. As a machine designed for both style and moving from place to place rapidly, the rear location of the vertical plane emphasized the forward thrust of its long flat hood. This is the same balancing symmetry and motion imagery utilized by tanks—and cars with CB whips. Imagine the analogy, in sensual terms, of a car backed against a brick wall, it can only move foreward. It's as if a giant foot were holding it back, ready to kick it forword. The feeling is even more pronounced in the later model Corvette Stingrays with their "snout" long and low to the ground and the small rear deck arched with the antenna jutting up. The object breathes.

Though the Corvette did not have an extended antenna, the same principles of balance are applied, as in CB, adding that vertical plane to the rear. Certainly the CB whip derives from these precursors, in both artistic effect and masculine emotive tradition as a guidon or a flag. While the CB mast is bare, it is a "flag" unto itself, as the oil painting depiction of George Washington; it advertizes its owner minus fabric. The whip, jaunty to itself, telling others "I am an individual, a CBer, member of America's last community, the society of the road, the quorum of the superslab."

In the mind's environs isn't the whip antenna reminiscent of the tanned tough, lean and victorious "desert rats" racing through the Libyan desert chasing Rommel? Like the tank's plummage, the whip conjures such images, as do other icons of similar nature: dune buggy whips, and the luminious whips on the rear of bicycles for visibility. The CB whip, even in its loaded coil truncated form, stands out and is as much a connotative banner as any flag or ensign.

Though it may have its ties to WW II cavaliers, and the long history of flags and other signs, CB owes its existence in present form to the pressures on technology via the exploration of space. In the 1950's there was emphasis in the consumer society on ostentation in goods—the cult of chrome, huge finned automobiles, glitter, the strut, and the glossy affectation of metal flake consciousness. The limitations of space demanded a shrinkage in bulk and a retreat into tiny, though complex, systems. Somewhere, perhaps vicariously punching buttons on tiny computers coasting back from the moon, the American people adopted the "little black box" syndrome, where less is more. Society placed magical powers in the little black boxes, much as other cultures imbue mystical qualities to a shaman's bones. Indeed, the majority of CB sets are predominately the "professional" flat black color. The modal leitmotiv here is "black." Black implies no frills, suggesting that the energy invested in the object, the scientific wizardry, is black, revealing nothing, hinting at some secret and hidden forces within. Like a magician's wand, the CB set with its wizardry can "throw" one's voice out into the ether, unseen, flying through space, reaching hundreds of listeners magically like some conjurer's illusion. It divides reality and the self, allowing one to be in hundreds of different places at once. The more the little black box is fitted with dials, knobs, and switches with odd names, the more it seems to resemble a miniature cosmos itself, and the more magical the nature of the object. The more complexity packed into the black box, the more inner sorcery it contains. The paradox of *looking* like less actually *is* more has been accomplished by microminiaturization: a pinhead size chip or circuit can contain 10,000 transistors. Fifteen years ago the criterion of excellence was displayed outside the object, today it is hidden and the small size is exalted. Technological achievements have altered our perceptions, now the simple flat black exterior of the CB set, with its myriad components, is a transcendantal vision in itself—a social icon of the space age.

"Junior Spaceman" the bubble gum card might read but it is not too far off the track as the CBer has the potential in his single sideband set to talk to the moon. When atmospheric conditions are optimal it is possible with a regular CB set to talk over a thousand miles via "skip." A single sideband CB set is allowed 12 watts power versus the regular set's 4 watts. Interestingly enough, the Apollo astronauts used a similar sideband system with the same wattage to communicate from the moon. To have a gadget with this potential power in one's car turns the shaman's bones to paltry pieces of junk rattling in the dust.

For technical reasons the mobile whip antenna is the most efficient of its kind, as most people know, and they also know that there is an infatuation with materials of the space age: "miracle" materials like the fiberglass of CB whips, kin of nose cones and mach II jet's honeycomb wing material. It is as if steel is passé, something Louis Sullivan used for skyscrapers at the turn of the century. The material acquires an immanent iconic quality now, just as stone or bronze marked an age's development plateau and social matrix. America seems to be at a point where materials more than signify the state of the art, but the state of mind.

Moving from the physical artifact to the state of mind, we find today there is a felt loss of a sense of community in our multifarious nation. We bemoan the loss and some see the erosion of regionality too, a sort of "flattening" of the land where we coalesce into a huge, bland, pedestrian nation of clones. CB has partly reversed that loss of community, and it has helped generate a rebirth of regionalism—a CB regionalism, the electronic drawl, a new language rooted in Southern wrappings. Mobile sets outsell base sets 3 to 1. Baron's financial weekly estimates that this year alone 10 to 12 million people will spend over $1 billion on CB sets.[2] The anomie, ennui, and malaise which once spread over the throbbing arteries of the land and its symbolic life style, the superhighways, have been replaced by a community drawn together through CB radio. Those sometimes routes to nowhere, ends in themselves, have strung us together, and CB is the collectivizing agent. A more human one, however, as CB has deflected and tempered the rootless, megalopical urban industrial sprawl with a new respect for civility and a willingness of people to reach out and communicate, care, and help one another. It is another subject to discuss in detail the argot and jargon of CB, yet most calls include the greeting "good buddy." This easy civil touch, framed in the southern patois of the air, gives a softening edge to the medium—a friendliness and feeling of neighborly concern for individuals. While not a concrete indication that society has become more cohesive, it is interesting to note that many people who feel that while they may be in the pestilential urban morass, they are among friends, not surrounded by crazed, sulking, silent maniacs ready to assault them at the drop of "hello."

That CB is now a definite sub-group is evidenced in the language and its specialized diction. To append one's self to this cultural community, one uses the proper terminology learned only from a few hours of listening, of trying to decipher and use it. Learning the vernacular and rituals of beginning and terminating calls is the initiation rite of this group. Plain English can be used, but one is looked upon as an outsider, an alien. Besides, much of the fun is the acting and imitation of the drawl and twang. And there is much of "game playing" to it also, as in spotting the "smokies."

(police.) (To those who make their living driving the road, this is not a game but an adversary relationship. To the "civilian" leadfoot it's the same, but to the rest of the CB motorists it's a game to keep interest much as the child's game of spotting different state license plates.)

The CB explosion has been canonized or iconized, in every form of the medium—even staid banks are offering CBs for large deposits. The White House once counted a CBer among its family—"First Mama." Is it a transitory phenomenon, a fad like hula hoops? The big names in electronics are now moving into the area: GE, RCA Motorola, Sony, Hitachi. Detroit now offers CBs as original optional equipment. Who knows where it will go or to what be transformed? The FCC is deliberating increasing the number of channels and conjointly authorizing a higher powered FM band. Will it become something like the telephone which once tied us together yet kept us apart? Will it still be the cohesive force it is now, reflecting the friendly atmosphere of the mobile community? Will it continue to make one feel as if everyone is from the same hometown and to "key" the microphone is just dropping in to say "howdy?" Who knows?

But as it has come from the folk heroes of the road to the true folk, the CB mast, the black box, with their iconic qualities, signify a massive egalitarian popular movement of vast and yet unquantified proportions. Whatever the meaning of this new community and its electronic sortilege, the answer lies somewhere out there—in the ether.

Photographic Credits:

All photographs by the author except those of the tank by the U.S. Army, released and OK'd for publication by U.S. Army.

NOTES

[1] I.O. Evans, *Flags of the World* (New York: Grosset & Dunlap, 1971), p. 5.
[2] Article, *The Washington Post,* June 19, 1976. p. C-7.

Pinball Machine: Marble Icon

Cynthia Packard
and
Ray B. Browne

With religious offerings clutched tightly in sweaty fists, the contestant is lured to the flashing lights of the electronic opponent. Plunk . . . plunk . . . kerchunck—plunk-kerchunk. Five balls. Four can play—two can play—one can play. Player up. The pinball game is on.

A strange place, perhaps, and an unusual icon, for a religious experience. But so it is. Standing at the foot and looking up at the head the player strokes and manipulates the icon in a strangely medieval sense—like the mythic wrestling match between Gawain and Lancelot, or that earlier match between eyeless Samson and the Temple in Gaza—and is joined in a personal contest with superhuman, perhaps satanic, forces.

This scene of the innocent but hopeful electronic antagonist-worshipper is common in numerous beer joints, arcades, bus stations, lunch counters and laundromats across the U.S. The eager patron directs the flippers, bumps the machine and awaits the outcome of his efforts, secretly praying that this time he—man—can triumph over technology and thereby be reunited with his personal god. The drive is addictive; one game never satisfies. The competitive urge, as in any athletic event, between contending players or between a single player and his score, is obvious. Yet the strongest urge transcends mere human competition. Player and machine, literally and symbolically, grapple in a bigger-than-life contest between human being and perhaps unknown supernatural force.[1]

In earliest times, great public games, like those in Greek,

177

Mexican, and Egyptian cultures—and present day Olympics—took place in connection with religious celebrations or ceremonies. Elaborate athletic events, races, contests, and dances became essential facets of religious ritual; man could verify his worthiness to his gods, striving to appease or equal them in some manner.[2]

One game in particular was popular in ancient Mexico, and was closely associated with the priesthood. Tlachtli, as it was known, involved players hitting a rubber ball with their hips and/or knees, attempting to drive the ball through one of several sculptured stone rings placed at the ends of a 150-foot walled-in court.

Tlachtli, according to folklorist Lewis Spence, may have "symbolized a struggle betwixt the powers of light and darkness."[3] More specifically, it may have represented the motions of some heavenly body, the sun or the moon, since the tlachtli ball was often half light and half dark in color. This ritualistic game might represent the myth, found in many ancient cultures, that contending powers toss the fortunes of the universe from light into shadow, in an eternal mythic ball game.[4]

It would be absurd to assume that pinball is a direct descendant of ancient religious games, tlachtli in particular. However, characteristics of each game point to some correlation, as far as ball movement and scoring are concerned. Each is played on a walled-in court, with balls being manuevered toward a goal. The tlachtli goal, a stone ring, could be compared to the various "extra ball" or "extra points" holes found on nearly every pinball table. Propelling the ball through the ring won the tlachtli player honor and fortune (the lighted universe); by tilting the pinball machine, the modern player loses fortune and fame, and plummets into universal darkness—the blinking lights cease to function, darkening the surface of the table. Ultimately, the god of light and darkness has been transformed into technology: the god of "on and off."

A second significant religious "game" which had similarities with pinball playing was the labyrinth ritual of Egypt and, most notably, Crete. This maze was, according to Spence, "associated with the worship of a deity whose image was concealed in the holy of holies at the centre of its complex passages."[5]

The Cretan myth of the labyrinth at Knossos tells how King Minos of Crete blackmailed the Athenians into sacrificing twelve youths and maidens to the half-bull, half-man monster-Minotaur, which lived in the maze. Through various schemes, the Athenian hero Theseus was able to find and slay the Minotaur. This "slaying" became a ritualistic dance, depicting the wanderings and gropings of Theseus in the winding passages of the maze. The ritual is most often associated with the cult of the sacred bull in several cultures, symbolizing man's strength over the powerful and most virile animal, thus reinforcing man's virility.[6]

While pinball is not specifically a "male" game, the fact remains that more males than females play it regularly and definite sex roles are reinforced in the playing.[7] It might follow, then, that threading the silver ball through the labyrinth of lights, buzzers, and traps, in competition for power over a machine is a virility reinforcement for male pinball players. In the wake of automation, computerized jobs, and feminism, playing pinball may be symbolically one of the few physical acts of power and/or virility left for the modern male: a sexual or physical prowess, god-like in nature, exemplified by the scoring of points against an electronic adversary.

Whether these connections are real or not is the province of the interpreter. What remains, is the basic idea that pinball is a game, no matter how uneven the odds of human victory, and any athletic event can be traced to religious ritual of some sort. The energies expended during such events, whether in playing tlachtli, chasing down the Minotaur, or competing with a pinball machine, are symbolically the outpourings of human vigor with the intention of further physical growth for the participant and for the culture, and ultimately for spiritual ectasy.

If modern man is left powerless by machines, then he is able to grow spiritually by defeating such devices, as in playing pinball. As Marshall McLuhan put it in *Understanding Media*,

The games of a people reveal a great deal about them. Games

are a sort of artificial paradise like Disneyland, or some
Utopian vision by which we interpret and complete the
meaning of our daily lives. In games we devise means of
nonspecialized participation in the larger drama of our
time . . . A game is a machine that can get into action
only if the players consent to become puppets for a time.[8]

McLuhan might have gone further and pointed out the
general iconic nature of games. Pinball, as we know it today,
did not flower until after World War II. But the seeds for
these marvelous contraptions were planted long before any
other technological device of reverence (i.e. automobiles,
telephones, airplanes, electric toothbrushes) in our culture.

Historically, pinball's nearest traceable ancestor is the parlor game bagatelle popular in the nineteenth century. As
mentioned in Dickens' *Pickwick Papers,* members of the Pickwick Club visited the Peacock Tavern and "beguiled their
time chiefly with such amusements as the Peacock afforded,
which were limited to a bagatelle board on the first floor."[9]

In this game, the player used a billiard cue to shoot balls
into holes located in the middle of the playing field. In the
late 1800's, a game closer to modern pinball, called "Log
Cabin," was introduced. This version of bagatelle was a table
top game which featured a large high-value "skill hole" located near the top, as well as numerous pegs, and several
smaller holes lower down, which counted for lesser point
values.[10] One political cartoon from 1862, shows the Union
Army defeated at Bull Run, while President Lincoln played
pinball (probably bagatelle). In the cartoon are rats and
slovenly dressed players, typifying the sleaziness long associated with pinball.[11]

It was not until 1930, however, that pinball was developed
and made widely popular. Although Leo Berman introduced
in 1930 an adaption of bagatelle which he called "Bingo," it
was David Gottlieb who became financially successful at
manufacturing the games. Gottlieb, founder of D. Gottlieb
and Company, a major manufacturer of pinball machines,
introduced his first machine also in 1930, which he called
"Baffle Ball." This simple and inexpensive game was a coun-
ter-top version of pinball, and had a playing surface that
featured four major scoring areas. For one penny, the player

could send seven balls onto the board with a wooden plunger. In less than a year, Gottleib sold 50,000 of these machines at an average price of $17.50.[12] Depression-heavy Americans were all too happy to purchase the ephemeral escape of seven clanking steel ball bearings for one cent.[13] In 1931, a second successful game was designed by a young Chicago business-man named Raymond Maloney. His version, "Bally-Hoo," was originally manufactured by Gottlieb, but as sales ap-proached the 70,000 mark, Maloney began making the machines on his own. His firm, now the Bally Manufacturing Corporation, equals Gottlieb's in the pinball field today.[14]

Howard Poe of Rochester, New York, introduced in 1932, what was to become the biggest selling counter game of all time, "Whirlwind." His success prompted many other pro-ducers of coin-operated machines to go into the pinball business. From all of these endeavors, features such as cur-ved loops, spring activated kick-backs, and other gimmicks were developed which added much to the action and appeal of the game. Many of these innovations from the early 1930's are standard components on modern pinball machines.[15]

One of the most important innovations in pinball history came in 1933, when Harry Williams, of the Pacific Amuse-ment Co. of California, designed a game called "Contact," which introduced electric circuitry into the pinball indus-try. "Contact" employed battery-operated gates and kick-out holes, devices which transformed this expanding industry. Williams, later to found another major pinball manufactur-ing firm, Williams Electronics, used four dry-cell batteries on his machine, which powered lights and rang an occasional bell; 24 volts is still the standard pinball current.[16]

The first solenoid was used on the playfield of "Fleet" in 1935, adding an essential element of action to the ad-vancing game. Other innovations such as electronic tilt de-vices, automatic scoring, free games, thumper-bumpers, and roll-overs were to evolve later.

By 1940, pinball machines were found in bars, cafes, soda fountains, and arcades all over the country. As with any popular entertainment that seemed to be growing into an obsession, pinball suffered the traditional lashings and criti-cism from decency leagues, PTAs, church groups, and crime commissions, as a corruptor of youth, addicting and expensive vice, and lastly a gambling device controlled by the "syndicate."

Much of the bally-hoo about pinball being a gambling device stemmed from the fact that Gottlieb and Bally both manufactured slot machines, which were gambling devices. In addition, early pinball machines returned money as rewards for high scoring games; prizes were given for attaining a certain score. Also, in 1940, the pinball player could control the outcome of the game, to a certain extent, only through bumping or jostling the machine with his body. This body English, or "gunching," was the only real human factor in playing pinball.[17]

So strong was the move to "stamp out" these youth-corrupting machines in the early 1940's that New York City's Mayor LaGuardia declared war against pinball machines, slot machines, weighing machines, etc.

Prior to the massive raids on establishments harboring the machines in 1942, the *New York Times* reported that, "One out of every three persons in the pinball business . . . has been arrested at least once . . . machines have replaced slot machines as a major industry and . . . the 11,080 machines now operated in New York bring in a gross 'take' of 20-25 million dollars per year . . . the average weekly gross 'take' per machine is between 35-40 dollars, of which 40-50% is paid out in prizes."[18]

When you consider that the machines were operated on nickles in 1941, the daily average income per machine reflects an obsessive interest by the general public in playing pinball.

LaGuardia condemned the pinball machines as, " 'an evil and a menace' to young persons because they develop the gambling urge in children"[19] This statement was the springboard for nearly a year of raiding of establishments, of arresting operators, and of axing up machines (ala Carrie Nation) in five burroughs of New York City. On January 22, 1942, war was declared against the so-called gambling machines, and in the first nightly raid, 1,802 machines were seized throughout the city.[20] By February 1, 1942, 3,261 machines had been taken and 1,593 summonses issued for possession of the gambling devices.

After World War II, the tables were turned, so to speak, with a historic development, the flipper. Designed by Harry Mabs in 1947, the flipper was not only to save the pinball machine from oblivion, but to remain as an essential device on all machines manufactured since that time. Gottlieb and Co. manufactured the first commercial machine to use flippers, "Humpty Dumpty" in 1947. The flipper, a rubber bat joined to a solenoid, could be controlled by the player by means of pushing a button on the side of the machine.[21] This small, but influential, device moved the pinball machine a little further away from a mere gambling device. In addition, manufacturers began altering their machines to award extra balls or free games instead of cash for a winning score.[22]

Now, skill—required only slightly on the older machines— became a significant part of the game, as one learned to manipulate the flippers.

Today, the pinball industry is flourishing, supplying machines to all parts of the world. Complicated machines with asymetrical playfields, drum scoring counters, messenger balls, captive balls, and electric comic book art are active once again throughout the smoke-filled bars and noisy arcades of America. The manufacturers of these "dream machines" produce six to twelve models per year, with each machine having a specific run of from one to four months. During that period, the company will be producing only one model; so in effect, each pinball machine is a limited edition.[23] Of the 50,000 or so games produced each year, 40% are sold in the U.S.[24]

In recent years, the brightly colored flashing machines have become popular as collector's items. Like Mickey Mouse watches, old comic books, and decoder rings, the older and more rare machines like "Contact", "Bingo", or "Bally-Hoo" are expensive and difficult to obtain. Most who buy machines for home entertainment purchase used ones from a distributor and pay from $500 to $900 for a four-player machine. They then treat the instruments as something far more important and "sacred" than mere machines.

Video games, such as "Pong," electronic tennis, "Gotcha,"

as well as air hockey, football, and various other electronic games have become popular bar and arcade machines, as well as home entertainment devices. More often than not those machines involve more skill and player to player competition as in a sporting event, than pinball does.

"Your community may be helping perpetuate one of the most vicious of all rackets—one that spreads gambling and corruption to practically every street corner, and has as its potential target every child."[25] No, it's not the slot machine, or even the local numbers racket, but merely the pinball machine. Articles like the one this statement was taken from were quite common prior to the inclusion of manual flippers on the various models of pinball machines manufactured in this country. Still, even after the human factor was admissible in court as evidence that the pinball machine was not wholly a gambling device (providing that it did not pay off in valuables for a good score), public opinion was most always unfavorable toward the amusement device. Quite possibly this public opinion against the pinball machine could be linked to the general attitude toward leisure activities in America, especially prior to the late 1950's. Wasting time was in direct opposition to the Protestant Work Ethic, where working hard was the sum and total within itself.

During the 1950's especially, the pinball machine was under heavy fire from nearly every small town decency organization and family magazine in the country. For instance, this statement from *Better Homes and Gardens*, typifies the middle class opinion of pinballing during this period, especially from the standpoint of community leaders and law enforcement officials:

> Be ready for the argument that pinball is a harmless little game. Here's what one of the country's leading crime fighters, James W. Connor, director of St. Louis Crime Commission says: "Pinball feeds on vast sums siphoned from the worn pockets of those least able to afford the sucker's game of rigged odds. If allowed to get out of hand, it can wreck the civic enterprise and economic well-being of any village, town, or city."[26]

At the same time that article appeared in *Better Homes and Gardens, Harper's Magazine* ran a story written by Julius Segal, entitled "The Lure of Pinball." Here, the middle class paranoia was mentioned, but the predominant tone was pro-pinball. This article is one of the first in major magazines to point out the differences between pinball of modern times and the slot machines of the 1930's and 1940's. As noted in the article, one pinball player's opinion of the game is much the same as present day views and demonstrates the gnawing-sexual-religious overtones of the game and the machine:

"If I could win on every try," he said
"there'd be no fun to this game; losing
every time would make me quit, too. It's
like chasing a woman. There's always that
chance you'll catch her. But if you knew
for certain, the chase would hardly be worth it.[27]

With computerization becoming more and more prevalent in business and industry, the assumption here might be that Americans were feeling the pressures of a mechanized society, especially where machines and/or computers were taking over human jobs. The idea of "beating the machine" was raised to an iconic level in the *Harper's* article:

In the pinball parlor, the player fancies, there is a machine he
can do something about, a contraption he can meet on equal
terms, an industrial challenge he can manipulate and master.
To prove it, he must deify the machine. Only then does the
practice of his crafty (but irrelevent) techniques become appropriate and satisfying.[28]

J. Anthony Lukas, Pulitzer Prize winning free lance writer, set forth part of what might be termed a "pinball philosophy" —again touching on the religious aspect—in a recent article in *New Yorker Magazine:*

. . . the game does give you a sense of controlling things in a way
that in life you can't do. And there is risk in it, too. The ball flies
into the ellipse, into the playfield—full of opportunities. But there's
always the death channel—the run-out slot. There are rewards, prizes,
coming off the thumper-bumper. The ball crazily bounces from
danger to opportunity and back to danger. You need reassurance in
life that in taking risks you will triumph, and pinball gives you that
reaffirmation. Life is a risky game, but you can beat it.[29]

In recent years the pinball machine has become the "in" thing to analyze in clinical psychology classes, to have in one's rumpus room, and to parallel to sociological patterns. As one psychologist, Ronald F. Balas, noted in a recent

Cleveland Plain Dealer feature:

> . . . Some are attracted by the pitfalls: the tile, the lost ball, the
> narrowly missed target. He is a loser who is "reinforcing his self-
> destructive anxiety" . . . the pinball player is much like the rapist,
> striving for power over the woman, forcing her into submission.
> The actual submission is not important, it's the process leading
> up to it.[30]

For the average player, perhaps, pinball does not control
his life. With some, however, the truly iconic characteristics
are obvious when, in biblical terms, the flesh and spirit meet
in ecstasy approaching religious experience, as explained by
one player in *Playboy:*

> Now I got a steady job, fixing pin machines. I'm 25, you know?
> Time I was settling down. I got my own apartment—just one'
> room, but I got three machines in it. Also a bed . . . About a
> month ago, my girl was playing one of my channies and I was
> balling her from behind, you know? We sometimes like it that
> way, while she plays the machines. She was playing Four Million
> B.C. and she had over 80,000 points on the first ball. Well, on the
> second ball she went over 100,000, and then, just as she hit the
> volcano—that's the big apple on Four Million B.C.—she came. She
> lost all three balls. They just drained right down; she never even
> flipped. I think she finished up at 120,000 or so. Not a bad score,
> but nothing great, either.[31]

Such contemporary thought on pinball drives one to conclude that many players indeed become "one with the machine." In seeking this togetherness some players seek the assistance of body and mind altering substances like liquor and
marijuana; many, however, feel that liquor or drugs adversely
affect playing skills. But of the people who like to take
liquor or drugs while playing, a large majority favor marijuana: liquor, they feel, dulls one's senses, while smoking
marijuana heightens them and allows the player to lose himself in the game, apparently the goal of nearly half the
people who play it. Such attitudes substantiate the assumption that players deify the game and indeed treat the machine
as an icon.

As with most religious experiences, the pinball player does
not remember occurrences from the middle of the experience.
Here, in other words, the player can recall after the game is
finished how the game started, and what caused the game to

end, but has no actual memory of the experience in between shooting the ball out of the gate, and losing the ball
down the run-out passage. The experience of actually playing
the game is nebulous; glimpses of points scored, gates
opened, and targets knocked down might come to mind, but
the experience as a whole is a blur.

Further total concentration is given to the act of playing
pinball. Talking, smoking a cigarette, drinking beer or any
other liquid refreshment and eating are next to impossible
while playing the game. There seems to be a need for isolat-
ing oneself from the immediate environment of noisy crowds
and interruptions, thus creating a different environment of
flashing lights and ringing bells closely related to a hypnotic
state, where the participant has no recollection of the inter-
mediate experience.

The belief of many avid pinball players that becoming
"one" with the machine enables them to play more effectively could be tied into the idea of the pinball machine communicating with the participant on a religious basis.

If the player's awareness is outside and "above" him, then
the entire process of playing pinball, especially the inter-
mediate aspect, is a religious experience. The only personal
awareness the player has or ends up with is the realization
that he has scored points, and here triumphed over the
machine.

Becoming one with the machine implies a loss of self, or a
loss of personal awareness for a period of time. Still, some
type of awareness exists. This communication with the
machine, for the player, is in a sense religious awareness,
with personal awareness only occurring when the quarter is
dropped in the slot and the player shoots the ball onto the
playing field. At that point, where the ball is no longer totally in the player's immediate control, the religious awareness begins. At the point where the machine stops communicating to the player, when the ball drops from sight, into the
"death channel", the personal awareness of the participant
returns. He has scored, and has a basis for judging his endeavor. The act of playing the electronic maze is anomalous,
and therefore a sacred or religious experience for the participant.

Evaluating a cultural artifact, like the pinball, under these terms and means is not always an easy task. Documenting assumptions is difficult and sometimes impossible, yet it must be concluded that pinball playing is not merely a game, nor is the instrument merely a machine. It involves altering one's environment to the point of blocking out immediate awareness, psychological readiness and inducing a pinball "state of mind" where one's hands become extensions of the flippers and one's eyes become analogous to the flashing lights. In such a state one is in a potential religious ecstasy far more intense than that associated with the usual lay icons. Indeed the feeling approaches that of the individual who lays his hands on the Bible or the altar or some other religious holy article.

The people who through the years have railed against the pinball obviously knew that they were combatting a powerful force, one strong enough to shape icons and religious ecstasy —and in more ways just as far-reaching.

NOTES

[1] Spence, Lewis, *Myth and Ritual in Dance, Game and Rhyme*, p. 4-5.

[2] Spence, p. 18.

[3] Spence, p. 19.

[4] Spence, p. 20-1.

[5] Spence, p. 55.

[6] Spence, p. 55-6.

[7] McMillen/McMillen, "Electronic Amusement Devices: Some Considerations of Sex Role Differentiation."

[8] McLuhan, Marshall, *Understanding Media*, p. 210-11.

[9] Laurence, Michael, "Great Moments in Pinball History," *Playboy Magazine*, Dec., 1972, pp. 162, 260.

[10] Sharpe, Roger C., "Boing! Buzz! Tilt!" *New York Times*, December 28, 1975, p. 29.

[11] Laurence, p. 163.

[12] Sharpe, p. 29.

[13] Laurence, p. 260.

[14] Laurence, p. 260.

[15] Sharpe, p. 29.

[16] Laurence, p. 260.

[17] Sharpe, p. 29.

[18] *New York Times*, December 28, 1941, 25:3.

[19] *Ibid.*

[20] *New York Times*, January 22, 1942, 19:5.

[21] *New York Times*, February 22, 1942, 30:2.

[22] *New York Times*, October 17, 1942, 17:2.

[23] *New York Times*, March 7, 1943, 34:1.

[24]Laurence, p. 260.

[25]Sharpe, p. 29.

[26]*Better Homes and Gardens,* October, 1957, p. 142.

[27]Segal, Julius, "The Lure of Pinball," *Harper's Magazine,* October, 1957 p. 142.

[28]*Ibid.*

[29]*New Yorker,* June 30, 1975, p. 81.

[30]*Cleveland Plain Dealer,* Sunday Magazine, January 11, 1976, p. 6.

[31]Laurence, p. 260.

The One-Armed Bandit: A Lasting Icon

Richard A. Kallan

CASE # 1: Tourist. Comes to Las Vegas and discovers its charm. Plays incessantly for days. It is an experience in life.

CASE # 2: Tourist/Resident: Dabbles only occasionally, but once started, cannot stop. Plays fast and furious when the urge overcomes. It is part of life.

CASE # 3: Resident. Plays almost every day at favorite spot. Nothing else really matters much. It *is* life.

Addicts all. Three kinds of people hooked on one of the most popular "drugs" of our time: the slot machine. Revered, respected, and sometimes personified, the slot machine as a popular icon symbolizes the fantasies of its fortune-hunting suitors. Yes, it is true that most "pop icons deal with the flux and impermanence of contemporary Protean Man," as Marshall Fishwick observes,[1] but the slot machine seems somewhat different; having endured a century of technological refinement, it appears less ephemeral than most products of popular culture. Perhaps because it reflects man's *timeless,* almost *spiritual* aspiration for material riches, the slot machine tenaciously survives.

Coin operated gambling devices first appeared in the 1870s.[2] These early pin-wheel or color wheel slot machines were ornately crafted out of wood and iron and usually stood five to seven feet tall and one and a half to two feet wide. By inserting a coin in any one of six colored slots, a handle was freed, allowing the player to place into spin an upright dial, similar to a roulette wheel but calibrated into colors represented by the coin slots. Winning meant guessing the correct color at which the wheel would stop. By century's end, these machines were extremely popular, with the Caille Brothers (Detroit), Mills Novelty (Chicago), and to a lesser degree, Watling Manufacturing (Chicago) being the three largest manufacturers.

Eventually size became a problem with the pin-wheel slots. The twentieth century saw many of America's newly arriving immigrants opening small businesses, usually in cramped quarters. These struggling proprietors had neither the money nor the space to house the massive pin-wheels. To meet this changing market, manufacturers began to develop smaller counter machines. Inexpensive and compact (which also made them easy to conceal from law enforcement agencies), the counter models were well received by owners and alluring to players; the old console slot machine soon would be obsolete. The slot machine as we know it today was born.

Some consider the first counter slot machine to be Charles Fey's Liberty Bell, which the young inventor introduced to San Francisco in 1895. Fey built, merchandised, and serviced his own machines for a rapidly expanding clientele. Although Fey's enterprising spirit never ventured beyond the San Francisco area, notice of his fame reached the Midwest. Herbert Mills wished to purchase a Fey machine, but Fey, who placed his Liberty Bells in local stores on a percentage basis while still maintaining ownership, refused. Some years later, Mills dubiously secured a model of the Liberty Bell which he copied; others then copied Mills. Compared to similar counter slots, Fey's Liberty Bell was lighter and simpler in construction, faster and more exciting in play. Understandably, it led to new interest among players and revolutionized the slot machine industry.

Slot machines enjoyed a prosperous period for the next several decades. O.D. Jennings and Edwin Pace, formerly associated with Mills, opened their own successful companies, and still others later would follow. The industry was burgeoning. But soon the moral fiber of many influential citizens was sizzling. States began to outlaw slot machines, and by 1951, the federal government had banned the interstate sale of slots to destinations where illegal. Bally Manufacturing, which had started slot machine production in 1938, halted its operations in 1951 because of local and state legal harassment.

By 1960, Nevada was about the only place where slot machines remained legal. There in large casinos, slots occupied much of the floor space given to gambling. Then in 1964, Chicago's gambling statutes having been liberalized, Bally reentered the slot machine business. They introduced an electric table model which made play faster, allowed for greater game variation, and kept a more accurate tally of jackpot winners. The Bally machine set the style for all future casino slots; today virtually all machines in Nevada casinos are electric.

Nickel slots remain the most popular, followed by quarter, dime, half dollar, and dollar machines; occasionally a five dollar or a penny slot can be found. Most machines allow multiple coin play in a variety of ways. But the basic contruction of the slot machine has not changed since Charles Fey's Liberty Bell. You still insert the coin, pull the handle, and watch the three or four adjacent cylinder reels spin your fortune. The wheels stop and a symbol combination is produced. Some are rewarded and others are not. It is that simple.

Nevertheless, there is a magic to slot machines. Sitting row after row, they beckon and fetch our attentions with their brightly flashing lights and their shimmering glow of multicolored wheels spinning amidst the plush, chandelier-illuminated casino. They beg us to come closer—to look, to touch, to play. So, so easy: just insert and pull. No rules to master, no etiquette to learn. No need to be rushed or bothered by the impatient veterans of Craps and Blackjack. All is very relaxed and low-keyed.

It is a private experience. No crowds, no onlookers. No disapproving, discouraging glances from smug peers. No one there to watch your mistakes—even if you *could* make mistakes. Slot machines are gentle and easy. Even the beginner, perhaps initially unsure and a little self-conscious, quickly learns. Before long the hands are working together, inserting coins and pulling handles at a staggeringly fast rate. Suddenly you are transformed into an expressionless, mechanical, but quite proficient robot. For a brief moment, the world has stopped, and you and slot machine are alone. The effect is mesmerizing.[3]

And always they await you. Strategically located, they are virtually everywhere. Situated where showroom, restaurant, and even restroom lines are likely to form, their columns stare at you from right to left as you stand idly waiting. And should you leave the casino, they form a grand departure salute at the door. Slot machines are found also in local taverns, restaurants, supermarkets, and discount stores. As if that were not enough, the battle fatigued cannot even leave Las Vegas without running into them at the airport or bus terminal. Escape is impossible: you are caught coming and going—and in between. Clearly the slot machine represents the most pervasive form of gambling in Nevada.

But why? Beyond the slot machine's obvious rhetorical dimensions, additional appeals—relative acceptance, associated myths, wish-fulfilling potential—make the slot machine Nevada's most popular risk.

Relative Acceptance. Slot machine play carries less of the "gambling stigma" than other forms of betting. In fact, to confess addiction to slot machines usually provokes laughter, rarely somber concern; no one takes the slot player too seriously. The passive acceptance of slot machines is owed to a couple of factors. First, slot machines are popular with women, whom many still consider the "purer" sex. Perhaps perceived as less vulnerable than men to "big city" vice, women by their "innocence" give respectability to gambling. Hence, a woman playing slot machines—even if an addict—might be tagged as frivolous or strange, but certainly not evil or wicked; neither woman nor machine is viewed as sinister. Second, slot machines, unlike other gambling games, are found not only in casinos but, as noted, in local businesses as well. To the Nevada resident (or familiar tourist for that matter), slots are part of the everyday, normal scenery.

Moreover, the All-American, commonplace aura of its surroundings—"Safeway," "K-Mart," "Bob's Big Boy"—lends
legitimacy to the slot machine and influences how we perceive its presence. Slots, you inevitably must conclude, are
harmless enough to prevail in even the most family oriented
of environments.

Associated Myths. As with any icon, there are many
myths concerning slot machines. It is thought, for example,
that because minimum and maximum bets are so small, slot
machines are never a serious threat to hard earned wages.
"You can't lose very much playing slot machines" is the common misconception, and the money does go a long way . . .
right?

True, only a small amount of money can be lost on any
single play, but considering that a machine can be played
600 times an hour on the average, money is lost amazingly
fast. And the cost dramatically increases when one moves
from nickel to dime, to quarter, to dollar machine. Noted
gambling authority John Scarne claims to know "a dozen
women players who have lost as much as $20,000 a year to
the machines."[4] However, since Scarne's circle of acquain-
tances is obviously limited (and hence his survey), his statistics are, no doubt, conservative.

In Las Vegas casinos, especially those oriented to local
residents, many on welfare or social security play slots
every day, losing whatever little "fortune" they have. They
cannot ultimately win, as anyone can tell them, but that does
not stop them. What with progressive jackpots and the
chance to turn small change into big bills with but a pull of
the handle, why not? After all, is there anything better to
do? Little else competing for their attentions, they befriend
all that is available: a complex mass of electrical circuitry.
The slot machine provides both an escape from boredom and
a dream excursion.

A second myth that we often hear is that a machine "is
ready" to pay off, as if the machine somehow were programmed to be generous at a precise moment in time. Not
the case. Payoffs are determined only by the laws of probability; machines are not "set" to pay off after collecting a
specific amount of money or after some specific number of

plays. People fall victim to the old gambler's fallacy—the mistaken notion that the odds of winning increase following a long series of losses. Theoretically, the odds of winning are equal for each single play of the machine. (Your overall chances of winning at least once do increase the more times you play, but so does your investment.) Similarly, there is no reason to abandon a machine after winning a jackpot, for the odds of winning again stay random. Although the chances are extraordinarily remote, it is even possible to catch as many as, say, three consecutive jackpots; but conversely, there is nothing about the machine's construction—beyond the probability created—that guarantees it must *ever* pay off.

Yet another fallacy associated with slot machines relates to the "house" or casino's winning advantage. Statements like "85% return" are usually interpreted by players to mean that the machine keeps 85% of all money deposited. Just the opposite is true. Slot machines in major Nevada casinos usually offer enough winning combinations that they return anywhere from 80% to 95% of all coins collected. Thus, for every twenty coins deposited, a machine in theory might return eighteen in winnings, if the percentage take is 10%.[5] But that does not mean, nor is it even likely, that most who begin with $20 will go home with $18. What happens is that the player empties $20 into a machine. after which he has $18 left in winnings; then he plays his $18 and ends up with $16.20 in winnings; and so forth. Because one usually keeps re-inserting his winnings, the 10% attrition rate eventually decimates the bankroll. Few slot machine players ever return home as victors.

The Dream Machine. Most casinos recognize that their best advertising is a winner. And people *do* win at slot machines, although not normally for long. Loudspeakers announce big winners, while smaller jackpot scores are broadcasted by sirens, buzzers, and flashing lights. Losing players . . . well, no need to remind anyone that you can lose. So you may not be doing well, but why give up? All around are the sounds of victory. It can be done . . . . Little victories spur you on—a dollar jackpot here, another there. You are still behind but not that much. *If I can win small, why shouldn't I be able to win big? Others are doing it. Am I any different?*

Play on. *I'm coming so close!* But the machine is tantalizing you, for it is the near misses that keep you coming back—*I can't leave when I'm this close.* But you are no closer than when you started. The possible symbol combinations are such that there will always be far more near misses than hits.

But *others* are winning, so, understandably, no one ever completely abandons hope. All believe in the possibility that their wildest dreams might be realized. After all, is not luck itself something strange and mystical—almost extra-terrestrial? Who knows what will happen next? Alright, so now you are down to your last dollars and you decide to convert to quarters. You will try to win the Chevrolet Corvette advertised on the casino marquee (many casinos offer automobiles as jackpot prizes on special quarter machines). It takes only one quarter. No one tells you the odds, but you can figure that if there are 25 symbols on each reel and one car symbol per reel, the chances are 25 x 25 x 25 x 25 to 1, or 390,625 to 1. Still, thoughts of winning . . . .

The dream? Always the same: a small bankroll, some skillful parlaying, a little bit of luck. Why not? The dream is reinforced by the "temporary" winners all around you and by the legendary stories of huge winnings. Equally persuasive is your own brief run of luck, for it sets you to wondering: *what if* I had played a dollar instead of a nickel machine . . . *what if* my streak had continued just a little longer. . . . If, only if. . . . Even penniless, the dream does not totally die. For while you were winning, you momentarily experienced the majestic exhilaration of victory. It was all so incredible, so uncanny . . . *maybe there is a CONTROLLER . . . and maybe I am the CHOSEN ONE. . . .*

Most people, of course, eventually learn that it is the slot machine, not the player, who is Lord and Master. Ironically, that may be the ultimate appeal of the one-armed bandit. Because deep down you know you cannot win, your expectations are more realistic . . . the dream is shaken but never shattered. You recognize and accept your fate, and your losses are palatable, so why be down on slot machines? Still offering hope—a durable commodity in any age—the slot machine remains an ageless, universal addicter . . . a welcomed hallucinogenic that may well be one of America's few, lasting popular icons.

NOTES

[1]"Entrance," in *Icons of Popular Culture,* ed. Marshall Fishwick and Ray B. Browne (Bowling Green: Bowling Green Univ. Popular Press, 1970), p. 3.

[2]For two good pictorial histories of slot machines, see David G. Christensen, *Slot Machines: A Pictorial Review* (Chicago: D. G. Christensen, 1972); and "Pictorial Hisotry: 100 Years of Slot Machines, 1875 to 1975," *Marketplace,* Dec. 1975, Jan., Feb., March, April, May, June 1976, pp. 1-98. (The series, already carried to seven installments, is still being written.)

[3]Says Charlotte Olmsted in her psychological study of gambling, *Heads I Win, Tails You Lose* (New York: Macmillan, 1962), p. 61, "The rhythmic movement and the monotonous sound of the machine also probably have a decided hypnotic effect, as witnessed by the glazed, vacant expression and lack of response to outside stimuli of the long-term player."

[4]*The Women's Guide to Gambling* (New York: Crown, 1967), p. 90.

[5]For an excellent discussion of slot machines and the percentages of winning at various casinos, see Jacques Noir, *Casino Holiday* (Berkeley: Oxford Street Press, 1968), pp. 39-60.

Postage Stamps As Icons

David Curtis Skaggs

When paper is so imprinted as to become currency or postage stamps, it becomes *iconic*. At that moment, the paper takes on a value—both economically and symbolically—which it could not have had before. In our book's terminology, the artifact-as-symbol has taken on a new dimension, and a new role in popular culture.

For years postage stamps were dominated by portraits of culture-heroes. In many instances (consider English stamps, for example) they were like classical busts of Roman emperors and generals . . . people who belonged on Olympus as well as on letters. And what power: they had the authority to take documents across the land, indeed around the world. Not only letters, but all important legal documents must be *stamped*. And what higher compliment than to say that a story "bears the stamp of truth"?

I propose to look at our Revolution, now entering its third century, through postage stamps, conceiving and cataloguing them as icons of America's birth.

No other governmental artifact so symbolizes the nation's popular self-image and no single event has been represented more often on these icons of communication than the American Revolution. The postage stamp became a vehicle for impressing on all citizens the reverence of the nation's founders and founding that the federal government felt necessary to create and to maintain a strong national identity. Moreover, because of the multiplicity of different philatelic icons used in the last one-and-a-third centuries, we can examine how that desired image changed over time.

From the first stamps of 1847 depicting Benjamin Franklin and George Washington until the "Spirit of '76" series that opened our bicentennial year, the ordinary postage stamp has made an important contribution to the creation and perpetuation of our patriotic image. An analysis of the past 130 years of postal iconology reveals five basic areas in which stamps relating to the Revolution may be categorized: (1) individuals; (2) battles; (3) events and documents; (4) symbols; and (5) groups.

In the individual category, Washington, Franklin, and Jefferson clearly predominate. Since 1861 they have been in every general issue series issued by the Post Office. Normally one of them, usually Washington, is on the stamp used for mailing letters and one of the others, usually Franklin, on the one for post cards. With the exception of patriots who became presidents—such as James Monroe, and James Madison—and such notables as the Marquis de Lafayette and Alexander Hamilton, whose major fame postdates the revolutionary era, few personalities of the era have either repeated often or been part of the regular issues. John Adams was not utilized until the regular issue of 1938-53. He never repeated.

Most of the honored individuals fall into the military category—John Paul Jones, John Barry, and Nathanael Greene, are good examples. No enlisted personnel merited such recognition until 1975 when Peter Francisco and Salem Poor were depicted in the "Contributors to the Cause" series. Among the political heroes are Patrick Henry, John Marshall, Albert Gallatin, and finally, in 1965, a radical like Thomas Paine. Other easily recognizable heroes are Nathan Hale, Paul Revere, and Daniel Boone. Francisco, a Portuguese-American, and Poor, a black, are members in an ethnic group tradition that dates back to the 1930s with stamps honoring Casimir Pulaski and Thaddeus Kusciuszko of Poland, and Frederick von Steuben of Germany. The latest in this ethnic imagery is Haym Salomon, a Polish-born Jewish financier. The Salomon stamp is another in the "Contributors to the Cause" series. No set of stamps so emphasizes the change of the Postal Service toward the bicentennial as compared with previous issues as does this one of 1975. The fourth stamp in this set lauds Sybil Ludington, a Danbury, Connecticut heroine who is hardly a household name in the pantheon of revolutionary figures. Actually she is the only woman depicted on a revolutionary era stamp whose career actually involved participation in the war effort. The first woman on a stamp, Martha Washington, has as her sole claim to fame being her husband's helpmate. Betsy Ross's claim to the design of the continental flag is somewhat tenuous. That leaves only "Molly Pitcher" who is honored by an overprint of the George Washington regular issue to commemorate the Battle of Monmouth in which she participated.

Another group of individuals frequently noted on the stamps are the artists of the era. Gilbert Stuart first appeared in self-portrait in 1940 as did Benjamin West in 1975. Charles Willson Peale was on a stamp honoring the Pennsylvania Academy of Fine Arts in 1954. Several of Peale's and John Trumbull's paintings have also been used as illustrations as did one by John Singleton Copley.

What is interesting about the entire series of individuals is not so much who is included, but rather who is excluded from the stamps. No stamp honors Horatio Gates, victor at Saratoga (later defeated at Camden), there is none for Richard Montgomery who took Montreal and died at the gates of Quebec, nor for Daniel Morgan the Virginia rifleman who fought with distinction in several major campaigns, nor for John Hancock and Henry Laurens, presidents of the Continental Congress, nor for the southern partisan leaders like Francis Marion, Thomas Sumter, and Andrew Pickens. Of course Benedict Arnold missed a stamp. Of the women of the era, one questions the omission of Mercy Otis Warren and Abigail Adams who actively participated in the intellectual ferment of the age.

The "Contributors to the Cause" series represents an important change in the postal iconography of the revolutionary era. Even though the Postal Service felt compelled to print identifying data on the back of these stamps, they constitute a revolutionary innovation. The government has used the postage stamp to recognize the "little people" rather than the "Founding Fathers." However much the official American Revolution Bicentennial Administration has chosen to ignore the unofficial Peoples' Bicentennial Commission, our postal authorities received a message and chose a new imagery in their representation of individuals on bicentennial era stamps.

Since no commemorative issues appeared during the centennial years, the issuance of stamps honoring battles of revolutionary age began with the sesquicentennial some fifty years ago. Three stamps commemorated the Boston campaign of 1775-76, single stamps honored Bennington, Saratoga, Valley Forge, Vincennes, the Sullivan Expedition into New York, and Yorktown, The omissions were glaring. Nothing on the victories at Montreal, Great Bridge, Virginia, Moore's Creek, North Carolina, Fort Moultrie, South Carolina, Trenton and Princeton, New Jersey, Stony Point, New York, Kings Mountain and Cowpens, South Carolina. Certain stalemates like Germantown, Pennsylvania, Monmouth, New Jersey, Guilford Court House, North Carolina and Eutaw Springs, South Carolina, lack philatelic remembrance. When one recalls that the defeat at Brooklyn received one stamp (depicting Washington's withdrawal, not his tactical miscalculations) and so did Washington's loss at White Plains, one wonders why the British successes at Manhattan, Quebec, Brandywine, Charleston, and Camden were omitted. This probably would have been too much to expect from the Post Office.

As the bicentennial begins we find Lexington illustrated with the same painting, this time in full color, that appeared on the 1925 commemorative. There is little to believe that a half century later the Postal Service will provide a different image of revolutionary combat than before. The second bicentennial battle scene depicted Bunker Hill, the second time in less than a decade that parts of John Trumbull's painting of the battle have adorned a United States stamp. Coupled with the Bunker Hill monument stamp of 1959, this engagement has been more celebrated in stamps than any other. Few historians would give such prominence to this battle.

Various events and documents of the revolutionary era have merited considerable attention from the Post Office imagemakers. The sesquicentennial brought stamps honoring the Northwest Ordinance of 1787, the Constitutional

Convention, the ratification, and Washington's inaugural. No stamp commemorated the Boston Tea Party, the Declaration, the Articles of Confederation, or the Bill of Rights nor any of the state constitutional developments that intrigue professional historians. Since the sesquicentennial, some of these deficiencies have been remedied. The Bill of Rights received postal recognition in 1966 and a quotation from the Declaration appeared in the Continental Congress series of 1974. A year earlier four stamps in a block depicted the Boston Tea Party. The Declaration, first commemorated in an issue of 1869, received a four-stamp strip on July 4, 1976. One might hope the Virginia Declaration of Rights of 1776 and the popular ratification of the Massachusetts Constitution of 1780 might merit stamps. Along with documents have been slogans like Henry's "Give me liberty or give me death" and Jefferson's "I have sworn . . . hostility against every form of tyranny over the mind of man" which appeared on the 1960 "American Credo" series. Here four of six quotations were by members of the revolutionary generation. A quote from the Olive branch Petition and one from the Declaration decorated two of the four "Continental Congress" stamps of 1974. More controversial are lesser-known events like the arson of the "Peggy Stewart" in Annapolis harbor in 1774 or the massacre of the Christian Delaware Indians in Ohio in 1782 are unlikely to merit postal commemoration. Although they have become more inclusive, the bicentennial stamps are no more controversial than earlier issues.

The "Continental Congress" series also marks the use of symbols in Revolutionary imagery, with two stamps representing the Congress' early meeting buildings, Carpenters' Hall and Independence Hall. Other symbolic edifices grace postage stamps, Mt. Vernon, Monticello, the Bunker Hill Monument, Washington Monument, and Gunston Hall (but who except a few Virginians or historians know the latter was the home of George Mason, author of the Virginia Declaratin of Rights?).

More typical symbols of nationhood have been the eagle, the liberty bell, and the flag. In 1851 a one-cent "U.S.P.O. Despatch" stamp with an eagle marked the beginning of an iconographic tradition long depicted on American coins. The liberty bell appeared first in 1926 and for the fourth time on the current 13¢ regular issue stamp, a denomination also depicting the eagle and shield and the flag with Independence Hall in other variations. Over thirty issues have representations of "Old Glory" in various ways. A special historic flags series of 1968 honored nine flags of the revolutionary era. The climax of flag symbolism came in 1976 with the issue of fifty stamps representing each of the states. The rise in postal rates in 1976 allowed the creation of an "Americana" series of patriotic symbols on all denominations. The capitol, the liberty bell, a drum, an old printing press, and Boston's Old North Church will become increasingly common postal icons in American households. The recent trend is to move from an iconography of individuals to one of symbols. Nowhere is this more apparent than in the current regular issue series.

Certain groups and meetings have also received philatelic honors. The Constitutional Convention in 1937, the Continental Congress in 1974, and the Continental army, navy, marines, and militia in 1975 are particularly representative of this rather limited aspect of postal depictions of the revolutionary age. A combination of symbolism and groups appeared in the opening issue of 1976—three stamps utilizing Archibal Willard's "Spirit of '76." Willard's painting of a century ago most graphically represents the popular image of the revolutionary soldier, the farm boy who picks up his musket or drum and marches off, somewhat haphazardly, to defeat the British regulars. However false this stereotype may be, it is one which Americans and the Postal Service cherish.

Two other bicentennial era series further denote the democratization of postage illustrations. The "Colonial craftsmen" of 1971 represent artisans of the revolutionary age and the "Rise of the Spirit of Independence" series of two years later showed popular means of communication via pamphlet, broadside, postrider, and drummer.These bicentennial era stamps mark a decided shift from heroic individuals to a concept of a popular revolutionary experience. Whether the general public recognizes the drift toward everyday illustrations in their bicentennial stamps is an entirely different matter.

Since the beginning of American postage stamps, the Revolution has dominated the depictions on this popular form of imagery. Whether the engravings represented individuals, events, symbols, or groups, all have sought to project the national origin in heroic terms. Most common have been the representation of individuals associated with the revolutionary age—Washington, Franklin, Jefferson, and Hamilton usually being the figures used. The bicentennial stamps show a trend away from this tradition. Is this because we live in an age without heroes but rather a time with transitory celebrities whose fuzzy images cross our television screens?

A new imagery has not yet been shown in the depiction of battles and other events. The test of any change here will come in the years after 1976. Will battles outside New England receive greater emphasis than previously? When one recognizes that the bloodiest fighting took place in the Middle Atlantic and Southern states, the distortion of historic truth represented in previous postal issues becomes increasingly obvious. Will the Articles of Confederation and the Peace of Paris be neglected as they were during the sesquicentennial? Only time will tell if iconography can approach reality.

We can expect the symbols of nationhood which emerged from the revolutionary era to continue to be emphasized. The latest general issue stamps in the nine, eleven, thirteen, and twenty-four cent denominations represent both the continued use of old symbols and the introduction of new ones in conjunction with cherished civil liberties. These new "Americana" stamps do not depict a single individual. While almost all these depict patriotic emblems of the Revolution, fo the first time in our national postal history the traditional icons of Washington, Franklin and Jefferson are not used to illustrate stamps.

Perhaps the most interesting aspect of the bicentennial stamps has been the drift toward representations of ordinary Americans of the revolutionary age. The revolutionary war uniforms, the "Colonial Craftsmen," the "Rise of the Spirit of Independence," and "Spirit of '76" series best exemplify this new emphasis. Although the "Contributors to the Cause" stamps illustrate individuals, they represent at the same time the contributions of all women, blacks, Jews, and ordinary enlisted men to the independence effort. The 1976 issuance of a joint Canadian-American commemorative honoring Franklin's role as British postmaster general for North America might allow for the joint printing of a stamp honoring the real losers of the Revolution—the Loyalists, many of whom went to Canada. If we could go that far, Americans would be going a long way toward making a popular representation of the usually ignored civil war aspect of our national birth.

When, about 1983, the last postage stamp commemorating the bicentennial is printed, we will have both a reaffirmation of traditional iconography concerning the Revolutionary experience and the introduction of new symbols depicting our nation's birth. Whatever the collective bicentennial postal image, it represents a continuation of the most common and most diverse of Uncle Sam's icons and describes our multifaceted infatuation with our national birth.

Postage Stamps Depicting the Revolution

Scott No.	Denomination	Date	Illustration
1	.05	1847	Benjamin Franklin*
2	.10	1847	George Washington*
12	.05	1851	Thomas Jefferson*
OC2	.01	1851	Eagle "Despatch"
116	.01	1869	Eagle and Shield
120	.24	1869	Declaration of Independence
121	.30	1869	Shield, Eagle, and Flags
143	.30	1870	Alexander Hamilton*
262	2.00	1894	James Madison*
306	.08	1902	Martha Washington
324	.02	1904	Jefferson-Louisiana Purchase
325	.03	1904	James Monroe-Louisiana Purchase
551	.00 1/2	1922	Nathan Hale
556	.08	1922	Martha Washington
562	.10	1922	James Monroe*
617	.01	1925	Washington at Cambridge
618	.02	1925	Lexington and Concord
619	.05	1925	Minute Man Statue
627	.02	1926	Liberty Bell

*Subsequent regular issue stamps illustrating this individual are not listed.

POSTAL ICONS OF THE AMERICAN REVOLUTION

INDIVIDUALS

Benjamin Franklin
Scott #1—1847

Casimir Pulaski
Scott #690—1931

BATTLES

Lexington and Concord
Scott #1563—1975

Surrender of Vincennes
Scott #651—1929

Washington Reviewing Troops
Scott #617—1925

Boston Tea Party
Scott #1480-1483—1974

GROUPS

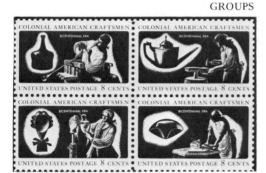

Colonial Craftsmen
Scott #1456-1459—1971

Revolutionary Uniforms
Scott #1565-1568—1975

SYMBOLS

Eagle
Scott #OC2—1851

Mount Vernon
Scott #1032—1954

629	.02	1926	Battle of White Plains
643	.02	1927	Battle of Bennington
644	.02	1927	Saratoga Surrender
645	.02	1927	Valley Forge - Washington Praying
651	.02	1928	G. R. Clark takes Vincennes
657	.02	1929	J. Sullivan Expedition in N.Y.

680	.02	1929	A. Wayne - Fallen Timbers
689	.02	1930	Frederick von Steuben
690	.02	1931	Casimir Pulaski
703	.02	1931	Yorktown - Washington, Rochambeau, de Grasse
704-715	.00½-.10	1932	Washington Bicentennial - 12 Stamps
727	.03	1933	Washington Headquarters-Peace Sesquicentennial
734	.05	1933	Thaddeus Kosciuszko
785	.01	1936	U.S. Army - Washington & N. Greene
790	.01	1936	U.S. Navy - J.P. Jones & J. Barry
795	.03	1937	Northwest Ordinance
798	.03	1937	Constitutional Convention
804	.01½	1938	Martha Washington
806	.02	1938	John Adams
835	.03	1938	Ratification of the Constitution
837	.03	1938	Northwest Territory
623	.06	1938	Bald eagle - air mail
854	.03	1939	Washington Inauguration
884	.01	1940	Gilbert Stuart
947	.03	1947	Postage Stamp Centenary - Washington & Franklin
1003	.03	1951	Battle of Brooklyn
1004	.03	1952	Betsy Ross
1010	.03	1952	Marquis de Lafayette
1011	.03	1952	Mount Rushmore
1032	.01½	1954	Mount Vernon
1034	.02½	1954	Bunker Hill Monument
1044	.10	1054	Independence Hall
1046	.15	1954	John Jay
1047	.20	1954	Monticello
1048	.25	1954	Paul Revere
1052	1.00	1954	Patrick Henry
C54	.04	1954	Eagle in flight - air mail

1064	.03	1955	Pennsylvania Academy - C.W. Peale
1071	.03	1955	Fort Ticonderoga
1073	.03	1955	Franklin - 250 anniversary
1086	.03	1957	Hamilton Bicentennial
1097	.03	1957	Lafayette Bicentennial
1105	.03	1958	Monroe Bicentennial
1108	.03	1958	Gunston Hall
1119	.04	1958	Freedom of Press
C57	.10	1959	Liberty Bell - air mail
1139	.04	1960	American Credo - Washington Quote
1140	.04	1960	American Credo - Franklin Quote
1141	.04	1960	American Credo - Jefferson Quote
1144	.04	1960	American Credo - Henry Quote
C62	.13	1961	Liberty Bell - air mail
C67	.06	1963	Bald Eagle - air mail
1273	.05	1965	J.S. Copley Painting
1279	.01¼	1965	Albert Gallatin
1292	.40	1965	Thomas Paine
1312	.05	1966	Bill of Rights - 175th anniversary
1345	.06	1968	Historic Flags - Ft. Moultrie (1776)
1347	.06	1968	Historic Flags - Washington's Cruisers (1775)
1348	.06	1968	Historic Flags - Bennington (1777)
1349	.06	1968	Historic Flags - Rhode Island (1775)
1350	.06	1968	Historic Flags - Stars & Stripes (1777)
1351	.06	1968	Historic Flags - Bunker Hill (1775)
1352	.06	1968	Historic Flags - Grand Union (1776)
1353	.06	1968	Historic Flags - Phila. Light Horse (1775)
1354	.06	1968	Historic Flags - Navy Jack (1775)
1357	.06	1968	Folklore - Daniel Boone
1361	.06	1968	John Trumbull
1387	.06	1970	Bald Eagle
1432	.08	1971	Revolution Bicentennial
1456	.08	1971	Colonial Craftsmen - Glassmaker
1457	.08	1971	Colonial Craftsmen - Silversmith
1458	.08	1971	Colonial Craftsmen - Wigmaker
1459	.08	1971	Colonial Craftsmen - Hatter
1474	.08	1972	Stamp Collecting - Franklin
1476	.08	1973	Colonial Communications - Printer
1477	.08	1973	Colonial Communications - Broadside
1478	.08	1973	Colonial Communications - Postrider
1479	.08	1973	Colonial Communications - Drummer
1480-1483	.08	1973	Boston Tea Party - 4 - stamp block
1509	.10	1974	50-Star & 13-Star Flag
1542	.10	1974	Fort Harrod, Ky. bicentennial

1543	.10	1974	Continental Congress - Carpenters' Hall
1544	.10	1974	Continental Congress
1545	.10	1974	Continental Congress - Declaration Quote
1546	.10	1974	Continental Congress - Independence Hall
1553	.10	1975	Benjamin West
1559	.08	1975	Contributors to Cause - Sybil Ludington
1560	.10	1975	Contributors to Cause - Salem Poor
1561	.10	1975	Contributors to Cause - Haym Salomon
1562	.18	1975	Contributors to Cause - Peter Francisco
1563	.10	1975	Battles of Lexington & Concord
1564	.10	1975	Battle of Bunker Hill
1565	.10	1975	Revolution Uniforms - Army
1566	.10	1975	Revolution Uniforms - Navy
1567	.10	1975	Revolution Uniforms - Marines
1568	.10	1975	Revolution Uniforms - Militia
1572-1575	.10	1975	200 Years of Postal Service - 4 stamps
1591	.09	1975	Right to assemble - Capitol
1593	.11	1975	Freedom of the Press
1596	.13	1975	E Pluribus Unum - Eagle & Shield
1603	.24	1975	Midnight ride - Old North Church
1615	.079	1975	Drum
1618	.13	1975	Proclaim Liberty - Liberty bell
1622	.13	1975	Independence Hall and 13-star flag
1629-1631	.13	1976	"Spirit of '76" - 3 stamp strip
1632	.13	1976	Interphil '76
1633-1682	.13	1976	State flags - 50 stamp sheet
1686	.13	1976	Surrender of Corwallis 5-stamp souvenir sheet
1687	.18	1976	Declaration of Independence 5-stamp souvenir sheet
1688	.24	1976	Crossing Delaware 5-stamp souvenir sheet
1689	.31	1976	Valley Forge 5-stamp souvenir sheet
1690	.13	1976	Franklin, Postmaster General
1691-1694	.13	1976	Declaration of Independence 4-stamp strip

For additional information on American stamps see the first volume of the latest edition of the SCOTT STANDARD POSTAGE STAMP CATALOGUE and the Postal Service's UNITED STATES POSTAGE STAMPS (Washington: Government Printing Office, 1972) with supplements.

Ladies And Liberation: Icon And Iconoclast In The Women's Movement

Edith Mayo

"Icons are images and ideas converted into three dimensions . . . external expressions of internal convictions. . . ." wrote Marshall Fishwick in the introduction to *Icons of Popular Culture*.[1] In our culture, where politics is the secularized religion, one of the more fascinating icons is the political icon — the political button. With interest in and study of the women's movement a major part of today's historical reinterpretation, it becomes important to examine the political icons of the women's movement as seen in the political button. What images of women, what issues affecting women have been projected into our cultural consciousness through the political button? What values have informed our way of life relating to women?

The earliest use of women in conjunction with political buttons dates from the campaign of 1856. This was the first campaign of the newly-formed Republican Party which ran John C. Frémont as its presidential candidate. Jessie Benton Frémont, daughter of the famous Senator Thomas Hart Benton, had eloped with John C. Frémont, marrying him against the wishes of her father. It was a tale to delight the hearts of Victorians who, despite protestations to the contrary, appreciated the triumph of love (and passion) over the conventions of daughterly submission to fatherly injunctions. Frémont's supporters issued a medal with the likeness of Frémont inscribed beneath, "Jessie's Choice."[2] (See figure 1). This was an early use in politics of what we would call today the "sex sell."

209

Figure 1

From this beginning at mid-century, and continuing until the end of the century, the wife of the political candidate is increasingly introduced into the campaign as the symbolic idealization of American womanhood — the epitomizing of the Victorian era's "Lady" syndrome — to be the candidate for "First Lady" (telling phrase). In trying to humanize the candidate and present him as Everyman in a campaign:

> . . . the center of the scene of the candidate's domesticity is the wife. Increasingly she has been developed as a candidate for First Lady. While still primarily a homemaker and companion to her husband considerably more attention is being paid to her as a potential mistress of the White House with all of the social obligations and public appearances this entails . . . . It is interesting to note that as her fitness for the 'public office' of First Lady comes increasingly to be emphasized, there is also an intensification of insistence on her domesticity. . . . Part of the process of humanizing the candidate is a gay little sally into the courtship in which he won his paragon of wifely virtue. . . . It seems particularly inappropriate that this emphasis on romance should begin with Cleveland. [While it is now evident from study of campaign materials that the emphasis did not begin with Cleveland, it certainly reached its zenith during his campaigns of 1888 and 1892.] Yet the middle-aged, corpulent statesman, the confessed sire of a bastard child, titillated the nation with his courtship of a young college girl that ended in a White House wedding. In his campaign for re-election, Cleveland's biographers had a field day describing the wedding in minute detail.[3]

Perhaps, in retrospect, this development is not so puzzling. With the nascent women's movement, the First Lady became the political symbolization of the permitted roles of American women — selfless helpmate, wife, mother, paragon of virtue, arbiter of morality, who set the social and moral tone of society and engaged in countless varieties of "uplift" (a legitimate term before it became identified with today's bra ads). Buttons, posters, ribbons, advertising cards, and sheet music were circulated in her honor. (See figure 2.) Essentially the First Lady iconography consisted of a recognition factor only — recognition of both personality and role. It was, however, an important political exercise in role enforcement carried out at a national level.

Figure 2

The Victorian "Ideal" of woman as paragon of virtue and queen of the home was touted as evidence of the elevated status of woman in society. No greater symbol could have availed itself for mass dissemination than Frances Folsom Cleveland, First Lady of the Land. Frances was hailed as young, beautiful, excelling in social graces; innocent. Nothing was mentioned about the double standard — indeed, public sentiment did not seem to notice there was one. These early political icons of First Lady exhibit many of the appeals and uses of campaign symbols which continued into the 1960's.

The only other women depicted in politics during this era were not represented as positive icons (revered symbols). Two women, Victoria Woodhull and Belva Lockwood, who ran for the Presidency on the Equal Rights ticket in 1872 and 1884 and 1888 respectively, were the distinct exceptions which proved the rule. Political materials exist which were distributed by their supporters,[4] but more numerous were those circulated by their detractors (See figure 3). Ridicule

Figure 3

to keep women in "woman's sphere" has always been a dominant means of social control which continues to the present. Politics was decidedly outside "women's proper sphere." Here, was seen operating the icon as destructive force.

With the decline of the Victorian Ideal of woman at the end of the century, and the serious drive for woman suffrage being organized at that time, no First Lady candidates appear on political buttons again until the 1930's. This suggests confusion over the role of women in society and, particularly, in political life. The only icon of woman to appear on political buttons (and even she disappears after World War I) is Columbia — mythical soul of the nation — endorsing candidates for the presidency.

The First Lady does not reappear in the spotlight until Eleanor Roosevelt. Very significantly no iconic First Lady buttons of Mrs. Roosevelt exist.5 Buttons such as "I Don't Want Eleanor Either," "Eleanor? No Soap!" (See figure 4) " 'My Day' When I Vote for Willkie" (referring sarcastically to Mrs. Roosevelt's newspaper column entitled, "My Day"), and "Washington Sweepstakes: 1st. Wendell, 2nd. Franklin, 3rd.

Figure 4

Eleanor" make explicit her position as the only woman in the traditionally-honored role of First Lady ever to receive the opprobrium of a large segment of public opinion. Because she stepped outside the traditional role of women and entered the realm of politics and was effective in it as well, particularly in political campaigning and social reform, Mrs. Roosevelt became an anti-icon. It is no accident that her image does not appear on political buttons, nor is the reason to be found in her lack of beauty. Edith Willkie, whose husband ran against FDR, appeared on campaign buttons, and buttons with "We Want Edith Not Eleanor," and "We Women Want Willkie"[6] give clear evidence that she assumed the iconic role in this instance because she conformed to the societal norm of political images for women.

The primary women's political issue which appears on political buttons during the late 19th and early 20th centuries is temperance. Buttons with the photograph of Frances Willard, head of the Woman's Christian Temperance Union,[7] appeared as did buttons with children's faces who pleaded, "Vote Dry for My Sake" and "Save My Home." (See figure 5). This type of political button was allowable for women

Figure 5

because temperance was a quasi-religious movement before it took on political overtones (and was, therefore within women's sphere) and because it was presented from the viewpoint of women's primary concerns — her children and her home. Also circulated in the genre of political buttons were hatchets, whose iconic association with Carry A. Nation and her essentially un-ladylike and activist forays into saloons, was forgiven perhaps in the belief that it was in the cause of a "higher good."

Neither the First Lady nor temperance icons ever hit the cultural consciousness with the impact of the political imageries produced by woman suffrage. In the early years of the 20th century the moribund suffrage movement was revived by a variety of factors: new leadership, infusion of imaginative political and promotional techniques adopted from the English suffrage movement, effective organization, the momentum of the Progressive movement, and the decision to concentrate efforts on passage of a federal amendment. With the re-awakening of the suffrage drive came a proliferation of political materials and buttons whose aim was to sell the movement. In doing so, women created an iconography communicating the vital essence of the movement both as they felt it to be and as they wished to present it to others. In an age prior to electronic mass communication, these political icons emphasized visual imagery and recognition, and personality recognition. Although the woman's movement was originally a broad and diverse one concerned with all aspects of a woman's life, by the early 20th century the entire ideology had been subsumed in the single phrase, "Votes for Women."

> To the suffragist the vote was a symbol of a whole intellectual reorientation. Throughout the nineteenth century she had seen her sisters gain the right to education, work, their own identity in marriage, and many other rights and opportunities. The right to vote alone was denied her, or so the movement stated, and without it it seemed impossible to turn women's attention from home and family out into the affairs of the world. However, the vote became not only the symbol of the basic change of attitude, but also was infused with the myth that achieving the symbol would achieve the reality. What was a means to an end became an end in itself.[8]

Though not a visual image, the phrase, "Votes for Women" (with variants such as "Ohio Next," or "Pennsylvania Next") became the primary political icon for the suffrage movement. It brought instant recognition of an entire movement, with all its associations and meanings, to those both inside and outside the movement. "Votes for Women" buttons far outstripped in number any other political button produced by the movement. The phrase appeared on buttons of every shape, size, and color; for national and local suffrage societies; on round and oval buttons; on pins shaped like shields, pins shaped like flags, and pins in the form of pennants (which immediately conjured the parades in which the pennants were used). (See figure 6)

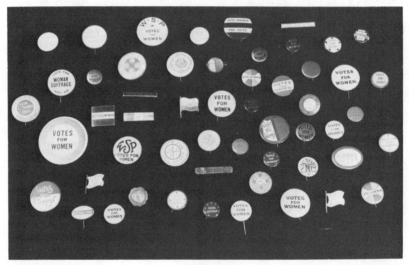

Figure 6

While "Votes for Women" buttons were the political mainstay of the movement, there were a variety of other iconic buttons produced. The images of several women within the movement achieved the status of icon: Susan B. Anthony (who, significantly, still retains her icon status in the new women's movement with buttons such as "I Love You Susan B. Anthony"), Elizabeth Cady Stanton, and Lucy Stone (whose button also advertised, "Take Her Paper." The paper

was the *Woman's Journal*, major organ of the suffrage movement for many years). These three women were immediately
recognizable and brought with that recognition the accumulated and shared experiences of organization, education,
selfless dedication, and frustration of fifty years of trying to
gain the right to vote. (See figure 7)

Figure 7

An icon which had the power to evoke instant identification was the "Joan of Arc" figure who appears variously with
sword or trumpet. She symbolized the leadership of woman
in a patriotic, "holy war," the leadership in a godly cause of
self-sacrifice for God and Country closely paralleling the suffrage movement's rhetoric. It is significant that Inez Mil-
holland of the National Woman's Party literally acted out this
imagery as she led suffrage parades clad in vaguely classical
garments astride a white horse, and that a statue of Joan of
Arc stands in the headquarters of the National Woman's
Party to this day. The Joan figure conveys at once unques-
tioned patriotism (as opposed to being "anti-system"), the

leadership by godly women of venal and bumbling men for the good of the nation, marching (the suffrage parades), and military discipline of a large corps of "troops" (if not outright militancy), (See figure 8.)

Figure 8

An allegorical figure widely used was that of a woman in classical robes, the herald, reminiscent of the idealized goddesses of Liberty and Justice, usually blowing a trumpet or carrying a torch. These figures are often backed by rays of sun, the symbolic meaning of which was heralding the dawn of a new day. Other motifs included female angels as well as the rising sun. (See figure 8.) In these motifs of "light" the sun or the torch always moves from west to east, signifying the enfranchisement of western states first and the gradual spread of suffrage across the country from west to east. This theme of "enlightenment" was a common symbolism used by both major suffrage organizations, the National American Woman Suffrage Association, and the National Woman's Party. The former used the woman with a torch enlightening the nation in many forms, while the official motto of the Woman's Party was "Forward Out of Darkness, Forward Into Light." The use of female figures in enlightenment and godliness was most consistent with the accepted roles for woman as teacher and moral arbiter. It is evident that the suffrage movement never challenged this role for women, rather used it to reinforce their claim to the franchise.

The suffrage buttons display excellent, imaginative graphics, yet they are "contained," sedate, and restrained — like the women themselves. Many buttons were personality oriented reflecting the great individual and charismatic leadership of the movement by such giants as Stanton, Anthony, Stone, and Carrie Chapman Catt. Suffrage icons admirably served the purposes, both psychological and objective, of the movement and perfectly reflected its tone. Their single theme, "Votes for Women" was calculated to appeal to the lowest common denominator — the single unifying factor in the myriad groups of reformist women who came together in suffrage as a means to achieve their goals. Their purpose was to attract all, to alienate none. They could not afford such luxury from a position of powerlessness. It was also a tactical stroke of genius which avoided having the suffrage tied to "entangling alliances" of other reforms such as prohibition, labor reforms and unions, or modification of existing sex roles.

There are two significant suffrage buttons which never became iconic. Both were distributed by the National Woman's Party and reflected their "militant" (though always passive and non-violent) tactics: the suffrage banner and the jail door (the "Jailed for Freedom" pin). Both were made of sterling silver and available only to party members. These buttons, too, reflected their origins: a small cadre of trained, disciplined, militant women, set apart from the crowd (the use of silver), who were willing to picket the White House and to be jailed for their beliefs. The "Jailed" pin was available only to those who had been incarcerated.

The suffragists, with a few important exceptions, never seriously questioned or attacked women's "ordained" role in society. No such suffrage buttons exist. Those who advocated "Votes for Women" went to great pains to assuage the fears of those who felt that voting might change women's roles in society. The suffragists correctly perceived, perhaps even believed, that demanding the vote to achieve "equality" with men would never bring them their desired goal. Only if their drive were couched in terms making the vote a necessary tool to carry out competently woman's (subervient) role in "her proper sphere" would the vote become reality. Woman's purpose was to unify, to lead the nation to greater godliness through uplifted politics, to protect home and children. Hence the iconic magic in the term "Votes for Women" for both women and men alike.

The modern women's movement has brought an enormous change in the style and rhetoric of women's political buttons. (See figure 9.) The buttons of the Women's Liberation movement have seen an explosion of subject matter oriented toward a multiplicity of women's issues and concerns, as well as

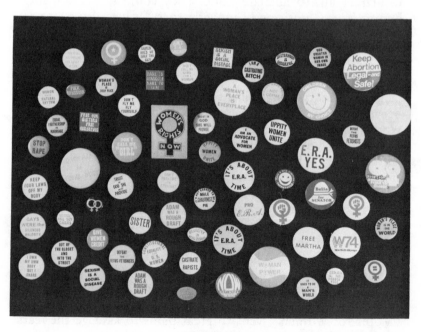

Figure 9

a dramatic increase in the political campaign buttons of women running for public office at all levels.[9]

The political buttons issued in the year 1964 give an indication of the transition of women's role in American politics. Campaign buttons were issued both for Senator Maragaret Chase Smith, the first woman in this century to run for the Presidential nomination, and for the First Lady, Lady Bird Johnson. While Senator Smith was a serious political candidate (whose campaign symbol was a ladylike red rose), she was overshadowed by Mrs. Johnson not only because Johnson was an incumbent First Lady but also because Mrs. Johnson's role was presented in a non-challenging light. She was not running directly for office — although politicking seriously — merely being the supportive helping hand that good wives should be. No one could really begrudge her that. Lady Bird Johnson made the transition from campaign symbol to active political campaigner with her tour through the South in the Lady Bird Johnson Special campaign train. Because the South was Goldwater Country and Johnson was unpopular, the device was used that no Southern gentleman would refuse to meet and greet a Southern Lady, no matter what her husband's politics. Lady Bird actively campaigned in partisan politics using the still-believed-in charm of Southern womanhood to accomplish the feat. (See figure 4.) It is a measure of how far we have come in First Lady images that in 1976 there can appear a button which reads, "Betty Yes, Gerry No!"

By the time of the Shirley Chisholm campaign for the presidential candidacy in 1972, the burgeoning women's movement had kindled enthusiasm for running for public office in one's own right — not as a worker for someone else. (Note the button, "Women Make Policy/Not Coffee.") Chisholm's campaign buttons reach a true iconic level, creating a symbol for women, black and white, of real credibility in national campaigns for public office. Chisholm had not only buttons with her photograph but catch slogans, a deliberate appeal to changed status for women ("Catalyst for Change"), and an appeal to the "reform" tendency still evident in most women's campaigns. "Unbossed and Unbought" referred to that aspect as well as to the title of Chisholm's own book. (See figure 10.)

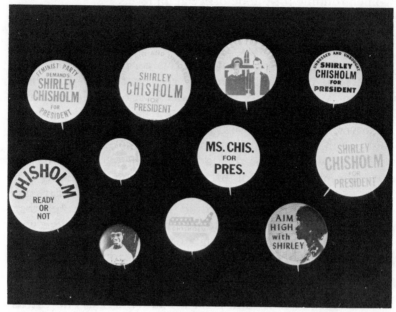

Figure 10

The political button continues to function in the women's movement as a primary icon, unlike other political areas, because women generally cannot afford access to electronic media dissemination of their message. It is critical, then, to see what use this icon serves.

There are many obvious differences in the women's liberation buttons from the suffrage buttons. Several are immediately apparent: the lack of recognizable leaders (other than those who are political figures such as Chisholm, Abzug, and Jordan); the variety of issues concerning women; the tone of the messages; the lack of visual imagery.

There is no monolithic phrase such as "Votes for Women" which sums up the philosophy and psychology of the entire movement. There is no monolithic movement, but one of variety and differences of approach and method.

The new movement is issue, rather than personality oriented. The lack of "personality" buttons, other than those which are campaign buttons for women running for public office, is indicative of the lack of dominance by personalities in the movement. The new women's movement is fed by many groups at the national and grass roots levels and has no outstanding leaders who speak for the entire movement. Issue oriented buttons are a sign of strength and growing up in the women's movement. They are reflective of the feminist assertion that women are capable of decision-making on facts and issues rather than following the lead of charismatic personalities.

The major difference between the suffragists and the current women's movement is that while the suffragists specifically sidestepped the issue of equality both philosophically and as a tactic for obtaining the vote, the women's liberation movement has as its major theme a direct, blatant, and insistent demand for total equality in every aspect of life. ("Equality Now," "Women's Rights Now," "August 26/ Women Strike for Equality," and a button with male and female symbols with an equal sign between, a button "W= M" i.e. women are equal to men. This latter button can be turned, but no matter how it is turned it always reads "W= M".[10] There are even statements of superiority to counteract the psychological effects of generations of subordinate and supportive roles. ("Adam Was a Rough Draft," "Trust in God, She Will Provide").

While there is similarity in the old and new movements in their drive for a constitutional amendment, and a wide variety of E.R.A. (Equal Rights Amendment) buttons exist, there is a vast difference in the approach of the two movements to making the amendment a political reality. The women of the liberation movement saw no reason to cloak their demands. Rhetoric is direct and blunt. These women are emphatically unlike the great body of ladylike suffragists. The movement assumed, perhaps mistakenly as the waning momentum of E.R.A. ratification and movements for recission indicate, that the time was more than ripe to speak directly about equality for women ("E.R.A. It's About Time"). While overt opposition to the change in women's roles was not blatantly evident, there remains a considerable residue of antagonism under the surface. Women today realize that no single political enactment will bring utopia as the suffragists thought. The Equal Rights Amendment is the main political goal of the movement, but not the single goal.

This approach has both strengths and weaknesses. Whereas the suffrage movement fell apart after the passage of the amendment (William L. O'Neill has stated that, for the suffragists, no defeat was ever so devastating as victory,[11]) the new movement has a multiplicity of purposes and does not see E.R.A. as the realization of all its goals. The movement will be less likely to disintegrate with ratification. At the same time, because many women are working on many different fronts to bring equality, it is considerably more difficult to mobilize a large, disciplined group of women to devote themselves to any single issue, as was done with suffrage, and the ratification drive suffers from a dilution of efforts.

Rather than seeking an appeal to everyone, the appeal of women's liberation is often a deliberately selective one — an appeal to an "in" group who already identify with feminist experiences, lifestyles, literature, and aspirations. ("Sister," "Sisterhood is Powerful," "Uppity Women Unite.") They have gloried in what set them apart (and therefore "elevated" them) from other women in the society, often to the detriment of support for the movement.

The lack of visual imagery in an object which serves as icon is, at first, puzzling. The new movement makes use of words, phrases, and slogans to conjure shared associations, concepts, experiences, goals, abhorrences. This, in part, reflects the generally well-educated makeup of the current women's movement.[12] The buttons are literate, sometimes literary, in their references to Biblical and feminist literature ("And God Created Woman in Her Own Image," "Ain't I A Woman?" referring to the speech by Sojourner Truth). Such references are an outgrowth of a movement which has produced a sizeable body of its own literature.

Few images, literally, have come from the new women's movement. The essential reason for this is that these women are deliberate iconoclasts: their purpose is to break the images of women in their traditional roles. The single recurring image, other than the female symbol which is an assertion of worth, personhood, and identity, is the strike fist — a symbol of power. Often the two symbols are intertwined with the strike fist rising from the bottom of the female symbol. ("Woman Power.") Such symbols of power speak meaningfully for a drive to obtain power individually over their own lives and as a class at all levels of public life. They also speak of the contempt of power and its use/abuse by the establishment to confine women in secondary status. Where the suffrage buttons were explicitly an effort to court the power establishment (thereby displaying their lack of power and control), the new women's movement buttons say "Fuck the Establishment" at every turn. It is a measure of the power women feel they have gained that enables them to say that.

Because of their iconoclastic purpose, the buttons attack every "sacred" image of women's formerly assigned role. Women's sex role is redefined completely: as to sex preference (lesbian buttons include intertwined female symbols, "Gays WERE the Silenced Majority," "Out of the Closet and Into the Street"); the control of her reproductive life (all buttons referring to abortion); control of her own body (rape and prostitution buttons which include "Stop Rape" in the shape of a Stop sign and "Castrate Rapists" and buttons from prostitution lobby groups such as C.O.Y.O.T.E.,Call off Your Old Tired Ethics and P.U.M.A., Prostitutes United of Massachusetts, as well as "I Own My Own Body But I Share" and "Keep Your Laws Off My Body"). Further breaking down of old images includes women's secondary status in both home and office ("Fuck Officework," "Equal Partnership in Marriage," "Equal Pay for Equal Work"); women's political coming of age (buttons for N.O.W., the National Women's Political Caucus, campaign buttons for women running in their own right, and "Political Power Now" with fist[13]); breaking down of women's religious conditioning by the churches to accept inferior status, and equal status in the church ("God Created Woman in Her Own Image," "Trust in God She Will Provide," "Equal Rites for Women"[14]).

Part of the iconoclasm of the new women's buttons is the tone of their rhetoric. They are often deliberately offensive, both because the movement believes women have been on the defensive too long and to enable them to break the "lady-like" image of "femininity." Ricidule, long used against women as a means of social control, has now become a feminist offensive weapon ("Adam Was a Rough Draft," "It Used to be a Man's World," "Sexism is a Social Disease"). There is deliberate "shock value" in many of the movement's messages — both to shock women from their former complacency and to shock a male establishment as a deliberate movement tactic.

Once women have completed the iconoclastic task of breaking the old images which have bound women for generations, the movement can then generate new and positive images of women to replace them. Perhaps then, visual imagery will return to the political icon. Meanwhile, the thrust of the movement is not merely destructive of the old but constructive of the new. "A Woman's Place is Everyplace" and "A Woman's Place is in the World" are powerful iconic messages. The image has just not yet come into focus.

NOTES

[1] Marshall Fishwick, "Entrance," *Icons of Popular Culture* (Bowling Green, Ohio, 1970), p. 1.

[2] Medal in the collections of the Division of Political History, Smithsonian Institution. (Hereafter abbreviated DPH,SI).

[3] William Burlie Brown, *The People's Choice: the Presidential Image in the Campaign Biography* (Baton Rouge, Louisiana, 1960), pp. 127-129.

[4] What appears to be a tintype of Victoria Woodhull and a campaign advertising card with her photograph and "Victoria Woodhull for the Presidency of the United States," and two ribbons advocating Belva Lockwood's candicacy in 1888 are pictured in: Dick Bristow, *Presidential Campaign Items, 1789 - 1892.* Santa Cruz, Calif.: Political Items Col., 1973), pp. 98 and 100.

[5] No such political buttons exist in the DPH,SI nor in any of the numerous campaign and political button books consulted.

[6] Many of the "Eleanor" buttons not pictured in this article appear in: Dick Bristow, *The Illustrated Political Button Book,* revised ed., (Santa Cruz, Calif.: Political Items Co., 1971), pp. 142-145.

[7] Otha Wearin, *Political Campaign Buttons in Color.* (Leon, Iowa: Mid America Book Co., 1969), p. 45.

[8] Jo Freeman, *The Politics of Women's Liberation.* (New York: David McKay, 1972), p. 18.

[9] Estimates of the increase of women running for public office state that 2000 women were candidates in 1972, and that the increase of women seeking election to Congress increased 74% from 1970 to 1974. Despite this, women elected officials comprise less than 4% of elected officials while women are 53% of the voting population. See Susan and Martin Tolchin, *Clout: Womanpower and Politics* (New York: 1974), pp. 15, 17, and 29.

10Buttons in the private collection of Frank Corbeil, Hartford, Conn.

11William L. O'Neill, *Everyone Was Brave: The Rise and Fall of Feminism in America.* (Chicago: Quadrangle, 1969), chap. 8.

12See Freeman, *op. cit.*

13Buttons in the private collection of Ms. Jo Freeman, New York.

14In the collection of Frank Corbeil.

Icons Of Popular Fashion

Valerie Carnes

> *"One should either be a work of art or wear a work of art."*
>
> Oscar Wilde

I

If icons are images and ideas converted into three dimensions, we confront them every time we dress. Fashion (in the sense of style or "manners") forms a visible, popular iconology, revealing much about our values, attitudes, and assumptions about "the good life."

Hence, the revolutionary change in fashions during the 1960's also represented a revolution in popular icons. Women of the 40's and 50's modeled their fashion-icons on movie stars and the Hollywood version of the female body beautiful. Greta Garbo, Vivien Leigh, Marilyn Monroe, Jayne Mansfield, and Brigitte Bardot all represented, for various eras, the ideal types that men desired and women emulated. Perhaps Gore Vidal's Myra Breckinridge was right when she commented that "in the decade between 1935 and 1945, no irrelevant film was made in the United States."[1] But by 1960, the dominance of Hollywood as icon-maker was over, and the reign of the new fashion icons had begun.

For the Sixties spawned not just a new era in fashion, but a whole new feeling, mood and significance for clothing. The ideal silhouette shifted from bosomy film stars to young, skinny teenagers with long hair, toothpick arms and legs — the English shopgirl type described by Tom Wolfe as "starved to near perfection." The new miniskirts fit these new girls to a T. The dresses were tiny A-lines, worn with white Courrèges, space-child boots or white knee socks and Mary Janes. Mary Quant was right to speculate that a new "idealized version of what a woman's shape should be" was indeed built into the clothes themselves. They were clothes by and for the young, and the whole look was 100-percent Lolita.

It is no accident that Nabokov's novel was just making its impact felt as our female icons were switching from *femme fatale* to nymphet. Humbert Humbert's rhapsodies over Lo's slightly unnatural beauty caught up America's new fascination with the childish Bardo-like sex-kitten. The new Sixties girl was not only childlike; she was kinky, kooky, adventurous, spirited. When in 1963 *Vogue* ran an article praising "unconventional" beauties like Streisand, Rita Tushingham, "platter-eyed" Carol Channing and "clawed-voice" Tammy Grimes for their very *lack* of conventional prettiness, we were well on the way toward a new pop iconology of youth, kinkiness and fun.

Interestingly, this characteristically Sixties interest in women as visual icons roughly parallels the rise of movies and of fashion photography as art forms. The screen heroine, the pinup girl, the *Playboy* foldout, the high-fashion mannequin all have one thing in common: they are all visual fantasies, eye-catching pop icons. The fashion model and the Playmate of the Month are both Orrin Klapp's true heroines of the surface: attractive, lacking in depth, "a model of bodily perfection, a secular ikon (sic) . . . [who] need not be a great lover . . . photogenic perfection is enough."[2] Neither model nor foldout is a living, breathing woman but instead, a stylization of an ideal type, as far removed from the actual as Venus de Milo or a Byzantine icon. Klapp names these pop idols our "heroes and heroines of the surface" and explains their appeal thus:

> The current secularization of values — the paring down of values to sensate qualities appreciated promptly through the senses and without complicated interpretation. . . Loss of value consensus in modern times has been so great that people can agree on little but what is obvious and on the surface. . . a sensate people move on when a surface is exhausted or a more attractive one looms.[3]

It was particularly interesting to watch the various popular and mass magazines change their advertising and editorial policies to fit the new iconology of fashion. Family magazines like *Post* by 1965 were already featuring young blonde models in Rudi Gernreich Op Art dresses, articles on discotheques and dope in the suburbs, and other milestones in the iconology of Switched-On. Several spring 1965 *Post* ads portray young blond models in Courréges space helmets and Gernreigh / Quant minis selling, variously, refrigerators, Dodge Polaras, Chevy hardtops and Dial soap. Ads featuring older women "of a certain age," like the famous Jolie Madam perfume ad, gave way by July 1965 to ads and features devoted entirely to teenage girls as sex symbols, and teenage interests like the Beatles and surfing. *Esquire* magazine (April 1963) even invented a name for the new pop icon: she was "The Golden Girl": "the girl on the train, cool in white linen, tennis racquets beside her; the girl in the sports car halted for one moment beneath the window of your bus."[4]

The Golden Girl was golden in more than one sense: she quickly became a wonderfully salable commodity. From teenage movies like "Beach Party" and other Annette Funicello features, she graduated to "The Endless Summer" and ads for expensive resorts. She walked over endless Kodachrome beaches with her bright bikini, her golden tan and flying hair, all careless and vacant-eyed surface: blonde, lean and very, very young. Because jet travel means sun, and tanned skin spells leisure, conspicuous sybaritism and wealth, the Golden Girl was usually featured in ads for exotic sports equipment, travel, vacations, fast-cars and sun-following. The equation of "golden" with money soon came to suggest sun, vacations, fast cars, sports, and jet-setting as a way of life. Increasingly, the Golden Girl was the composite pop icon who sold resorts, hotels, travel, tours, sun-tan oil, while her high-fashion equivalent leapt through the pages of *Vogue, Bazaar* and *WWD,* and her Jet Set version was pictured skiing in Gstaad or sunning in St. Tropez.

It is a testament to Nabokov's genius that *Lolita* ends with its child-heroine pregnant, for little Lo's symbolic progeny in the 60's were more numerous than even the luckless Humbert could have predicted. Feminine charm, *panache,* mystery, allure — all were forgotten in the interest of sheer surface shimmer. And in response to this new iconology of surfaces the press, the fashion industry, the slick magazines, the entertainment media, bred a new succession of new icons: Realgirls, Swingers, Gamines, Ingenues, Kooks, Chicerinos, Littlegirls, Jet Setters, Surfer Chicks, Hippie Girls, Beautiful Creatures, Free Souls. All, despite their superficial differences, were impeccably packaged, pretty, kinky, kooky, and young. They were our new celebrities, our new secular goddesses, and together they would usher in an era of popular fashion iconology.

II

If the women themselves — the professional models, rock stars, "fashion groupies" and consumers — comprised the new icons of pop fashion, then fashion itself, in the newer, more abstract sense of "lifestyle" or simply "style," was also developing into an elaborate pop iconology of the surfaces. In the politically-saturated 60's, fashion became more than itself. More than ever before, it was a code, a secret system of signals, a highly complex and subtle iconology that both shaped and reflected the volatile social values and ideologies of the decade. John Corry, in a 1970 article called "The Politics of Style," comments that the obsession with style began when Robert Frost rose up and read a poem at John Kennedy's inauguration. This was the signal, Corry believes, for the stylish and style-obsessed Kennedy era and the subsequent half-decade when "from then on it would not matter so much what you said, but how you said it."[5] What the popular iconology of fashion did, in effect, was to identify the style with the substance and make an equation between the two. In this media-created environment, clothes no longer made the man; they *were* the man, and vice-versa.

A further set of clues is provided by an article entitled "Growing Up in the Forties."[6] Richard Schnickel describes the two worlds that were familiar to every child of the 40's. There was the corner grocery, the drugstore, ones family and friends; and then there was the Other Place—a mysterious realm somewhere just beyond the lights of Broadway; the world of Sherman Billingsley and the Stork Club, Walter

Winchell and Lux Radio Theatre. What happened in the 60's, quite simply, was that for a number of complex cultural, social, political and ideological reasons, the Other Place began to merge with the real world. The result was a media-created environment of surfaces whose preoccupations were image and style, and which thus generated whole new pantheons of pop icons and deities.

In an environment: of surfaces, theater becomes reality. Fashion, style, "flash," the ability to change, chameleon-like, with the changes in the environment: these are the ingredients of success in the world of surfaces. For fashion is the epitome of surfaces; it is the surface *par excellence.* The right clothing, the right style, means the right coloration that allows us to fit into the current, constantly shifting scene. The high-fashion model paints herself to hide the blemishes; the *Playboy* foldout is an airbrushed nude, also with blemishes hidden. Either way, the surface must be pleasing, for it is the surface that counts, not the real woman underneath.

There were several major steps in the development of the concept of fashion as "lifestyle" and thus as popular icon. Significantly, the revolution in fashion in the 60's began with Carnaby Street and the boutiques which Mary Quant opened in London in the late 50's. Quant was quick to grasp the sense that fashion was coming to signify much more than simply the clothes one wore. In *Quant by Quant* she sums up this new significance to fashion:

> What a great many people still don't realize is that the Look isn't just the garments you wear. It's the way you put on your make-up, the way you do your hair, the sort of stockings you choose, the way you walk and stand, even the way you smoke your fag. All these are part of the same feeling. . . [Fashion is] a whole host of elusive ideas, influences, cross-currents, and economic factors, captured into a shape. . . .8

Thus for the youth-oriented and upwardly mobile consumer of the 60's, buying clothes became an instant passport into the iconology of the Jet Set, the Cat Pack, Radical Chic, the hippie world, the earth movement, depending on her whim and inclinations. Whereas once the world of fashion had been open only to the wealthy and elite consumer, the patroness of the grand *salons,* now the housewife, secretary, or businesswoman found entrance into this burgeoning realm.

She could herself, with a little help from various friends, become a popular icon.

When Diana Vreeland became editor of *Vogue* in 1962, the magazine's whole format and editorial policy changed, however subtly. The greatest shift was from fashion in the old narrow sense of current clothing styles to fashion as a whole amorphous set of objects, ideas, values. "Fashion" became a sort of shorthand for a contemporary, fast-paced, *au courant* style of life: Gucci, Pucci, Hermes or Vuitton luggage and clothes, opening-night seats at *Hair*, Angelo Donghia fabrics, Rigaud chandles, Gernreich dresses, loft parties with Andy Warhol and Tigermorse, dancing in the Peppermint Lounge, summers in the Hamptons, David Webb animal bracelets and Cartier love chains. It was the Beautiful Life, *la dolce vita,* and the American public missed its irony as surely as they had overlooked the bittersweet irony of Fellini's film.

The myth of Jet-Setters and Beautiful People, the "implausible sybarites" of Marylin Bender's phrase, thus forged one more link between the cult of obsessive style and the new pop iconology of fashion. Tom Wolfe attributed their development to the growth of Pop Society and the tendency of New York socialites of the early 60's to borrow their styles increasingly from pop groups: to dance the Jerk, the Monkey and the Shake, listen to rock, wear teenage styles like stretch pants and decal eyes, and follow "underground" and *avant-garde* art. In Baby Jane Holzer, Wolfe found the perfect pop icon of the switched-on 60's: "a living embodiment of almost pure pop sensation, a kind of corn-haired essence of the new styles of life. . . . Baby Jane is the hyperversion of a whole new style of life in America. I think she is a very profound symbol."[9]

With the canonization of the Beautiful People, Jet-Setters and super-consumers as fashion's newest secular deities, a curious shift took place in the source and direction of fashion influence. No longer were trends dictated by the Parisian salons, to move from the *couture* downward to knock-off mass houses and thus into the streets. Now, unlike the situation in 1947 when the New Look was thrust upon a reluctant mass market, fashion did not originate on Seventh Avenue or in Right Bank Parisian *salons*. Rather, the new iconology of fashion started in Greenwich Village, on Carnaby Street, in the discothèques and bistros of Paris and St. Tropez, and worked its way up with dizzying speed into designers' workrooms, store windows, and at last into the pages of *Elle, Bazaar,* and *Vogue.* No longer did mass fashion "knock off," or copy, the couture; now the couture was in the curiously ironic position of knocking off mass fashion. Pop couture, the Great Leveller, had a marvellous way of erasing class distinctions. Contessas and shop girls could now jostle one another past Biba's or Bendel's racks in pursuit of the same dress. And Jane Holzer could say, in 1964, that "There's no class anymore. Everybody is equal," and find the corroboration for the statement in her own wardrobe.

Examples of this reverse direction of fashion iconology—from streets to salons, not vice-versa—are almost too numerous to mention. For example, the much-maligned midi was not the exclusive invention of John Fairchild and *WWD:* it was a conscious attempt at copying fashionably the cheap, ankle-length cotton dresses of the young girls in St. Tropez, Cannes and Rome. Paradoxically, American women, not understanding the street origins of the midi, rejected it as an elite and artificial fashion which became acceptable only when popularized by the young French *pret-a-porter* designers like Sonia Rykiel, Dorothee Bis, or Kenzo for Jap. And the *avant-garde* style of outrageous dress that Tom Wolfe called Radical Chic caught on only after *Vogue,* in a fall 1969 issue, praised the "*looks,* the fascinating and beautiful ways of putting themselves together, that the young wore during the Woodstock Rock Festival,"[10] while *WWD's* Bill Cunningham hyped the tremendous style and *panache* of New York Black and Puerto Rican fashion in July of 1970.

Aristocrats dressing as workers and peasants is as old as the French Revolution, but it took the 60's to institutionalize this popular trend into a look and style of its own. "Radical chic" in late 1969 and early 1970 began gaining ground with the affluent fashionables as well as with the young. At its inception it reminded Wolfe of the *nostalgie de la boue* that flourished in the era of the French Revolution, when the court of Louis XIV amused themselves by dressing up as farmers and shepherds, or the English court during the Regency period, when London socialites aped the dress and manners of coach drivers and tavern girls. But 60's Radical Chic became a constant costume parade of outrageous mixing and matching — a hippie fringed vest over a Halston pantsuit and silk blouse, or "a pair of faded, patched jeans with an $80 silk shirt, and $800 Indian belt, and a $350 velvet blazer."[11] No wonder John Corry commented in a 1970's *Harper's* article that "this generation of radicals may end up being distinguished from others only by its style, and by its marriage with the world of fashion."[12]

The pop icon of Radical Chic Tom Wolfe christened the Debutante in Blue Jeans. She was found in the pages of every large city newspaper in the country — "blue jeans and her blue work shirt open to the sternum, with her long preraphelite hair parted on top of the skull, uncoiffed but recently washed and blown dry."[13] She was usually handing her interviewer such inanities as Amanda Burden's famous gaffe: "The sophistication of the baby blacks has made me rethink my attitudes about fashion." Wolfe quite correctly saw 60's fashion, politics, ideology and the *avant-garde* in the arts interacting in a complex and fascinating way. Instead of fashion serving as the embroidery of history, Wolfe claims that in the late 60's, the movement was quite the other way around: that once Radical Chic or "ethnic" sympathies became fashionable, the fashions acquired their own momentum, formed their own iconology, and thus had the power to generate social change on their own.

Jeans were, of course, already standard student and bohemian fare long before the fashion world discovered denim. But designers began knocking off jeans, starting first with hamburger chain owner Errol Wetson who, in the late summer of 1969, began to copy the sun-faded jeans worn on the French Riviera in a lightweight, pre-bleached cotton fabric imported from Africa. The couture, in turn, copied the enterprising Wetson's designs in suede, ciré, and studded leather. Designers like Calvin Klein and Oscar de la Renta responded to the new spirit of democracy in fashion by sending street photographers out into Central Park, Harlem, and the Lower East Side to shoot up rolls of candid shots of

The miniskirt, the first *bona fide* "youth fashion" to capture the mass market, produced a standard silhouette: long hair, short A-line dress, hips accentuated by a chain belt, legs covered in opaque tights.

This "hippie dress," made of pre-printed panels of African fabric, could be bought in kit form through the *Ladies Home Journal* for the capitalistic price of $9.95.

The long cotton swirl skirt, worn with gauze tie blouse and big straw hat, was seen in resorts such as St. Tropez and later spawned the midi fiasco of the early seventies.

The midiskirt, worn with high stocking boots, wide belt, and "dog collar," was the fashion establishment's most notable failure at creating a mass market for a style still considered avant-garde by most American women.

"Ethnic" and fantasy looks, a strong undercurrent in fashion since the mid-sixties, continue as a strong influence. They range from outrageous Radical Chic mixing and matching to the toned-down gypsy influences of this outfit: printed voile skirt, fringed shawl, and scarf-wrapped turban head.

Tom Wolfe's pop icon, "the Debutante in Blue Jeans," mixed worn denims, work shirts, silver and turquoise American Indian Jewelry and expensive luggage to achieve an authentic Radical Chic look.

For hundreds of women, pants and a sweater became a safe uniform for both work and leisure. In a time of drastically changing hemlines, they offered both comfort and a classic casual look. And for many women, they spelled the liberation of the female wardrobe from the complexity and fuss of skirts.

The modified "Big Look," complete with shawl, gaucho boots, and mid-calf skirt, was the first spin-off from the midi which appealed to the American mass market.

Army fatigues, once a part of the "Radical Chic" look, have enjoyed a revival in the last few months as part of the renewed interest in "funky chic" work clothes.

For fall of 1976, the Big Look is toned down into a slimmer "tube" or tunic shape, here worn over bloused pants and straight leather boots.

"street fashions." One of Klein's best-selling 1971 designs, a denim vest and jean-cut pants, was said to have been inspired by a street costume and went from snapshot to runaway in about ten days.

The denim craze continued from the 60's well into the 70's. In 1972 alone, the sales of Levi-Strauss and Blue Bell, respectively, reached $504 million and $344.5 million — in both cases, roughly a 17 per cent increase over the previous year's sales. But it was not until 1973 that the American Fashion Critics presented a special award to Levi-Strauss for "a fundamental American fashion that has endured for 120 years and now influences the world." Levis also won the coveted Nieman-Marcus award for distinguished service in fashion for 1973. The special citation ranks Levis as the single most important contribution to worldwide fashion, widely copied in every land and "extensively used for inspiration by the haute couture of Paris."[17] With these two awards, the relationship between street and salon fashion seems, both literally and symbolically, to have come full circle: the couture was indeed knocking off the streets with jeans, the most native American, perhaps the most complex and ironic, fashion icon of all.

III

Walter Weisskopf, in *Alienation and Economics,* provides one last important clue to the role of fashion in the last decade. Weisskopf points out that given a "value empty" society where all the old absolutes — manners, morals, religion, faith — have lost their authority, it is not surprising that the measure of all things in the consumer society has become the self. For the value-empty and value-relativistic culture turns the individual inward upon his own resources which he is then free to embellish in any way he sees fit. Thus the self and its personal style — its personal iconology or "lifestyle" — becomes both the literal and symbolic centers of the universe. Given the consumer orientation of our society, buying, shopping, and acquiring become important ways to fill the self's value-empty void, as well as to establish its uniqueness and individuality in a world where all the surfaces are beginning to look much the same. Buying, then, shifts mere exchange of goods to become the supreme act of self-expression, the ultimate self-assertion and, perhaps, the ultimate iconographical gesture that the consumer society affords.

Thus 60's (and 70's) clothing offered instant identification that was less important as body covering, sex signal or status symbol than as emblem of a personal style. Nowhere was the growing emphasis on visual surfaces, appearances and styles so apparent as in the various fashion icons of the 60's. The visual symbolism of the new youth cult came, as we have already seen, to dominate film, advertising, television, photography, mass entertainment, magazines, newspapers and the arts and grew, in time, into a total pop iconology, mass-produced, mass-packaged, easily salable. For the young and would-be young of the decade, fashion was theater in the streets, an instant lifestyle and often an instant politics and ideology (Left = Hip; Right = Straight). It provided an easily accessible image, an identity statement, a way of "coming on" that transcended its immediate practical or even aesthetic value. It was human pre-packaging for that most salable of 60's commodities: the elusive Self. It also provided a viable iconology for a generation for which authentic existence had become a major obsession. Suddenly, once-neutral items took on hidden sexual, political and social connotations. The miniskirt suggested and symbolized the New Morality, the new freedom of lifestyles and the new adoration of youth and prepubescent body types. Ethnic clothes reflected subtle, often specious, sympathies with radical revolutionary movements and minority groups, sympathy with the Third World, scorn for straight WASP fashion, and a romanticization of the exotic and primitive. Denim jeans became the ultimate no-fashion put-down style — a classless, cheap, unisex look that stood for, variously, the frontier values, democracy, plain living, ecology and health, rebellion *a la* Brando or Dean, a new interest in the erotic import of the pelvis, or, as Charles Reich suggests in *The Greening of America,* a deliberate rejection of the "artificial plastic-coated look" of the affluent consumer society. Ecology, women's liberation, the pollution of our streams and land, the plight of workers, the problems of consumerism are real dilemmas; their fashion equivalents, however, are earth clothes, the no-bra look, $75.00 peasant calico dresses, and pre-bleached workers' smocks. A philosophical position on racial discrimination, economic oppression, the morality of war or the brotherhood of man takes years to develop, perfect and mature. But the iconology of fashion solves the problem with an Afro wig, a set of Army fatigues, a poster, a mechanic's jumpsuit, tie-dyed workers' clothes.

Where is Seventies fashion going? It is difficult even to hazard a guess, given the fluctuating political and economic situation. The In signals have all changed, of course; now they tend toward co-ordinated get-ups by Halston, Sonia Rykiel, Missoni, or John Anthony; Elsa Peretti silver and ivory jewelry; Bobby Breslau leather pouch bags; bare rooms dressed down in white Haitian cotton and wicker, or layered with carpeted platforms in the style of Joseph d'Urso; tennis lessons; dancing at New York's Regine; Cuisinart food processors; Calvin Klein signature jeans; backpacking; work clothes, jumpsuits and the western look; Frye boots; EST and meditation; Mandarin cooking, fasts, and vegetarian diets. But the essential purpose served by fashion remains the same: the clothes, the accessories and furnishings (now subsumed under the catch-all term "environment") remain the iconology, the code symbolizing a total lifestyle of the self surviving in an environment of surfaces.

Grace Mirabella, editor of *Vogue,* suggested in a recent interview that as women become more secure in their sense of self and career, fashion will not disappear but instead will shift from clothing exclusively to a combination of clothing, home, food, and surroundings — the total lifestyle, the total image, in other words. As if to bear out this prophecy, already interior design and gourmet cooking, widely featured in fashion magazines for the last three years, show signs of developing into popular iconologies in their own right. For example, *W's* April 13, 1976 issue lists among its "in" signals white cookware, down-filled comforters or *duvets,* bare bleached floors, herringbone and white cotton pillows, and uncurtained windows. Too, fashion itself seems to be taking a new turn or two: recent straws in the wind include well-tailored classic clothes, menswear suits for women, the western look, and a new and refreshing disdain for signature clothes that flash their designer's name.

Overall, the current mood is a somberly anti-fashion one. We deprecate fashion, deplore artifice, spurn cosmetics, claim to be honest, natural and up-front. Yet paradoxically, we secretly still adore, envy or emulate the Kook, the Kink, the Free Soul, the Jet Setter, the Debutante in Jeans, the Golden Girl. They are our secular icons, our pop deities; and the fashion world that spawned them will continue to serve us for what it is — a rich and suggestive popular symbolism of styles, costumes, manners, images, surfaces. It is a true iconology: highly conventionalized, mass-directed, but paradoxically catering to an elite of initiates and *cognoscenti*, laden with cultural ciphers that help unlock the mysteries of our most cherished assumptions. Like the religious images of Byzantium, that once served as physical memoranda of something beyond, fashion is the window through which we glimpse something beyond workaday existence: the chameleon-colors of the Other Place, the kaleidescopic flux of our style-obsessed and image-conscious age.

NOTES

[1] Gore Vidal, *Myra Breckinridge* (New York, 1970), p. 13.

[2] Orrin Klapp, *Heroes, Villains, and Fools* (Englewood Cliffs, N.J., 1962), pp. 38-9.

[3] *Ibid.*, pp. 99-100.

[4] *Esquire*, April 1963, 12-13.

[5] John Corry, "The Politics of Style," *Harper's*, Nov. 1970.

[6] Richard Schickel, "Growing Up in the 40's," *New York Times Magazine*, Sun., Feb. 20, 1972.

[7] A model for the dynamics of popular culture, developed and elaborated by Ralph L. Carnes in "Survival in an Environment of Surfaces" (with Valerie Carnes), forthcoming in *Creativity, Consciousness and Human Ecology* (State University of New York, Fall 1976).

[8] Mary Quant, *Quant by Quant* (New York, 1965-6), p. 102.

[9] Tom Wolfe, *The Kandy-Kolored Tangerine-Flake Streamline Baby* (New York, 1963), p. xv.

[10] *Vogue*, October 15, 1970, 250.

[11] *W*, Oct. 5, 1973, 2.

[12] Corry, *op. cit.*

13Tom Wolfe, "Funky Chic," reprinted from 1974 *Rolling Stone* in Oct. 1974 *Cosmopolitan,* 182-6.

14Chicago *Sun-Times,* Sept. 9, 1973 and Oct. 8, 1973.

15Walter Weisskopf, *Alienation and Economics* (New York, 1971).

Paradox In Paradise: The Icons Of Waikiki

Edward Whetmore & Don J. Hibbard

> Puka shell neckware of paper and plastic
> Flower print PJ's bound up with elastic
> T Shirts and short sleeves to wear in the spring
> These are a few of my Waikiki things . . .
> (Sung to the tune of "A Few of my Favorite Things")

FADE IN: *Waikiki, Hawaii, U.S.A.*

Kalakaua Boulevard in mid-August, bright reds, greens and yellows. Shimmering sunshine, the street is filled with thousands of restless tourists pounding the pavement with the "thunka-thunk" of their rubber sandals. There are over 100 shops lining the boulevard and each displays hundreds of items designed to let you take a little of Hawaii back home. An icon hunter's paradise!

"You'd never know to look at it now," (Lou is my native guide and photographer, a half dozen Nikon lens cases draped around his neck), "but this whole Waikiki area was once a swamp."

"Uh huh."

"Sure, they still have to bring in sand once a week from the other side of the island—it comes by truck—trouble is most of the people take a little home, ya know, a handful here, a handful there it adds up. They have to bring tons of the stuff. It's the only thing here that's free . . . ."

Lou lives in Waikiki with a beautiful oriental lady and takes pictures of the tourists for a living. In his spare time he gets in a few classes at the University.

"You know over a million people come here every year, but only a few of them ever get any further than Waikiki—it's all here—the sun—the discos—the surf—the ladies. . . Wow!

A tall blonde lady strides by in a bikini bottom and a clinging wet T-Shirt with "Hawaii-76" embossed in large red, white and blue letters.

"I wouldn't live anywhere else," he adds enthusiastically.

DISSOLVE TO: *Interior of the Aloha Shirt Shop.* Lou is snapping away and I'm asking the proprietress about the icons of Waikiki.

"Which ones are the biggest sellers?"

"Oh, da blues, da polyesters—wash and wear—dey sell big—especially to Japanese, dey buy lots. One Japanese man—he buy 50 shirts. 50 shirts! He going to send dem home as presents—but he ne-vah weah one himself—dey never do."

"Are there really noticeable ethnic buying differences?"

"What?"

"Who buys the most?"

"Ya, oh ya, da Japanese, dey buy most—den da Canadians —dey buy good, ya."

"What about the mainland people, you know, caucasions?"

"Oh—Haoles? Haoles don't buy too good—dey look a lot mostly—but don't buy aloha wear."

She points to a rack of Hawaiian print shirts.

"Dese cost five, maybe ten dollah each—Haoles wear T-Shirts dey buy for two dollah."

DISSOLVE TO: *Interior of the 1001 T Shirt Shop.*

The proprietor is in his mid-50's, greying side-burns and a paunch. Noticeable east coast accent:

"What sells? What sells? That all ya wanta know? Hell anything with Hawaii written on it, ya know, they want the name—it's a not so subtle reminder for the folks back home ya know—we've *been* to Hawaii. We sell some "Primo" shirts, that's the local beer—you know that, don't you, are you from around here?"

"I teach at the University."

"Oh yeah, well we sell some T-Shirts with "University of Hawaii" on em, for sure, anything with Hawaii. The big sellers have been the "year" series, you know Hawaii 77, Hawaii 76 and so on. They really got big during the Bicentennial, I wish I had some of the old Hawaii 75's left, they're scarce now, practically collector's items ya know?

DISSOLVE TO: *Interior of the Waikiki Superette-Shop of Memories.* Paper shells, puka shells, aloha shirts and muumuus, miniature surf boards, color postcards, key chains, and little hula dolls made of plastic which do their thing when the car comes to an abrupt stop. There are also some large wooden salad tongs with small labels that say: "Made in the Philippines."

"Oh they don't like that," (Bob, the super-salesman has his hair slicked back, he wears an aloha shirt and rubber sandals.), "they don't like that at all. Let me tell you what I mean, take those wooden bowls here, these are made in Hawaii, they say so right here, see?"

I nod.

"These run $12.50. Now look at these, same thing, same wood, but made in the Philippines—$3.95 tops, and I couldn't give em away. But there's a lot of things like—take these barrel novelties, they're fantastic movers, I can't keep enough of 'em in stock. He points to six rows of identical wooden carvings. It's an old oriental man with a bamboo hat. Instead of clothes he's wearing a wooden barrel, and his head is bent down as if he were looking for something in the barrel. It reminds me of those old editorial cartoons of the taxpayer after April 15. Each row of Oriental men and their barrels gets progressively larger. The price tags too.

"These are great," Lou says—"Have you seen these?"

"Uhh—no."

Bob, the super-salesman lifts up one of the little barrels and the little wooden man's erect wooden penis pops out from underneath. Bob laughs.

"It's funny you know—everybody reacts differently to these—the Japanese women, they giggle and are real embarrassed and turn away—the haole women, they love it—they'll lift the old barrel up and down 30 to 40 times and laugh and laugh and laugh. . ."

FADE OUT

****

SATURDAY'S NOTES FROM WAIKIKI:

1. The traditional Hawaiian "Lei greeting" is supplied by a number of companies who enter bids with the tour organizers. Tour organizers then take a traditional 30-40% kickback from Lei Company profits. Lou says tour organizers also take about 30% off the top for letting him snap their tourists.
2. I notice a tremendous similarity from shop to shop, not variations on the same products, but *exactly* the same products. I spotted the little Oriental man and his barrel in a dozen places.
3. Marshall Fishwick has noted that "Hawaii is marvelous territory for the icon hunter. Where else can a surf board support an entire lifestyle?" But, all the surfboards here are rented and for $1.44 anyone can purchase a T-shirt that says "Waikiki Surf Instructor."
4. Paper products like color postcards have a markup of 200% but they sell for 10 or 15 cents each and it takes a lot of them to make it worthwhile. Still, Bob, the supersalesman, says he can move 2500 a week when the Canadians come, which is in October and November.
5. Bob also points out that any wooden statue of a woman with naked breasts is a terrific seller. Part of the Polynesian ethic he says. Poor man's Gauguin. Same size statue of a male with bare breasts brings half as much. Also, wooden masks and samurai swords don't move too quickly, but when they do it's good business. Each brings in over $100.
6. Everyone agrees and Lou confirms that there are three "bestsellers" on Waikiki:
   a. Aloha *shirts and dresses.* Hawaiian blues and deep greens are best. Next is red or tangerine orange. There are identical prints in various sizes so that papa bear, mama bear and baby bear(s) can look alike.
   b. *Paper shell and Puka shell neckware.* Popular with males and females long before the choker became acceptable attire for the mainland male. Hawaii is surprisingly androgynous in that respect. There is little room for macho here. These go for 99 cents and up. The original "paper

shells" were found only on Oahu (the island that contains Honolulu) but the supply ran out and most are now made of synthetic material and shipped over from the Philippines. Lou notes that the bottom has fallen out of the market. A year ago they went for $5.00 and up.

   c. *T-Shirts* go for $1.44 and up. They *must* say "Hawaii," the bigger and bolder the letters the better. Lou notes that the bottom has fallen out of the market. A year ago they went for $5.00 and up. . .

FLASH INTO ANY DRESS SHOP: "My these dresses are so pretty! But they are so colorful I could never wear them back home." But the brave do plunk down $40-50 for a muu-muu. Wear it one or two nights, neatly fold it into their suitcase, and then hang it in their closet.

Leisure is escape—traditional tastes do not apply—step out of yourself, let yourself go, be bizarre. This goes beyond muu-muus. Check out any summer cabin or beach house, or even the ski lodges and golf courses, and don't forget dad in a chef's hat and apron in front of the barbeque. Leisure activity has its own set of icons, all of which may be distinguished by a sense of the extraordinary or unusual, when placed in the normal set of life. The question is, do these icons primarily function to identify a certain endeavor to others, or to assure the participant of his/her role?—"Yes, I may now do as I damn well please!"

See plenty of matching aloha shirts and muu-muus too— "We are a pair." The Japanese tourists really get off on this. But then the Japanese get off on everything. The tourist par excellent, coming to America to divest it of its treasures, all too reminiscent of the British pillaging of Egypt and India etc., or the American quest for European objects d'art. The Japanese know where its at. While most tourists photograph Ala Moana shopping center's fountains, palm trees and koi pools, the Japanese make sure not to exclude shots of themselves or escalators, some with no steps.

THE TOURISTS' TOURIST: They get off a JAL plane, (served Chateau Lafite 1959, in first class), are greeted by the tour company, shuttled onto a bus which will take them to one of the many Japanese owned Waikiki hotels. But first stop is the aloha wear factory. White shirted, dark pants tourists with Nikons swinging from their necks, disgorge from the bus, enter the factory, and emerge clad in aloha attire. All wear the same print, the same color.

For the Japanese tourist the group is sacred. Following the cultural stress on familial hierarchy, so well adapted by large Japanese corporations, the tour group becomes a family away from home. Group pictures are in. Get off the bus, see the site, snap individual scenes (usually recording the same scene repeatedly with new faces) and then the inevitable group photograph. "These people made up the tour with me."

The Japanese buy more aloha wear than the haoles, and a lot more. Must bring back gifts when you travel, old Japanese custom. So perfume, postcards, and other small items are consumed by the gross. But that's not all—while we go to Japan for cameras and stereo equipment, the Japanese come here for golf clubs, Johnny Walker Black, and pornography. Specialty shops catering to these desires have sprung up in all sections of Waikiki.

The Japanese tourist has further changed the face of Waikiki with okazu stands (Japanese delicatesan) and saimin stands, the largest of the latter, stands in the middle of Kalakaua, and while appearing exotic to the mainland traveler, it is a reassuring icon for the Japanese, their McDonalds.

When not in their matching aloha garb the Japanese tourist adds another dimension to the Waikiki scene, especially the ladies—wide rimmed hats, slippers decorated with plastic flowers, 1930's art deco outfits with make up to match. If you ever wish to excite the wrath of a local Japanese, just mistake them for one of these peculiarly clad tourists with their strange ways.

And still the graffiti inquires: "Has anyone laid a Japanese tourist."

Enter any hotel: jet lagged tourists everywhere, forgetting the traditional purpose of a tropical vacation: rest and relaxation, get away from it all. Off on a whirl-wind three islands in eight days and seven nights tour of the fiftieth state. Consuming the islands with a hectic flood of Kodak photographs, seeing all they are shown, so once back home they can claim, yes, we saw that, and maybe even add to their community's

folklore of Hawaii. Picking up souvenirs as tangible evidence
—they really did Hawaii. Stands abound, with a plethora of
items on display, much not even related to the islands—just
international tourist style, popular everywhere: Mexican
trinkets, turquoise jewelry, Spanish, Phillipine and Taiwan
wood work, attire from India—anything you might not be
able to get back home. And then there are the potted plants,
sealed in their plastic bags to get them through California's
agriculture inspection. Place a bit of Hawaii greenery in
your kitchen window to get you through the long winter
ahead.

A casual hecticness is ever present. The middle class bar-
gain hunter cannot down. The fear of not getting what you
paid for thumps away at the back of the brain. . . .

FLASH TO A RENT-A-CAR STAND: "Now with our
flight to Maui we get this rent-a-car for half price, right? The
cost is normally this much per day, right? Does this include
insurance? Gas? Mileage? And the car has an air conditioner
and power. . ." and on and on. Confirm, reconfirm, inform,
re-inform, until the client gives a satisfied harumph and another business transaction is completed.

New uniforms, same players. They think they have escaped
the daily routine, the race of the rats; amazing what a shift in
set and setting can accomplish. But there is another side to
this particular set and setting: The mainlanders step off the
giant 747 and are greeted not only by a new location, but
also a new time. Welcome to Waikiki, Flash Gordon with a
tropical backdrop.

It all started with the Ilikai in 1960. The steel and concrete monolith was heralded as the uncompromising view of
the future. Hawaii was about to alter its image—we must
show the American public that we are not just another
Tahiti or Fiji, but are just as attractive as Chicago or Las
Vegas.

[This is just an amazing quote, unfortunately the exact
wording and citation is in storage with my lecture notes in
Hawaii—never thought I would have occasion to refer to
them in Boise.] While some people bemoaned the destruction
of Hawaii's scenic vistas with the advent of the highrise, the
builders of the Ilikai proudly proclaimed, "For every view we

destroyed we have given man ten new ones which he never dreamed possible before." Another article advised the tourist that when the hustle and bustle of the streets got to be too much, they could just hop in the elevator and whiz to the privacy and serenity of their penthouse apartment.

The article failed to mention the Ilikai's elevator is glass walled on one side in order to give the tourist a few of those highly acclaimed ten new views. Flash Gordon land now claims three such elevators in the heart of Waikiki. Add to that the revolving restaurant at the Top of Waikiki, the Sheridan Waikiki's mysto globes standing in front of the elevator banks on every floor, surrounded by garish green hued tropically inspired carpet, potential passengers huddled around the object, waiting for the glow which will indicate the elevator's arrival, and you are all set for Space 1999. Once in the elevators don't touch the buttons. They are heat activated, just wave your hand. How can the people from Peoria not be impressed? They probably won't even make it down to the Sheridan's chrome plated discotheque—The and probably won't even be able to handle the multi-media presentation—Hawaii Now!

All is a blur, and hopefully some guide will point out what is supposed to be seen. The tropics merge with the future as Jimi Hendrix cried out, "IS IT TOMORROW OR JUST THE END OF TIME?" Sensory overload is the name of the game, perceptions are no longer believed and must be verbally reconfirmed. Leads to incredible conversations:

"Where can I buy stamps?"

"In the machine directly in front of your nose."

"How does it work?"

"Read the directions." They feign to, but really don't. Place their coins in the slot, push the coin return, and claim the machine is malfunctioning. A typical shop clerk's evening. Giving directions is just as bad. After confirming you speak English, all directions must be repeated at least three times: "Yes, that's right, go down the hall to the right."

My girlfriend's now off work. Not a bad evening. Only two stamp machine scenes, she's pissed though. Someone called her a "native." Nothing could be lower, anyone who watches television and the movies knows natives carry spears and eat

Christians. Another small image gap.

I start up the machine, we hop on and head out for Rainbow Drive-in and a plate lunch. But that's another story.

FADE IN: *My office at the University* which overlooks the University Avenue parking lot. It's about nine p.m. here, midnight in Los Angeles, three a.m. in New York. The tradewinds are blowing through the window but JoNell and I have the fan on anyway—it's the humidity. Lou's pictures are scattered across my desk.

Wilber Schramm, probably the most prolific of all communication writers, was a mile up the hill at the University's East-West Studies Center until he retired. He began his *Men, Messages and Media:*

> As I write these lines I can look up from my paper at the jagged green mountains of Hawaii. If i look down the horizon to the seacoast, I can pick out the place where man is supposed to have first stepped ashore on these islands. He came out of the Stone Age, twelve hundred years ago, riding in an outrigger canoe that he had fashioned with the crudest of instruments. He came to Hawaii at the end of an incredible 5000-year journey from Southeast Asia, carrying his gods, his children, his foods with him hopping from island to island over thousands of miles of open sea, living in a rapport with wind, water, and earth such as we could hardly expect of modern man. He landed on a lava island, planted his seeds and his culture, and made the land his.[1]

The process is now complete. Modern men (and women) travel those thousands of miles in great winged canoes to return the seeds of Hawaii to their homelands in Asia where, according to Schramm, it all began. The gilded image of a Hawaii that no longer exists is preserved in the samurai sword shipped home to grace a Japanese fireplace, or a wooden caricature of a man in a barrel, sitting on a kitchen windowsill somewhere in suburban Cincinati.

Hawaii *is* a series of still pictures which begin "Hawaii 5-0" every Friday night; a grass skirt, an aloha shirt, a wooden salad fork made in the Philippines. The cultural seeds of the "lava island" have born fruit: the Waikiki Icon!

At the same time, the eager tourist is greeted by a red neon sign proclaiming "Ramada Inn" before the plane ever touches down. "Jack in the Box" may be found here too, comfortably tucked away between two of the large Waikiki hotels. Employees can actually watch the waves break over the sands of one of the world's most famous beaches while they prepare a "Jumbo Jack."

Perhaps it is a fair exchange. The Waikiki icon makes "their land ours" and in our rush to procure it we have made "our land theirs" as well. The jet plane and electronic communication have forever banished the national ethnic boundries of popular culture. This curious mixture of Hula and Disco is only one example of the "icon sandwich" of a new international culture.

NOTE

1Schramm Wilbur, *Men Messages, and Media,* New York: Harper & Row p. 1.

Mine Mules and Coal Tipples: Icons of the Coalfields

David A. Corbin

The men and women of the American coalfields developed a distinct working-class culture. For decades they lived in towns owned and controlled by corporate officials, worked in the nation's dirtiest and most dangerous occupation and endured and resisted company exploitation and oppression. Their history is a brutal one, filled with bitter and bloody warfare and murderous explosions, but it produced a culture that has been patronized, romanticized, maligned, condemned, sometimes praised, but rarely understood. In their world, the miners came to treasure things which had little meaning to so-called sophisticated, middle-class societies. And because their culture was in-bred, self-sufficient, self-contained, intense, the artifacts in their lives took on powerful meanings. Two—the coal tipple and the mine mule—were so powerful that they became icons—perhaps the most powerful type of icons, because at the same time they were revered they were also hated.

The tipple was omnipresent in the camp. By far the most visible and conspicuous object, it towered over the small, dingy shanties the miners lived in. One observer, awed by the breaker noted:

> The whole monstrous thing—the huge building two hundred feet high perched above the shaft through which the cars of coal were hoisted from a thousand feet below, surrounded by great culm-banks, hills of slate and refuse from the mines—screeched its inexorable omnipotence.[1]

253

The tipple's powerful figure and its thunderous, mysterious sounds dominated the coal camps. In contrast to the looming tipple, the mine was inconspicuous; it was simply a small hole in the ground, several hundred yards "up the hollow" which was, by superstition, off-limits to women and, by law, off-limits to their children.[2]

The coal tipple never developed the mocking or hated image of the other central structure in the coal camp — the company store, symbol of the coal company's exploitation — labeled the "pluck-me-store." In the company store, the miner saw his paycheck drained by monopolistic prices and the infamous scrip system. In contrast, the breaker was the place where the miner was rewarded for his daily labor. As Archie Green noted: "since the tipple was the place where coal cars were unloaded and weighed, it was the site where miners could feel their sweat translated into pay."[3]

In addition to its size and conspicuous location, the breaker dominated the coal regions by its booming and mysterious noises. The sounds of coal rushing through chutes, coal cars banging the tipple's sides as they were raised and lowered, the roar of the processing machines set the pace of life and work. The booming, nerve-wracking noises were not only tolerated by the coal diggers, they were appreciated — for the most dreaded noise in the coalfields was the silence of the coal tipple. When the coal tipple ceased to roar, it meant there was, at least temporarily, no market for coal, no mining, no work and no pay for the miner. The miner knew there would be "hard times" until he again heard the breaker thunder.

In their homes and on the steps of the company store, the miners waited to hear the roar of the tipple. When it did come it meant, according to an old miners' song, "me troubles are over." The ballad claimed that "when the breaker starts up on full time," the miner would be able to "throw his calico shirt into the dirt" and buy a new suit for himself, "put Jimmy in pants," buy an "organ for Ritchie," and a "turkey" for Sunday dinner. All of this was possible, the song explained, because "coal was scarce down in New York and the breaker will start up on full time."[4] Hence, the coal breaker also represented the economic tragedy of the miner's industrial life, as it symbolized the miner's income and the dignity that could only be bought with money in a bourgeois society.

The breaker symbolized not only the miner's pay and well-being but also his rites of passage to adulthood. From the "moment he left the cradle," the young boy in the coalfields looked forward to the day when he would enter the breaker, as a slate-picker, and thus enter the world of his father, uncles and grandfathers. Though still a youth, his job in the breaker gave him status in the community; it caused him to be recognized as a man and a miner.[5]

> At eight years of age,
> to the breaker I first went,
> to learn the occupation of a slave,
> I certainly was delighted and on pushing slate was bent,
> my ambition was noble, strong and brave.[6]

The youthful slate-picker also realized that once he had entered the breaker, it was only a short time before he would enter the mine, his destined world of reward and dangers.

> I'm pickin' slate in the breaker,
>   But it ain't the place I'll stay,
> I'm gonna be found way underground
>   A-drawin' a miner's pay,
> An' takin' a miner's chances
>   An' plenty of them there be,
> It's me for the hole where they dig the coal
>   A miner-you-bet-that's me.[7]

And during his life as a miner, the coal digger knew if he survived, he would return to the tipple. When he no longer possessed the strength and ability to pick, shoot-down, shovel coal, and then push the loaded coal car, the tipple would be his last occupational home. It was in the breaker where the miner began and ended his career. As the "old and feeble" miner who had laid his "rusty mining tools away" recalled:

> I started in the breaker
> and went back to it again,
> But, now my work is finished
> for all time.[8]

But even in his old age and facing death — "waiting for the

signal at the door" — the "old and feeble" miner's concern remained for the whereabouts and welfare of those who had entered the world of mining with him:

> Where are the boys who worked with me
>   in the breakers long ago,
> Many of them now have gone to rest,
> Their cares of life are over, they have
>   left this world of woe,
> And their spirits are roaming with the blessed.[9]

The tipple towering and thundering over their lives, carried even a deeper meaning for the hundreds of thousands of southern blacks, European peasants and Appalachian mountaineers who entered the coalfields. The coal tipple stood as a "statue of serfdom," welcoming the immigrants and migrants to industrial slavery and tolling, and the passing of their old, agrarian ways of life. It was their introduction into the world of industrialization with the anxieties and problems which accompanied it.[10] The coal tipple represented a new way of life and work, new friends, new habits, new traditions, a new culture.

The industrial life in the coal mine was a lonely as well as a dirty and dangerous occupation. Working in the dark for ten to twelve hours a day, often without seeing another person, the coal digger came to respect and value all living things. Outside the mine, the coal miner, of course, cherished his family most, the concern for which lay behind the protracted, brutal strikes for higher wages to support his family and shorter hours so that he could spend more time with them. Their families reciprocated, a protective oasis in some of the most violent and bloody conflicts in American labor history.

Inside the mine, the miners learned to appreciate any and all things which made their work safer, easier and more enjoyable. One of the most congenial, efficient and valued animals in the coalfields, and one that has inspired much folklore, was the mine mule.

Until the introduction of mining machines, such as shuttle cars, Joy loaders and conveyor belts, mine mules were used to haul loaded cars from the miner's workplace through the mine to the tipple. For hauling coal, the powerful, sure-footed mine mule was the ideal work animal. It was preferred over other animals, such as the horse, because it required less food, could pull a heavier load, withstand more abuse and was free from excitability. As one observer noted, the mule "faced danger with a philosophic coolness that was short of amazing."[11] As a result, the mine mule fit into the miners' culture, with its emphasis on hard and efficient work and thereby became a working icon.

To the miner, the mine mule was worth its weight in coal. Paid on a piece-rate basis, miners appreciated anything which increased their coal production, including their mine mules. The mine mules delivered coal cars to the miners and then pulled the loaded cars to the tipples without delay, enabling the miners to work steadily without interruption. Consequently the miners recognized the hard-working animal in spirit and in song.

> Old Jim had toiled in Dalton mine
>   for many a weary year,
> He had drawn his car on its narrow track,
>   nor showed no sign of fear.
> Not one murmur of complaint had his
>   fellow workers heard
> Him never make; and he was always ready
>   to start at a word.
> He received no wages, just his food - Old
>   Jim was only a mule;
> But a patient, gentle animal that never broke
>   a rule.[12]

The miners realized that the mule was no "lazy ass," but the fulfillment of the work ethic.

The miners further realized that the mule was no "dumb ass." Because of the dangers the miners faced — the deadly slatefalls and murderous gas explosions — the miners respected the safe, intelligent worker. Here again the mine mule excelled. His knowledge of the tunnels and extraordinary sense of coming danger saved many a miner's life. Stories are legion about how mine mules alerted miners to a forthcoming cave-in, enabling them to find shelter, of mine mules leading trapped miners out of the honey-combed mines, of mine mules, while pulling loaded coal cars ducking overhanging rocks hidden by the darkness of the mine, and warning the miner of the rock's deadly presence.[13] Such acts of wisdom earned mine mules nicknames such as Moses and Daniel Webster and created a special affinity between the miner and the mule.[14] Many a miner came to regard the mule as his "best friend."

The miners demonstrated their devotion and loyalty to their "best friend" in a number of ways. They condemned and ostracized any person found mistreating a mine mule.[15] In southern Illinois miners voted to have the company withhold an amount of money from their paychecks so that a retired mule could be provided a pension of "oats and green pastures."[16] The most startling illustration of the miners' concern for their mine mule occurred in Dalton, Ohio, when the miners struck in behalf of their mine mule — an incident that shows the miners not only accepted the mule as a friend and workman, but as a fellow unionist. According to a ballad written about the event:

> There came a day when the faithful mule was
>   sent to another mine,
> And when the news had reached the shaft
>   it flew along the line.
> Then every lip in protest moved, and every
>   heart was sore,
> For now they thought that they might see their
>   favorite no more.
> "What made them take that mule away, we'd like to
>   know," they said.
> "We want him back, let's strike for him" and
>   thus the feeling spread.
> Four hundred picks were laid aside for the sake
>   of one old mule.
> Four hundred sturdy miners struck, nor would
>   they lift a single tool.

As a result of the strike, the ballad claimed

> It was not long before the mule's familiar form
>   was seen
> A-coming down the road, two of his partisans
>   between.
> And as he neared the shaft, Old Jim gave
>   one bray, long and loud,
> While a rousing cheer of welcome wafted from
>   the waiting crowd.
> And in that shout the strike dissolved like

fog before the sun.
  Next morning found the men at work, quite
    conscious they had won.[17]

The place of the mule in the miner's life and imagination was not entirely one of loyalty and devotion. The miners also used the mule to denigrate and ridicule the coal company's lack of concern for its workers. Conscious of the fact that the company hired men but bought mules, they realized that if a miner was killed in the mine, the company simply hired another at no cost, whereas if a mule was killed it cost the company. According to the miners:

Kill a man, have to hire another,
Kill a mule, have to buy another.[18]

Many an elderly miner tells the story, which can probably be officially classified as folklore, that when an explosion occurred at a mine where he was working, the first question the company superintendent asked was not if any men were hurt, but "did they get the mules out?" Therefore, the miners believed that in the eyes of the coal company, according to another expression, "miners were not worth the price of a mule."[19]

George Korson collected a story in eastern Pennsylvania about a mule that caused its driver to be run over and killed by a coal car. A week later, the same mule was hauling a car when it stumbled, fell over and was killed. When the coal company promptly fired the driver responsible for the mule's death, the miners appropriately asked "Why the discrimination?"[20]

The use of the mine mule to mock the coal company's attitude toward its miners was not derogatory to the mule. Rather, in these slogans the mule was the means of expressing the miner's class consciousness and antagonisms toward his employer and the owner's lack of concern for their miners' health and safety.

The miners were right. Coal companies spent considerable amounts of money for the care of the mules, such as building them lavish underground stables and pastures.[21] Company officials constantly wrote articles advising other companies on how best to care for their work animals and warning against their abuse. "The overloading or overworking [of] a mule cannot be too strongly condemned," claimed one coal operator, who stressed the need to give the mule proper care, enough rest, good food and clean stables. But the operator's interest in the health of the animals was the same as his interest in his human workers, that is, related only to their profit-making ability. According to the same coal operator, proper care would make the mule "more efficient and effective at a lower cost . . . because the renewed vigor with which the mule would attack its work and the resulting gain in efficiency would amply repay the loss of time and money, if any . . ."[22]

The miners also idealized the mule's stubbornness as a symbol of his own tough independence. The pride they took in the humble humbling the proud was a prototype of their own dignity. For example, the miners told the story of an obstinate mule named Katie, that humbled an arrogant braggart who had claimed he could tame any animal. Also, there was "Temperamental Liz" who drove an "eddicated precher" to swearing and cursing.[23]

The occasional fierceness of the mule could also be used to prove the miner's courage and ability to defeat the socially or physically stronger. It is not surprising that a story arose of how the greatest miner of all, John L. Lewis, bare-handedly defeated Spanish Pete, a temperamental, man-killing mule. Legend has it that Spanish Pete cornered Lewis against the wall of a mine and tried to kill him, when Lewis "smashed the animal off its feet with a right-hand punch and with a quickly grabbed piece of timber met the mule's return charge and drove the club with pile driving force through its brains." The legend records not only Lewis' strength, but his ingenuity and ability to outwit the coal operators, even as a rank-and-file miner. The story concludes that Lewis, aware that killing the mule might cost him his job, covered the gaping head wound with clay and reported the death of Spanish Pete as the result of heart failure.[24] Vicious mule and exploitive owner both could be beat by the miner willing to fight and to plan for his life.

As mentioned earlier, the coal tipple symbolized the economic and social tragedy of the miner's industrial life, his captivity in and subordination to a competitive bourgeois society. The coal miner's life and work revolved around the coal tipple; he lived and worked under its roar, and his income, welfare and pursuit of happiness depended upon its functioning. The miner may have failed to understand his subordination to the mechanical monolith, which he held in awe, but he clearly understood the harsh, competitive world it represented. At times, his understanding of his captivity caused him to lash out and engage in the most bloody industrial conflicts in American labor history, but he also found more subtle ways of making life endurable in the coalfields.

In the coal camps the miners came to idealize the work animal, the mine mule, which demonstrated to them that it was possible to maintain one's rugged independence in an industrialized, bourgeois society. The miner envied the mine mule and cited its integrity to deride not only the coal companies but himself. His conception of the mule went beyond regarding it as a companion and fellow workman and unionist when he sang, perhaps somewhat facetiously, but certainly with a strain of sincerity: "My sweetheart is the mule of the mines."[25] But there was no facetiousness in his belief that:

> He is the best, our friend, the mule,
> > Better than man.
> In work and rest he observes the rule,
> > Better than man.
> He wastes no time in laugh or sob,
> He never takes a fellow's job,
> > He beats the man.[26]

Hence, the personal tragedy and disgrace of life and work in industrialized America: the worker held a four-footed beast in higher esteem than himself.

NOTES

[1]Owen Lovejoy, *In the Shadow of the Coal Breaker* (New York: National Child Labor Committee, 1917), Bulletin 61, p. 4.

[2]For the discussions of the superstition about not allowing women inside the coal mine, see: George Korson, *Coal Dust on the Fiddle* (Philadelphia: University of Pennsylvania Press, 1943), Chapter 11, "Craft Supersitition and Legends," pp. 201-211.

[3]Archie Green, *Only a Miner* (Urbana: University of Illinois Press, 1972), p. 51.

[4]George Korson, *Minstrels of the MIne Patch* (Philadelphia: University of Pennsylvania Press, 1933), pp. 29-31.

[5]For an excellent account of the prestige a child felt when he entered either the mine or the breaker, see: John Brophy, *A Miner's Life,* ed. by John O.P. Hall (Madison: The University of Wisconsin Press, 1964), pp. 36-50.

[6]"The Old Miner's Refrain," transcribed by Melvin LeMon, cited in Korson, *Minstrels,* pp. 273-274.

[7]Berton Braley, "The Breaker Boy's Ambition," *United Mine Workers Journal* (hereafter cited as *UMWJ*), June 12, 1913, p. 4.

[8]"Miner's Refrain," Korson, *Minstrels,* pp. 273-274.

[9]*Ibid.*

[10]The anxieties and problems which came with the adjustment of workers to industrialization is a current topic among labor historians. For the best treatment of the topic see: Herbert Gutman, "Work, Culture, and Society in Industrializing America, 1815-1919," *The American Historical Review,"* (June 1973), 531-588.

[11]Korson, *Coal Dust,* pp. 187-189; Phil Conley, *History of the West Virginia Coal Industry* (Charleston, West Virginia: Education Foundation, Inc., 1960), p. 35.

[12]Henry Jeffries, "Old Jim," *UMWJ,* February 15, 1931, p. 7.

[13]Jacob Tennant, "Daniel Webster," *West Virginia Folklore,* XII (Spring 1962), 46; Bill Price, "Moses and the Mule Driver," *West Virginia Folklore,* XII (Spring 1962), 47: "Whoa Mule," *UMWJ,* December 1, 1924, p. 7; also see Korson, *Minstrels,* pp. 151-152.

[14]Tennant, "Webster," p. 46; Price, "Moses," p. 47.

[15]See for example, "The Driver Boys of Wadesville Shaft" cited in Korson, *Minstrels,* pp. 117-122.

[16]"Pension for Mule," *UMWJ,* December 1, 1924, p. 7.

[17]Jeffries, "Old Jim."

[18]Korson, *Coal Dust,* p. 190; The author also collected the expression from several sources throughout southern West Virginia during summer 1975.

[19]The author collected the story from several sources including Columbus Avery, Williamson, West Virginia, July 13, 1975; George Hairston, Eckman, West Virginia, August 20, 1975.

[20]Korson, *Coal Dust,* p. 190.

[21]"The Mine Mule," *UMWJ,* December 1, 1925, p. 13.

[22]Matthew Davies, "The Care of Mine Mules," *Coal Age,* I (May 11, 1912), 1021-1022; Also see, E. Hogg, "Care of the Mine Mule," *Mines and Minerals,* XXVI, 1905/1906, p. 149-151, and I.C. Newhard, "Care of Mine Mules," *Mines and Minerals,* XXVIII, 1907/1908, pp. 56-58.

[23]"Temperamental Liz," Korson, *Minstrels,* pp. 80-82; "Katie and Pat," Korson, *Minstrels,* pp. 82-83; Also see, Korson, *Coal Dust,* Chapter Nine, "Whoa, Mule!" pp. 187-191.

[24]Saul Alinsky, *John L. Lewis* (New York: Putnams, 1949), pp. 8-9; Also see "The Grateful Mule," *West Virginia Folklore,* VIII (Summer 1958), 61-62. This is a story of a "grateful mule" reciprocating the miner's kindness by killing a sadistic company official who is about to hurt a miner.

[25]Korson, *Minstrels,* p. 122; The author collected the song from Nimrod Workman, Chatteroy Hollow, West Virginia, July 15, 1975.

[26]Korson, *Coal Dust,* p. 187.

Comicons

Harold Schechter

Of all the festivities that take place in New York City over the July Fourth weekend, perhaps the most intriguing is the annual Comic Art Convention. Thousands of people congregate in one of the big midtown hotels — usually the Commodore or Statler-Hilton — and devote three or four days to the celebration — and veneration — of the comic book. These people constitute a kind of congregation — an assembly of devotees — and it is suggestive that they refer to their gatherings as Comicons. The name contains two meanings: first (the intended one), "comic conventions," and second (inadvertent but no less valid), "comic icons." For it is at these conventions that the comic book's function as popular icon becomes particularly plain.

As Marshall Fishwick points out in his introductory essay to *Icons of Popular Culture,* one basic definition of icon is "an object of uncritical devotion."[1] In other words, an icon is defined, most simply, by the effect it produces. If an object — a thing — is regarded with reverence, we may say that, *by virtue of that fact alone,* it serves as an icon. The power of comic books to generate reverence is nowhere more apparent than at these conventions, where fans will jostle each other for a glimpse of a *Superman #1* or stand — almost breathlessly — before an early *All Star Comics* exhibited under glass.

A significant fact about such behavior is that for many of these people the contents of these comics are virtually immaterial. What is of primary importance is the object itself.

When a Batman fan sees a mint-condition copy of *Detective Comics # 1* in a display case, he doesn't want to take it out and read it: the story has been reprinted in a dozen different places, and some of the reproductions are of far higher quality than the original (e.g., the one that appears in Jules Feiffer's *The Great Comic Book Heroes*). But, for the true devotee, there is a special potency — magic, numinosity, call it what you will — about the original. It's enough for him just to stand nearby and gaze at it, to be able to go home and tell his friends — veneration in his voice — that he actually saw a copy of *Detective #1*.[2] Some comics books have so much of this potency that they even endow their possessors with mana, so that, at the comic conventions, the owners of especially rare issues are themselves regarded with a certain kind of awe. Though his use of the phrase is rather precious, Stan Lee, the chief executive at Marvel Comics, hits on something essential when he addresses his readers as "True Believers", as he does, for instance, in the introduction to his book *Origins of Marvel Comics*: "So read on, O True Believer. May this small but salient slice of living history now serve to nourish thine awestruck, hungry eyes."[3]

But comics serve as icons not simply because they inspire devotion. Like all icons, the comic book is an embodiment of both societal and spiritual values: a symbolic object whose meaning arises from the interaction of archetype and culture.

The notion that a comic book might possess archetypal significance, perform an essentially religious function, might strike some people as absurd, if not downright offensive. Nevertheless, the mythological power of the comics was recognized over twenty years ago by a British psychotherapist named Alan McGlashan, who pointed out that the characters in certain comic strips were modern-day incarnations of primordial figures:

> Garth and Jane, Jimpy and Captain Reilly-Ffoull: is it possible that someone on the staff of the *Daily Mirror* chose these grotesques with full understanding of what he was doing? It is wildly unlikely. Yet beyond this, and the even less likely explanation of pure chance, there lies only one other possibility — that they were chosen by the uncannily accurate processes of unconscious selection, operating at the deepest level of the human psyche. If this were so, they would

be found to exert a curiously compulsive power, overriding rational repudiation, on the minds of multitudes. Which is precisely what they do.

For these figures are no casual products of the imagination. Faintly, through all their exploits, vulgar and puerile as they usually are, sounds the echo of something unimaginably archaic: the adventure cycle of the early gods.

. . . .

Unpalatable though it may be to modern taste, the truth is that we cannot live without the early gods. . . . If cast out in the forms of Man's profoundest apprehensions of them — if Christ and Buddha and Mithra, if Ashtaroth and Pan are disowned — they nevertheless come back. However meanly and unrecognizably, they come back to the human heart whose inevictable tenants they are. And "there all smothered up in shade" they sit, radiating that strange compelling power which is Man's unconscious tribute to the Unknowable. In the comic strip may lie concealed the indestructible germ of natural religion.[4]

What McGlashan perceived about the English funnies is equally true of American comic books: they are strikingly rich in mythic imagery — in large measure, their "curiously compulsive power" springs from archetypes. Since an extensive archetypal analysis of the comics is not possible here, a few examples will have to suffice.

Among the most important of the "primordial images" identified by Carl Jung are the hero, the wise old man, the shadow, trickster, and anima — and these are the very images that we find again and again on the comic book page. There are, of course, countless incarnations of the hero archetype in the comics; if Joseph Campbell had included the domain of the comic book in his classic study of the hero myth, he would have been obliged to call it *The Hero with Two Thousand Faces.* That "the great comic book heroes" are, in fact, directly descended from the great mythological ones is acknowledged in a rather interesting way by the publishers of a text entitled, simply, *Mythology* — a book which includes contributions by Ernst Cassirer, Edmund Leach, and Claude Levi-Strauss. The cover of this anthology is a collage of comic book and classical art: a full-color torso of Superman topped with the head of an ancient Greek god.[5] In their book *Comics: Anatomy of a Mass Medium,* Reinhold Reitberger and

Wolfgang Fuchs draw some provocative parallels, comparing Superman to both Achilles and Siegfried ("all three are invulnerable, except for Achilles' heel, the spot on Siegfried's back, and Superman's susceptibility to Kryptonite"), the Flash to Mercury, Hawkman to Icarus, and the Green Arrow to Philoctetes.[6] The mythological heritage of the modern-day superhero is made explicit in some of the comics themselves. Captain Marvel is a prime example. The magic word which transforms Billy Batson into "the World's Mightiest Mortal" is an acronym derived from the names of the Captain's archetypal ancestors:

Solomon . . . . .wisdom
Hercules . . . . .strength
Atlas . . . . .stamina
Zeus . . . . .power
Achilles. . . . . .courage
Mercury . . . . .speed

Shazam is also the name of Billy Batson's mentor, the "ancient Egyptian wizard" who teaches him the secret word, thereby endowing him with the wisdom of Solomon, etc., etc. With his flowing robe and long, white beard, Shazam is a fascinating embodiment of the archetypal figure that Jung calls the wise old man. Other manifestations of this primordial image include "the Ancient One" — the venerated master of Doctor Strange — and Mr. Natural, the flipped-out guru of R. Crumb's *Zap Comix*.

A third mythological figure that often appears in the comics is the shadow. A personification of the hidden, unacknowledged side of the psyche, the shadow traditionally assumes a variety of forms: the alter ego, the doppelgänger, the dark brother. Comic books are filled with such symbols. The superhero's "secret identity" is perhaps the most common representation of the shadow: almost every costumed crime-fighter in comicdom has an alter ego — Batman-Bruce Wayne, Spider-man—Peter Parker, Captain America-Steve Rogers, etc. Sometimes, the shadow takes the shape of a grotesque double. A good example is Bizarro Superman. In a fiendish (though predictably futile) plot to destroy the Man of Steel, Lex Luthor — Superman's perennial arch-enemy — constructs a duplicator ray which he trains on his foe. The result is (in

Luthor's words) "your imperfect double, Superman. I created him so that he can battle you with his super-powers! Ha, Ha!"

A form of the shadow archetype very closely related to the sinister double is that of the dark or hostile brother. Several recent comic books contain very striking examples of this motif. In *Master of Kung Fu #16*, Shang-chi, the hero of the series, is forced to fight his evil foster brother — "the man-menace called Midnight" — to the death. Midnight is a horribly scarred black man who hides his deformity behind a sable cowl. In fact, his combat outfit is entirely black — flat black — so that, in the fight scenes, Shang-chi appears to be battling a silhouette. The language used to describe Midnight's arrival at the battleground is significant: "He steps out solidly, a living shadow in a realm of shadows." Another comic book structured around the archetype of the hostile brother is *Kobra,* which first appeared on the stands early in 1976. Its plot revolves around the rivalry of two young men — Siamese twins separated at birth — who end up following rather different paths in life: (one) becomes an undergraduate at Columbia University, the other (less conventional) the leader of a cult of New Delhi snake worshippers and, in the words of Lieutenant Perez of the N.Y.P.D. Special Weapons and Tactics Force, "one of the world's deadliest criminals."

Two final archetypes that are frequently met with in comic books are the trickster and the anima. Trickster figures are particularly prevalent: all the compulsive pranksters that abound in the comics, the mischievous tykes and anarchic animals, are embodiments of this archetype. Best known, perhaps, is Bugs Bunny, whose mythological lineage extends back to Br'er Rabbit and, beyond that, to the Winnebago trickster god Hare. The trickster archetype is common, not only in humorous comic books, but in superhero series as well. Two of Superman's long-standing adversaries, for example, are trickster figures: the Prankster, who commits crimes by means of elaborate practical jokes, and Mr. Mxyztplk, the imp from the fifth dimension. The Green Goblin, one of Spider-man's most formidable foes, is an extremely disquieting character. With his demonic Halloween garb and bagful of lethal tricks, he is a true descendent of the primordial trickster gods — malicious, savage creatures who do "the most atrocious things."[7]

In comic books, the anima — the archetypal feminine — is usually portrayed in her negative aspect as lamia or succubus. One of the most popular characters in comicdom is Vampirella, the bloodsucking cutie from the planet Drakulon. A more serious and genuinely unsettling embodiment of the bad anima appears in *Conan #32*. In this story, the brawny barbarian follows an enticing blonde into a bottomless pool. As they dive deep into the "watery blackness," the "sloe-eyed wench" turns toward the hero and wraps him in her arms — whereupon she abruptly changes into a "creature spawned in some nether hell," a loathsome thing with the head of a woman and the body of an octopus. Enclosed in her tentacles, Conan can only stare into her eyes — "eyes not really those of even a half-woman, but of some monster which has assumed human form to ensnare him." Finally, the Cimmerian manages to close "his mind to the image of haunting deadly beauty," free his sword arm, and slice off her head. This hypnotic she-creature, whose power nearly pulls Conan into a watery grave, has many mythological cousins: the sirens, the Lorelei, the Rusalka, the nixies:

> Half she drew him down,
> Half sank he down
> And nevermore was seen.[8]

An iconological analysis of the comic book, then, reveals a profusion of primordial imagery. But it is not only the collective unconscious — the "timeless and universal" realm of myth — that finds expression in the comics. Like all icons, comic books are, in Marshall Fishwick's phrase, "cultural ciphers," embodying the values of the particular society in which they are produced. And this is why the Fourth of July is such an appropriate time to hold a comic convention, for, in a very real sense, the celebration of the comic book is the celebration of the American spirit.

After all, though Superman et al. are clearly manifestations of mythological figures, they are uniquely *American* manifestations — heroes engaged in a never-ending battle for Truth, Justice, and the American Way. The epitome of the patriotic superhero is, of course, Captain America, whose career began in 1941 when the brilliant Dr. Reinstein innoculated a frail 4-F named Steve Rogers with a "wonder serum" and transformed him into the Sentinel of Liberty. "Don't be afraid, son," said Dr. Reinstein as he administered the injection. "You are about to become one of America's saviors," and thirty-five years later, Cap is still doing battles with freedom's foes:

> A *man* can be destroyed! A *team,* or an *army* can be destroyed! But how do you destroy an *ideal* — a *dream*? How do you destroy a living *symbol* — or his indomitable *will* — his unquenchable *spirit?* Perhaps *these* are the thoughts which thunder within the murderous minds of those who have chosen the way of *Hydra* — of those who face the *fighting fury* of freedom's most fearless *champion* — the gallant, red-white-and-blue-garbed figure who has been a towering source of *inspiration* to liberty-lovers everywhere! How can the fearsome forces of *evil* ever hope to destroy the unconquerable CAPTAIN AMERICA?[10]

Like Cap, most of comicdom's flag-waving heroes were born during WW II: Spy Smasher; Minute-Man, the One Man Army; Boy Commandos; the Shield (who once received the following tribute from a beaming F.D.R.: "My son, you are a true courageous American. You have saved America from the slimy clutches of master spies and saboteurs. The youth of our country can well look upon you as a model American!"). But even the less blatantly chauvinistic superheroes, Batman, Green Arrow, the Human Torch, are American prototypes. Boyishly modest, misogynistic, pious and proficient in killing, they possess all the qualities that have characterized the American hero since he first appeared in the Leatherstocking Tales.

But it's not only the content of the comics, their stories and characters, that give expression to American ideals. The comic book — the object itself — is unmistakably American. You don't have to read through a comic to get a powerful sense of our society; you don't even have to open one up: our national traits are revealed right on the cover. It's all there: the gaudiness, the violence, the vitality, the materialism ("52 Big Pages for Only 25¢"), the strain of puritainism ("Approved by the Comics Code Authority") and something else, what Leslie Fiedler calls "the regressiveness, in a technical

sense, of American life, its implacable nostalgia for the infan-
tile, at once wrong-headed and admirable. The mythic America is boyhood," Fiedler goes on to say. In some countries,
France and Italy, for example, comics are prized even more
highly than they are over here and for the very reason that
they embody the spirit of that mythic place. We are known
throughout the world for our comics. Like the Coke bottle,
Kodak, and Cadillac, the comic book is much more than a
commodity; it is a universally recognized symbol of our
culture, one of Uncle Sam's most potent icons.

NOTES

[1] Marshall Fishwick, "Entrance," *Icons of Popular Culture,* ed. Marshall Fishwick and Ray B. Browne (Bowling Green, Ohio: Bowling Green University Popular Press, 1970), p. 2.

[2] Unless, of course, he's extremely rich, in which case he might buy it. My
point remains the same, however: he wouldn't spend a small fortune to read the
story but to possess a sacred object — a comicon.

[3] Stan Lee, *Origins of Marvel Comics* (New York: Simon and Schuster, 1974),
p. 18.

[4] Alan McGlashan, "Daily Paper Pantheon: A New Fantasia of the Unconscious," *The Lancet,* 31 Jan. 1953, pp. 238-239.

Jung himself was aware of the mythological content of the comics. In his
essay "On the Psychology of the Trickster-Figure," he refers to McGlashan's article and notes that "the figures in comic-strips have remarkable archetypal
analogies." See *Archetypes and the Collective Unconscious, Collected Works* IX,
part I (Princeton: Princeton University Press, 1959, Bollington Series XX), p. 260.

[5] Pierre Maranda, ed., *Mythology: Selected Readings* (Baltimore: Penguin
Books, 1972).

[6] Reinhold Reitberger and Wolfgang Fuchs, *Comics: Anatomy of a Mass Medium* (Boston: Little Brown and Company, 1971), p. 100.

[7] C. G. Jung, "On the Psychology of the Trickster-Figure," *Archetypes and the
Collective Unconscious, C.W.* IX, part I, p. 264.

[8] Quoted by C.G. Jung, "Archetypes of the Collective Unconscious," *C.W.*
IX, part I, p. 25.

[9] Marshall Fishwick, "Entrance," *Icons of Popular Culture,* p. 1.

[10] From *Captain America #113.*

The research for this essay was supported in part by a grant from the Faculty
Research Award Program of the City University of New York.

The Plantation : Southern Icon

Earl F. Bargainnier

> *The past is never dead. It's not even past.*
> *William Faulkner*

If a region of the United States can be said to be represented by an icon, the states of the Confederacy are represented by the plantation of the Old South, a plantation
which has resulted from regional pride, idyllic memories, a
lost cause with bitter after-effects, and a consequent sense
of self-righteous alienation. These deeply held emotions have
shaped the image of the South, for Southerners and non-
Southerners, through the various forms of popular culture.
Whether one examines a Mississippi brochure aimed at tourists, the names and architecture of an Alabama sub-division,
tours of "historic" homes around Charleston, Tallahassee or
Richmond, such amusement parks as Carowinds in South
Carolina or Six Flags Over Georgia, a rack of the latest sex-
and-slavery paperback novels, Colonel Sanders, the hundreds
of "Old Plantation" motels and restaurants, Jimmy Carter's
peanut farm being called a plantation, or the phenomenon
of a sequel to *Gone With the Wind* (as well as the unpara-
lled publicity given to the 1976 television showing of the
film), the evidence is that the plantation of the antebellum
South has become the central image — however inadequate
or inaccurate — of what the South has been and, for many,
still is. The continued dominance of this icon of Southern
life in the America of the 1970's raises several questions: In
what ways did it develop? What are its characteristics? How

271

close is it to reality? Why does it have such appeal? And most importantly, What are its effects?

It has been noted that since "the South is, in many ways, the product of an overactive imagination, both regional and national. . . . the distinction between a *historical* and a *fictitious* South becomes a particularly difficult one."[1] This overactive imagination, in the South and elsewhere, has created *Dixie,* "a monolithic region of popular legend."[2] At the center of Dixie, the myth of the Old South, stands the antebellum plantation, and around it cluster numerous related images which form most people's ideas of the South. As John Richard Alden has said, "We Americans who are not too familiar with our history harbor a haunting memory of an Old South — an Old South of broad plantations; of their gracious masters and charming mistresses; of humble, cheerful, and loyal slaves who rose occasionally in ferocious revolt; of poor whites fearing naught but the wrath of Heaven; of cotton, magnolia, and Spanish moss — an Old South menaced and at last overwhelmed and demolished by Northern masses and machinery."[3] This romantic icon of the South has been building since the 1830's and is the result of popular culture in its broadest sense.

When the Abolitionists began their attacks on the South's system of slavery, Southerners in their resentment and regional patriotism, "a peculiar mark of the Southerner,"[4] began not just to defend but to glorify their way of life, and the idealization of the plantation, which employed most of the slaves, was their basic method. Southern apologists presented the planter aristocrat as the descendant of either the English country squire or Sir Walter Scott's medieval knights — Scott being the antebellum South's favorite writer. In either case, the planter was a gentleman, benevolently ruling his vast domains, succoring those less fortunate, and upholding true civilization: a model of innate gallantry and rectitude. "Not everybody by any means was a planter, but the myth holds that everybody wanted to be and that all had the same chance to rise to that pinnacle of grace — all save the noncitizens with dark skin."[5] The plantation became the icon of success to Southerners, and non-Southerners accepted this view, even when disapproving of it. Paul M. Gaston has expressed the irony of both sides in the slavery controversy contributing to the perpetuation of the plantation myth: "The defenders, for obvious reasons, exaggerated the grandeur of their civilization, while the abolitionist assault had the ironic outcome of adding credibility to the myth. In drawing pictures of the horror of Southern society, abolitionists invariably had their dramas of exploitation played on enormous estates presided over by wealthy planters who lived on the grand scale."[6]

By the beginning of the Civil War (in the South: The War Between the States), the concept of the Southern plantation as the epitome of "the good life," at least for the masters, was *an idée reçue*. The war's destruction of plantation life based upon slavery fixed the icon in time. The antebellum South became the romantic "before the war," a golden age; the war itself became that period of heroism, when the Cause was lost but the South was not beaten on the battlefield; and Reconstruction was the vengeful rape by the vulgar North of the beautiful South. As Clarence E. Cason has said, "Defeated on the actual ramparts of Virginia, the southerners retired to the ramparts of the mind. Here the glories of the old South became an impregnable castle over which was flown the invincible banner of 'the Lost Cause.' Since reality was unbearable, mythology became supreme."[7] The refusal to accept post-war conditions, which compared so badly with memories of the antebellum period, led earlier plantation life to become in the late nineteenth century a sentimental dream of lost glory and magnificence. At the same time, slavery was now a thing of the past; it no longer had to be defended. Only the romantic icon of the "good old days" on the plantation remained: "by 1880 nothing remained of the abolitionist tradition except the exaggerated accounts of plantation splendor."[8] In 1888 Albion W. Tourgee, Ohio-born novelist and hated Federal judge in North Carolina during Reconstruction, could lament, "Our literature has become not only Southern in type but distinctly Confederate in sympathy."[9] Southern writers of fiction, led by Thomas Nelson Page, set out to convince the North of the South's honor and the justness of that Lost Cause, and the plantation was their favorite setting. Their success was phenomenal;

their stories filled late 19th-century magazines, once and for all imprinting the image of a Romantic South of moonlight and magnolias on the public consciousness.

Page wrote in the Preface to his novel *Red Rock* that "it seems that even the moonlight was richer and mellower 'before the war' than it is now."[10] In this novel and in such stories as "Marse Chan" and "Meh Lady" of *On Ole Virginia,* Page contrasted the glory that was with the despair of the South after the war, often using as narrator an ex-slave who looked back on his days as a slave on the plantation as the happiest of times. For instance, in "Marse Chan," Sam says, "Dem wuz good ole times, marster—de bes' Sam ever see! . . . Dyar warn' no trouble nor nothin'."[11] If even ex-slaves remembered with nostalgia life before the war, obviously the masters had even fonder memories—along with a corollary bitterness at the passing of that life—which embedded the icon even deeper.

The effect of Page's works on Southerners is clearly seen in the statement of Grace King, the Louisiana writer who was later herself to contribute to the romantic image of the South: "It is hard to explain in simple terms what Thomas Nelson Page meant to us in the South at that time [1880's]. He was the first Southern writer to appear in print as a Southerner, and his stories . . . showed us with ineffable grace that although we were sore bereft, politically, we had now a chance in literature at least."[12] Many Southern writers, such as King, followed Page's lead, becoming hugely popular from the 1880's to the early 1900's, but practically all are forgotten, George Washington Cable—a special case— and Joel Chandler Harris being the only major exceptions. Such writers can be found in profusion in the seventeen-volume *Library of Southern Literature* (1907), edited by Harris and Edwin Anderson Alderman, "Compiled under the Direct Supervision of Southern Men of Letters." This monument to moonlight and magnolias presents the plantation icon in its full splendor. These writers created the image of The South in popular literature which was to last at least through Margaret Mitchell's *Gone With the Wind,* an image which is still not completely obliterated. However, in the 1940's Frank Yerby, a Black writer no matter what his attitude, became a popular novelist by keeping the setting and paraphenalia of the plantation and adding the attraction of invading its previously sacrosanct bedrooms. Since then there has been a floodtide of sex-and-slavery novels, each declaring itself more "scorching" than its predecessors. Though the images produced in these works are closer to the pre-Civil War abolitionist novels and often seem pornographic parodies of the moonlight and magnolias tradition, they still contain at their core the icon of the plantation.

While popular literature provides the outstanding examples of the prevalence and longevity of the icon, other forms of popular culture have also contributed to its development, particularly in the twentieth century. Films, of course, appropriated the plots of the novels and stories from *Birth of a Nation* through *Gone With the Wind* to *Mandingo*. (Strangely, television has ignored the romantic South, preferring the comic grotesquerie of *The Beverly Hillbillies* or the "homey" domesticity of *The Waltons*.) The use of the icon in advertising has been widespread. The Southern states themselves have exploited all aspects of the romantic image to lure tourists, and they have been successful. At the same time, commercial concerns have used the same image, either straight or burlesqued, to sell anything and everything.

However, next to popular fiction, the most significant form in developing the icon has been popular music. Tin Pan Alley, that catch-all term for the American song-publishing industry, has produced nearly one thousand songs about the South, almost all conforming to the established icon.[13] The mammy (and pickaninny) songs, the songs of Southern activities, of the Southern belle, of places, and of praise all present a nostalgic picture of the South as remaining a 19th-century world, which has never gone beyond the simple pleasures of that time, and many are directly related to plantation life: "Down Where the Cotton Blossoms Grow," "She's the Fairest Little Flower Dear Old Dixie Ever Grew," "Roll Them Cotton Bales," "Plantation Days," "Bandana Days," "Mammy's Little Kinky Headed Boy," "It's an Old Southern Custom," and on and on. Such songs have generally been written by non-Southerners (the same is true of the earlier minstrel shows, which also contributed to the icon).

The successful lyricist Leo Robin has commented that "you could fault some hack Tin Pan Alley songwriter back in 1925 who was writing second-rate mechanical songs about how sweet it would be to be back in dear old Dixie with his dear old mammy or his lovely little tootsie-wootsie baby. Maybe he was doing a professional job, but he was peddling a totally false picture."[14] False or not, the images of happy "darkies," beautiful belles, a leisurely existence, honeysuckle, mint juleps, watermelons, and dear old Dixie were what popular music presented of the South in the first half of this century. The general view of such songs is summed up by three: "Away Down South in Heaven," "Anything Is Nice If It Comes from Dixie Land," and "You're Living Right Next Door to Heaven When You Live in Dixieland."

Some of the characteristic features of the plantation icon have already been mentioned, but a catalogue of its major constituent images indicates more clearly its "mixed-bag" nature:

hoop skirts & tight bodices	moonlight
mint juleps	sunny skies
cotton	Uncle Remus (& Uncle Tom)
white columns	the black mammy
gracious hospitality	pickaninnies
bourbon (& sherry for the ladies)	field hands (devoted or otherwise)
"master's" Townhouse	house servants (always devoted)
leisure (& laziness)	white suits & string ties
barbecues & picnics	chivalry & gallantry
family reunions	feminine chastity
magnolias	aristocracy
oleanders	Christmas feasts
azaleas	broad lawns & formal gardens
honeysuckle	Spanish moss
verbena	levees
banjos	huge oaks & tall pines
ring tournaments	family loyalty & pride
duels	slave cabins

noblesse oblige
gambling
the overseer (usually a Yankee)
Mississippi steamboats

crinolines & pantaloons

horse racing

the planter-colonel
the cavalier-cadet

hunting
regional patriotism
dancing
bandanas & starched
 aprons
verandas, porches, &
 piazzas
"plantation Greek" or
"red-brick Georgian"
mansions
the plantation mistress
the plantation belle

These various characteristic images fall into distinct groups: stereotypical characters (white and black), buildings, activities, flowers, food and drink, dress, scenery and concepts and codes of conduct — providing all of the elements needed for embodying the icon. At the center is the plantation itself, whether called Level Green, Oxmoor, Oak Valley, Silver Bluff, Woodlawn, Rosedown, Casa Bianca, Cypress Grove, or Peach Point. With either a plantation Greek "big house on the hill" or just a large rambling countryhouse surrounded by oaks or pines, each is the locale for the characters and their activities: where Colonel Taliaferro (pronounced Tolliver) greets Beauregard Claghorn from Pleasant Hill in the next county, who has come to court crinolined Miss Alice Sue Ellen, while Miz Taliaferro is rushing Aunt Zeba and Uncle Nicodemus to prepare roast pig and juleps for the handsome guest, and grinning pickaninnies get in the way. It is easy to mock this rose-colored view of the antebellum South, but it is the icon which has endured.

One of the South's major historians, Francis Butler Simkins, has stated, "A majority of Southerners believes that the nearest approach to heaven this side of the grave is that aristocratic perfection known as the Old South," and yet a host of historians have proven, "through the collection of multitudes of facts, that things were not what they were supposed to have been."[15] There were, of course, plantations — and even millionaire planters — in the Old South; however, the myth of the South being practically covered with vast plantations is hardly accurate. There were many more small farms and yeoman farmers than plantations and gentlemen-planters, and even a medium-sized plantation was only 1000 to 1500 acres. The large plantations were located mainly in four areas: tidewater Virginia, lowcountry South Carolina and Georgia, the Mississippi delta region, and Louisiana. Certainly, there were few in upcountry Georgia, in Tennessee, North Carolina, or Arkansas. Yet the public concept of slavery has come from the popular portrayal of life on enormous plantations as *the* mode of existence in the Old South. With a few significant facts, Clement Eaton has succinctly shown the inadequacy of such a view: "The plantation has come to stand for the characteristic element in the civilization of the Old South. Nevertheless, there were only 46,274 persons out of a white population of approximately eight million people in the slave states in 1860 whom the census officials classified as planters, i.e. owning as many as twenty slaves. In this priviledged class slightly less than three thousand persons held as many as one hundred slaves, and only eleven individuals possessed over five hundred slaves."[16] The truth of the agricultural system of the Old South is that most often both whites and blacks worked together in the fields to scrabble a living from the land.

Also, the image of white columns or red brick, the dominant one of plantation "big houses," is exaggerated and romantic. Except for a very few areas, such classic homes were rare in the country (they were more common as rich planters' townhouses in such cities as Charleston, Natchez, and Mobile). In the country, wealthy "planters often lived in plain farmhouses with no pretensions to architecture. Their houses had evolved from the double log cabin with its breezeway or 'dog run,' to which a porch in the back and front had been added," and even when there were white columns, "the spacious colonnaded porches were often cluttered with saddles and bridles, piles of loose cotton, agricultural implements, and a washstand, wash bowl, pitcher, towel, and wash bucket."[17] Such a scene does not have the noble beauty and exalted magnificence of Washington's Mount Vernon or Jefferson's Monticello nor, more significantly for the icon, of the two representations of the antebellum plantation known to more people than any others: the O'Hara's Tara and the Wilkes's Twelve Oaks of *Gone With the Wind,* and since it does not, it has been erased from the icon.

The appeal of the plantation icon is that of a supposed world of beauty, leisure, gallantry, and hospitality, which—however untrue to actuality—once was and is no more. It is a "different," even "exotic," world, which has become a part of the American historical consciousness. William R. Taylor ends his study of sectional stereotypes, *Cavalier and Yankee,* with the statement that "for the great mass of Americans, . . . the Old South has . . . become an enduring part of our sense of the past. At odd moments probably even the most skeptical of us allow our thoughts to play over this lingering social image, and to concede with mingled pride and wonderment: 'Once it was *different* down there.' "[18] This difference and the disappearance of the society whose social structure made it different are the major factors in the romantic appeal of the icon.

What began as the South's polemical defense of its "peculiar institution" in the 1830's and continued so until the Civil War became after the war a glorification of what was considered by white Southerners to have been the pinnacle of Angle-Saxon civilization. No longer was it necessary to answer Harriet Beecher Stowe's *Uncle Tom's Cabin* as did, among others, Mary H. Eastman in *Aunt Phillis's Cabin; or, Southern Life as It Is* (1852) or J.W. Page in *Uncle Robin in His Cabin in Virginia and Tom Without One in Boston* (1855); rather Thomas Nelson Page could ignore slavery as such and compose fictional rhapsodies to "the purest, sweetest life ever lived" — life on the antebellum plantation. Grace King's comment on the effect of Page's works has already been quoted; it indicates the comfort and pride that such works provided Southerners at a time of physical and spiritual deprivation. Page and his followers had equal success with Northern readers. The stories of Northerners crying over the death of Page's Marse Chan, as recounted by his faithful Sam, are legion. The North could not accept an idyllic view of slave society until it was past, but after the war and emancipation, it was fascinated by that different, now-gone world of its defeated kinsmen. The often used "reconciliation theme" — the marriage of a Union officer and plantation belle or of an impoverished Confederate veteran and Northern lady symbolizing the end of sectional strifle — of Page, Harris, and numerous others reassured Northerners that Southerners were willing to rejoin the Union and be loyal Americans. Facile as the symbol may seem today, it did aid reconciliation. As previously stated, by the late nineteenth century the plantation as icon of the South was firmly established. Jay B. Hubbell has said, "The Northern concept of Southern life was by 1890 a strange blend of somewhat incongruous elements drawn from Stephen Foster's songs, *Uncle Tom's Cabin, In Ole Virginia,* and the Uncle Remus stories."[19] "Incongruous elements" or not, they are all from and of the plantation.

The appeal of this different and past world has continued in this century. W. J. Cash has written in *The Mind of the South* that though "nobody any longer holds to the Cavalier thesis in its overt form, it remains true that the popular mind still clings to it in essence."[20] Cash is undoubtedly right, for Southerners cling to the "Cavalier thesis," i.e. the romantic icon of the Old South, as their distinctive heritage, which sets them apart from — and, for some "Southron" diehards, above — people of other regions. This reaction is prevalent even when paradoxically the South of the 1970's is becoming more and more powerful in national affairs. On the other hand, Northerners and Westerners are still entranced by the differentness of the Old South icon, while often being infuriated by the "New South" of the present day. The reason is that, as has been indicated, the various forms of popular culture have kept the icon within the public consciousness, and there is little indication that it will fade in the foreseeable future.

As an epigraph for this essay, I have quoted the remark of Gavin Stevens in William Faulkner's *Intruder in the Dust:* "The past is never dead. It's not even past." this statement by the South's greatest writer encapsulates the meaning and effect of the plantation icon. A society that vanished over one hundred years ago remains the icon of a fourth of the United States for both the inhabitants of that region and others. One native son has said bluntly, "We Southerners are, of course, a mythological people. Supposed to dwell in moonlight or incandescence, we are in part to blame for our own legendary character. Lost by choice in dreaming of high days gone and big houses burned, now we cannot even wish to escape."[21] Though some today are only too happy to escape from the dream, the majority of white Southerners still accept as fact, and cherish, the romantic icon of gracious plantation life. It has caused the South to look to a "golden past" rather than toward a "golden future." Destruction of antebellum society also provided an excuse for later deficiencies in the South — economic, political, and social; the argument is that if the South had been "left alone," the slavery issue would have "worked itself out" and the South would have been a major force in all aspects of American life during the years of its economic impoverishment and lack of national power. Needless to say, such views have been debilitating to the South for years. Equally so has been the view of the South by non-Southerners as a result of their acceptance of the icon. In one sense, the South has been thought of as "quaint," i.e. backward, in its fidelity to a society that has "gone with the wind." The acceptance of the icon by non-Southerners has separated the South from the remainder of the nation. Also, the icon has prevented others from seeing the South as it really is. It is not a monolithic entity: North Carolina is not Florida, Louisiana is not Georgia, and Mississippi is not Virginia. But the myth supporting the icon treats the South as if its geography, culture, and people are all the same: a moonlit, magnolia-scented plantation of the 1850's.

The response to icons is reverence by the many and mistrust by the few, and such is the case with that of the Old South plantation. Though historians may continue to point out the exaggeration and sentimentality present in the icon and warn of the dangers of its total acceptance, the icon's romantic appeal to the producers of popular culture and their audiences is unlikely to abate. The further away in time the reality of Old South society becomes, the more romantic it appears. The planned sequel to *Gone With the Wind* — whether a success or failure — is bound to re-stimulate interest in the Old South myth. The coffee commercials under the columns, the imitators of the planter to sell whiskey or fried chicken, the ice cream parlors and concession stands at amusement parks in mock plantation style, and other commercial adaptations will undoubtedly continue to proliferate. (After all, with the election of a Georgian to the presidency, "Southern chic" is in.) And so, the different, past world of that epitome of "Heaven down yonder," the plantation and its way of life, will remain the popular icon of Southern culture.

NOTES

[1]Patrick Gerster and Nicholas Cords, eds., *Myth and Southern History,* Chicago, 1974, p. 307.

[2]Henry Steele Commager and Richard Brandon Morris, "Editors' Introduction," Clement Eaton, *The Growth of Southern Civilization: 1790-1860,* New York, 1961, p. xi.

[3]"The First South" in Gerster and Cords, pp. 57-58.

[4]Richard B. Harwell, "The Stream of Self-Consciousness," *The Idea of the South,* ed. Frank E. Vandiver, Chicago & London, 1964, p. 19.

[5]Frank E. Vandiver, "The Confederate Myth," in Gerster and Cords, p. 148.

[6]*The New South Creed: A Study in Southern Mythmaking,* New York, 1970, p. 169.

[7]"Middle Class and Bourbon," *Culture in the South,* ed. W. T. Couch, Chapel Hill, 1934, p. 493.

[8]Gaston, p. 172.

[9]"The South as a Field for Fiction," *Forum,* 6 (December 1888), 405.

[10]*Red Rock,* New York, 1898, p. viii. For an analysis of the roles of Page and other popular Southern writers of the late nineteenth century in creating the sentimental, romantic view of plantation life, see Earl F. Bargainnier, "The Myth of Moonlight and Magnolias," *Louisiana Studies,* 15:1 (Spring 1976), 5-20.

[11]*In Ole Virginia,* Chapel Hill, 1969, p. 22. This edition is a facsimile of the original of 1887.

[12]Quoted in Edmund Wilson, *Patriotic Gore,* New York, 1962, p. 605. A later and quite different attitude which also shows Page's influence is that of James Branch Cabell: in the period 1910-1925, "the ghost of Thomas Nelson Page still haunted everybody's conception of the South, keening in Negro dialect over the Confederacy's fallen glories" (*Let Me Lie,* New York, 1947, p. 241).

[13]For a study of such songs about the South, see Earl F. Bargainnier, "Tin Pan Alley and Dixie: The South in Popular Song," forthcoming in *The Mississippi Quarterly: The Journal of Southern Culture.*

[14]Quoted in Max Wilk, *They're Playing Our Song,* New York, 1973, p. 11.

[15]"Tolerating the South's Past," in Gerster and Cords, p. 316. It is impossible to list here all of the historians who have examined the romantic tradition of the plantation, but a few require mention. Already noted are Eaton, Gaston, and the essays gathered by Gerster and Cords. Others of importance include Paul H. Buck,

The Road to Reunion: 1865-1900, Boston, 1937; Francis Pendleton Gaines, *The Southern Plantation,* New York, 1924; Rollin G. Osterweis, *Romanticism and Nationalism in the Old South,* New Haven, 1949; Anne Firor Scott, *The Southern Lady: From Pedestal to Politics,* Chicago, 1970; William R. Taylor, *Cavalier and Yankee,* New York, 1961; and C. Vann Woodward, *Origins of the New South: 1877-1913* (Vol. IX. *A History of the South*), Baton Rouge, 1951.

[16]Eaton p. 98.

[17]Eaton, pp. 121 and 122.

[18]Taylor, p. 341.

[19]*The South in American Literature,* Durham, 1954, p. 735.

[20]*The Mind of the South,* New York, 1941, p. 4.

[21]Jonathan Daniels, *A Southerner Discovers the South,* New York, 1938, p. 1.

Iconology Of The
Western Romance

Michael T. Marsden

Icons are objects in our environment that evoke uncritical and deeply felt emotional responses from those for whom they have a special, shared meaning. These magical items also function in formularized popular art as a type of shorthand and provide both the creator and the audience with a series of shared touchstones that carry with them a deep and meaningful significance that far outreaches their physical reality. Each formula in popular art can be identified with its own set of central icons which both limit and, paradoxically, expand the story form.

At their base icons have, of course, a type of religious significance. It is this religious significance which endows them with their basic power. A few years ago there was a short Associated Press wire story about a silver chalice brought to the town of Belem in Brazil by a visiting American priest which bore the following inscription: "In memory of Marilyn Monroe."[1] A remarkable mixture of the sacred and the secular, a fusion of the strengths of both into what can only be described as a super icon.

The Western formula, in both the literary form and the film form, is at its very basis religious in its implications. The hero, standing between the wilderness on the one hand and civilization on the other, mediates, much like a priest, between the powers of light and darkness because he can synthesize the strengths of both and use them against the weaknesses of the wilderness. The hero-priest functions as a nineteenth-century messiah by combining New Testament mercy with Old testament justice.[2]

In the Western genre there are no more central icons than the gun, the horse, and the landscape. While the horse enables the hero to move easily about the virtue-laden and vice-ridden landscape, the gun aids him in the final arbitration between good and evil. The hero's gun must, of course, be special, almost magical; it needs to be empowered with the forces of life and death, right and wrong. The hero's gun is not a tool, but a real extension of the manhood and the "rightness" of the hero-messiah. For the Virginian in Owen Wister's novel of the same name, the six-gun becomes a true extension of his manhood. Shortly before his wedding to Molly Stark Wood, he takes her for a ride and they happen upon a rattle-snake in some sagebrush. The ensuing dialogue is significantly revealing:

> "Can I hit it?" he inquired.
>
> "You don't often miss them," said she, striving to be cheerful.
>
> "Well, I'm told getting married unstrings some men." He aimed, and the snake was shattered. "Maybe it's too early yet for the unstringing to begin!" And with some deliberation he sent three more bullets into the snake. "I reckon that's enough," he said.
>
> . . . And then, with one leg crooked cow-boy fashion across in front of his saddle-horn, he cleaned his pistol, and replaced the empty cartridges.[3]

The phallic nature of the six-gun is all too obvious in the above passage as it is in many other Westerns.

The six-gun, however, is also a divine instrument of justice. Who can erase the image of William S. Hart's two six-guns delivering proper justice to the depraved townspeople who have corrupted the minister and forced him to burn his own church down in *Hell's Hinges* (1916), or the magic of the six-gun in other silent Westerns from *The Great Train Robbery* (1903) forward? With the advent of sound came the six-gun's other characteristic, its ominous aural power. When Ringo twirls his rifle at the stagecoach in *Stagecoach* (1939), we know we are dealing with no ordinary man, but rather with the man and his weapon who will restore civilization to its throne in the land of murdering outlaws. Just as the Virginian must use his gun to kill Trampas and thus cleanse himself before his marriage to Molly, so Ringo must avenge

the deaths of his father and brothers before he can marry
the reformed Dallas and settle on a green ranch to put down
roots.

The ways of the gun are learned and perfected in the
wilderness, away from civilization. For it is there that the gun
functions best, unobstructed, true to its target. In the romance of the West, the gun takes on magical powers as its
owner becomes supernatural. For *Shane* (1949), the gun is a
divine tool. He instructs young Bob Starrett:

> "Listen, Bob. A gun is just a tool. No better and no worse than any
> other tool, a shovel — or an axe or a saddle or a stove or anything.
> Think of it always that way. A gun is as good — and as bad — as
> the man who carries it. Remember that."[4]

During the 50's and 60's the Western genre flourished on
television screens across the land, spreading the six-gun's
iconic power to the young and old alike who watched in-
tensely as Wyatt Earp or the Rifleman dispensed justice. But
Gunsmoke, with its twenty-year run, certainly represents the
archetypal television Western. Marshall Dillon's huge six-gun
stood out as a large icon on that small screen, a magnificent
symbol of the forces of civilization at work on the streets of
Dodge City. But, as more than one critic has noted, Dillon
was more trigger-sorry than trigger-happy on our television
screens week after week.

For the Shanes and Dillons of America's imaginary West,
the six-gun was a way of maintaining one's individuality, or
of establishing oneself in the heroic mode, while at the same
time joining with the forces of civilization to fight the forces
of the wilderness. The hero finds, ironically, that once the
battle has been won, his magical weapon and he are no longer
welcome in the now secure society and that he is consequently alienated from both the wilderness and civilization.

One strain of Westerns glorifies the six-gun's violent power.
The six-gun in the hands of a Louis L'Amour Sackett, for example, is a skillful but violent weapon, as evidenced in this
passage from *Ride the Dark Trail:*

> Well, he'd started. So I shucked my old hog-leg and let 'er bang.
> He taken |sic| two of them through the middle button on his vest
> and just for luck I put another through his Bull Durham tag, where
> it hung from his left vest pocket.[5]

In some revisionist and anti-Westerns, the gun is viewed with disgust. But disgust with the six-gun is not the common-place. *High Noon* (1952) was a turning point in Western film history because Gary Cooper views the Western Choice with a question mark as he throws his badge in the dusty street after realizing that he has killed for a populace that isn't worthy of him.

The traditional view of the six-gun as positive Western icon continues into the mid-1970's. It is a powerful icon, as strong in the romance of the Western as Robin Hood's silver-tipped arrows are in lore. The gun to the Western hero is more important than his physical body, for it gives him life:

> Three of the men, including the man in the lead, apparently their leader from the way he gestured them forward, were heavily bearded. The rest had shaved sometime within the past week. They may have washed sometime within the past six months. They'd cleaned their guns, though, within the past hour.[6]

The image of the Western six-gun cherished by American audiences is that best expressed by Gary Cooper in a docu-mentary entitled *The Real West,* in which he said that the five bullets in the cylinder of the Western six-gun were for law and order and the one in the chamber was for justice! The finality is seductive and the catharsis artificial, but satis-fying. The icon of the six-gun, powerful and unmistakable, will continue to function as a central type of iconographic shorthand in Western mythology for generations to come.

The icon of the gun has made the transference from the Western in film, television, or print form to the urban Wes-tern, best exemplified by *McCloud,* to the detective genre on television with ease. While the transference has been in pro-cess for generations, the iconic significance of the gun in gen-eral is highlighted in the technologically-centered television series *S.W.A.T.* The more personal hand weapon, however, still remains the most popular icon among the maverick de-tectives who fill our television screens week after week.

The Western hero-messiah's horse is no less an extension of his persona, for the horse is his link to the landscape, to the wilderness from which he draws his strength and to which he owes his instruction. The particular horse is more often than not part of the wilderness, a mustang, for example, who is durable and can be counted on.

Historically, the horse as icon has been most important in Western film. The list of famous Western horses is legion, but a few names are worthy of mention. There were, of course, William S. Hart's Fritz, Gene Autry's Champion, and the Lone Ranger's Silver. But Matt Dillon rode a durable buckskin which had no name, a horse more consistent with its counterparts in popular Western fiction. The horse is individualized in the "kiddie" Western, but universalized in the adult Western. As an icon, the horse is representative of the force of nature, mute evidence of the hero's mastery over nature, of his ability to command respect from nature's forces.[7]

Of particular interest in the analysis of the horse as icon in the shorthand of the genre is the characters' treatment of horses. The villain, for example, is the only character type who will mistreat his horse or mule. A notable example of this occurred in *The Virginian* in an episode entitled "Balaam and Pedro" where the villainous Balaam tortures a pony and incurs the wrath of the Virginian.[8]

While mistreatment of horses is a signal of the character's lack of moral qualities, horses go generally unnoticed and are part of the landscape, except when the hero is in jeopardy of losing his mount. In Zane Grey's *Code of the West,* young Cal Thurman finds himself faced with the dilemma of modern life:

> Cal Thurman loved horses, and as a rider he was second only to his famous brother Boyd. But he hated automobiles and simply could not understand what made them run or stop or get out of order.

It is only in the film Western, though, that the horse can assume its fullest iconic power. For like the landscape, the horse is visual and therein lies its most important iconic significance in advancing the story. In a romance it is the action that predominates, not character development. And it is possible through the use of the horse to suggest an adequate amount of information about a character for the action to continue. For example, if the horse is tall of stature, the audience is led to assume that the man riding him is tall as well. If the horse is of race horse stock, then the character riding him is lately of another part of the country, having only recently arrived in the West. If the horse is a buckskin, a mustang, or a cowpony, then the man riding the horse is probably practical, hard-working, and hard-riding — the type of man it is best to stay clear of unless you are in the right.

Consistent with the iconic significance of the gun and the horse is the landscape itself, which finds its most complete expression in film. The landscape is not just a backdrop against which the story is set, but rather an integral part of the action. The landscape is the wilderness in all of its positive-negative completeness. The landscape is able to provide spiritual and physical healthfulness for the flapper-corrupted Georgiana May Stockwell in Zane Grey's *Code of the West*. And it is able to provide solace and strength for the Virginian and his bride, Molly Stark Wood, after the spilling of Trampas' blood and their union in marriage. It also can teach man the ways of the savage wilderness and provide a home for the undesirable elements of society as well. In many ways, the landscape serves as a kind of iconic metaphor for the feelings and emotions of the characters.

There is, of course, the romance and the appeal of the Western landscape that appears in Westerns of all media. Perhaps the following passage from Louis L'Amour's novel *Tucker* illustrates this as well as any:

> Frost had turned the leaves, and the mountainsides were splashed with golden clouds of aspen. Great banks of them poured down the steep slopes as though the earth had suddenly decided to give up and pour all her gold out to the waiting hands of men, only this gold was there for everyone to have — they had only to look. It was the kind of wealth that stayed with a man down the years, the kind you could never spend, but the memory of it waited in your mind to be refreshed when another autumn came.[10]

But it is primarily in the film Western that the landscape becomes an iconic force crystallizing the essential moment of decision between the forces of the wilderness and the forces of civilization which hang in suspended tension. In *Stagecoach* (1939), for example, the landscape of Monument Valley seems ready to pounce down upon the frail stagecoach at any moment, thus making not the vehicle but the social relationships developing within it the focal point. In *Shane*, the landscape of Jackson Hole functions iconically as well. The farmers are shown on a hill outside of town burying one of their own who was killed by the gunfighter Wilson. Between them and the mountains in the background is the town, stark and vulnerable, suggesting how frail their bid to establish civilization is. But Shane, who at the beginning of the film rides down from the mountains and into their valley, is part of the landscape, understands it, and is able to use the forces of the wilderness in the cause of the farmers and their families who want to establish a new society.

The icon of the landscape in technicolor and cinemascope is almost overwhelming and continues to function as a powerful force in the audience's experience with the national ritual that Americans invented and export to other cultures whose members welcome the story form.

The Western romance has its basis in reality, but as Marshall Fishwick points out in *Icons of Popular Culture,* history begets mythology and mythology begets ritual and ritual begets icons.[11] Popular Westerns depict a moment in our national American past when the American Choice was made and when we decided who we were and where we were headed. That moment never existed, of course. But we believe it did, and as John Cawelti points out in *The Six-Gun Mystique,* every Western is a type of Fourth of July Celebration where we relive our national past.[12] It is the icons associated with this important cultural ritual that give it depth and meaning.

While the television Western has diminished in popularity from numerous examples of the genre each season in the late 1950's to one in the 1976-77 season, (*Quest*), it has remained a viable story form in both print and film. Its icons in these media continue to work their magic on unsuspecting audiences as well, functioning as a powerful shorthand that is likely to remain viable in our society for generations to come. On television, the three key Western icons have been transmuted into the detective's pistol, the squad car, and the urban landscape. The Western icons have simply taken on disguises, extending themselves into the world of the American Nightmare until the audience is once again ready for the Romance of the West. For in the words of John Ford, the Western is not about the West as it is, it is about the West as it should have been.

In the popular arts, icons provide a most important bridge between the artist and the audience. They form part of the rich, shared cultural traditions which the popular artist and audience share and out of which the artist creates new works. Icons are conventions; the true popular aesthetic may lie in the ability of the artist to utilize conventions in a new way, retaining a large audience while at the same time entertaining them and enlightening them with a work which becomes part of the shared cultural traditions in a way that is paradoxically old and new.

The Western genre is just one of many story types in popular culture that utilizes icons to move the formula from the planes of enjoyable story telling to the level of significant cultural ritual. Iconology may well be the single most important approach to a study of popular culture, and as such deserves close attention in any popular art form. Icons move people; that is their strength. And for the serious student of popular culture, they are a magical force to be reckoned with.

NOTES

[1] *The Toledo Blade,* December 29, 1973.

[2] I examined this point in some detail in my article, "Savior in the Saddle: The Sagebrush Testament," *Illinois Quarterly,* Volume 36, Number 2 (December, 1973), 5-15. (The article was reprinted in *Focus On the Western,* edited by Jack Nachbar. New York: Prentice Hall, Inc., 1974, pp. 93-100.)

[3] Owen Wister, *The Virginian* (Boston: Houghton Mifflin Company, 1968), p. 272.

[4] Jack Schaefer, *Shane* (New York: Bantam Books, Inc., 1966), p. 44.

[5] Louis L'Amour, *Ride The Dark Trail* (New York: Bantam Books, Inc., 1972), p. 69.

[6] Jed Cross, *Vengeance Is Mine* (New York: Popular Library, 1975), p. 16.

[7] John Cawelti discusses this point in *The Six-Gun Mystique* (Bowling Green, Ohio: The Popular Press, 1971), p. 57.

[8] This episode is Chapter XXVI in the Houghton Mifflin edition cited above. The episode was apparently based on a real life experience Wister had witnessed in Wyoming in June of 1891, but did nothing about at the time. This chapter may well have been his reparation. ("Introduction," p. ix.)

[9] Zane Grey, *Code of the West* (New York: Grosset and Dunlap, 1934), p. 22.

[10] *Tucker* (New York: Bantam Books, Inc., 1971), p. 181.

[11] Co-edited with Ray B. Browne (Bowling Green, Ohio: The Popular Press, 1970), p. 3.

[12] Cawelti, p. 73.

Academicons–Sick Sacred Cows

Ray B. Browne

Icons, though historically and generally three dimensional objects or artifacts, can in fact at times be somewhat less tangible. They can be concepts and philosophies by which people have lived that have been compressed, as it were, into palpable objects for worship and uncritical following. Unexamined philosophies grow into aphorisms, then are elevated to truth, are enshrined in the museum of holies and thence grow into icons. As such they become realities by which people live and for which they will kill and die. Icons exist best in societies that will not examine their beliefs closely, for icons thrive best in semidarkness. To paraphrase Plato, the unexamined icon lives the fullest life. So over-whelming is the urgency to have icons that even the most "enlightened" groups in a society cherish many. Further, it is axiomatic that the more unsure a society or a group in a society becomes, the more icons they develop and the more blindly they worship them.

Academics in general, and those who profess the Humanities in particular, constitute a sub-society in America that live by their own academic rules and laws. Like other groups in America, academics when they are criticized for some of their beliefs and practices, even by respectable members of the inside core of the group, tend to form a circle, like the moose in the wild when attacked by wolves, and present a thorny circle of antlers to the attacking enemies. The more besieged they are, the more they automatically cling to their practices and ideologies. Their thinking becomes knee-jerk and reflex, and their beliefs are raised to the power of icons. But icons, as the Catholic Church so completely recognizes, must occasionally be reexamined and the dead ones cast out of the temple if iconology is to prosper. Some old discarded icons may be remembered with real affection, like St. Christopher, patron saint of all travelers, but they must not remain as officially approved members of the iconography.

Though the group may be smaller than those of other societies, academics maintain a set of icons in their higher education temple that are private, self-serving and generally as impervious to re-examination as those in any other section of our society. These academicons are in effect sacred cows that clutter and dirty the streets of academia and, because the flow of traffic is generally from the college campus outward to the world, therefore they spread out and all over non-academic communities. Although there are numerous incubi and succubi offshoots, the major academicons consist of a kind of secular holy trinity: the Ivory Tower, the curriculum and "standards."

Of these icons the holiest is, of course, that which represents the belief that the Academy is and of right should be separate and distinct from the world in which it resides, which supports it, and which supposedly it serves — an island entire unto itself. Like the monks in medieval days who retired to their monastaries to separate themselves from worldly obligations so that they could prepare themselves for the next world, many present day academics are almost priestly in their feeling that they must maintain their distance from the world so that they can pursue "disinterested" and "pure" research and scholarship, thereby rendering to society the best possible service. This position, if it was ever totally sound, is in our day only partially defensible. It may cause more trouble than it settles. Harold Howe, then Commissioner of the U.S. Office of Education, attributed most student unrest in the late 60's to professors' indifference to the real world;

> Students are disaffected and disgruntled with what is going on in the universities; and they cannot understand why university professors who are responsible for the reach into space, for splitting the atom, and for interpretation of man's journey on earth seem unable to

find a way to make the university pertinent to their lives.

In the 70's society at large is disaffected and disgruntled with the attitude of the universities and colleges. Yet the institutions of so-called "higher" learning remain largely indifferent and complacent. As Gene Lyons in an essay called "The Higher Illiteracy" (*Harper's,* Sept., 1976) bitingly points out, "Our universities have become ingrown, so self-contained that most of their faculties believe that what is good for them is good for the culture at large." Such an attitude grows from the assumption that the university is indeed an Ivory Tower and its own reason for being. The evidence for such an attitude is the widely held notion that American education must be nearly perfect because America has developed so beautifully for the last 200 years. It is a truism: America is the greatest country in the world; a nation grows on its educational system; therefore America's educational system is the greatest in the world. There are numerous flaws in this exercise in philosophical narcissism. And many inherent dangerous consequences.

One flaw is tragically evident in the richness and lasting quality of the humanities in society at large. In our colleges and universities the humanities presumably are those profound philosophical studies that enrich our lives, make us superior to mere machines, and ultimately make life worth living. Yet the lasting effect of most of the humanities taught in our universities and colleges is short. Most alumni give the lie to the boasts of the professors. In many ways the most shattering refutation comes from those alumni who eventually come to control the first twelve grades of our school systems. These people tend to be conservative, penurious, and more interested in creating schools that are mere extensions of what the people remember from their own school days than any really educational institution that is *building* on yesterday's progress not *imitating* it. At no time has this rearview vision been more frightingly apparent that at this moment, when educators, disturbed by what they are being told about the high rate of illiteracy in our schools, want to ditch the whole system and, throwing the baby out with the dirty water, go back to McGuffey.

Another flaw in education's faith in its own infallibility is seen in the professors it has created. Again, in the humanities, which should teach openmindedness, inquisitiveness, altruism and, even, unselfishness, what the professors teach by their behavior if not their mouthings is genuine and not very enlightened self-interest and the drive for self perpetuation. Instructors in the Humanities tend to teach how people can get more from other people than they give. Scratch the professor of Humanities and you often find an inhumane person. Such professors do not teach the mind to think independently and search out new truths and new richness to life. Instead they are more likely to teach students to remember facts and to be safe by searching only along fairly well known paths.

Undoubtedly such attitudes are not all bad; one has to live. But flashed on the screen of non-academic life, articulated from the powerful sound box situated in the Ivory Room, sometimes they reverberate like sounding brass or worn-out cymbal.

The second leg in the Academic holy trinity is the conviction of the sanctity of the Curriculum, which many professors think is chiseled in stone. To a large extent academics are not so concerned with what they *should* be professing as they are in worshipping and in perpetuating those things that they are and have been teaching. Criticism of the Curriculum often is considered an assault on the Ark of the Covenant and therefore restricted to as little change as possible. Consequently modifications of the Curriculum tend to be extensions of the present program rather than real and full scale revamping of the whole program. Few things are considered more irreverent than the suggestion that every course on a Curriculum should be thrown out every two years unless it can justify its existence. In the Sixties McGeorge Bundy, head of the Ford Foundation, stated what virtually everyone knows: ". . . The American university Curriculum and the American pattern of the organization of courses is badly out of date and is the product of custom and inertia much more than of rational examination of the learning process, and I think that great improvement can be made." If anything the thinking in the 70's is even more conservative.

Today with taxpayers' insistence that the University

modernize — or at least move into the twentieth century — the battle on the field of humanities curriculum has become almost a Holy War. The study of literature, generally considered one of the most humanizing of the humanities, has become something of an exercise in worship. Many critics feel that only the aesthetic is worthy of study. The plea for relevance is considered irrelevant. Many literary scholars insist that no literature since Beowulf or Shakespeare or the New England Transcendentalists should be studied since there have not been any "good" things written since that time. Historians still subscribe to the percolation theory that one should not bother with events until time has separated the "important" from the "trivial." Philosophers prefer the Ancients to contemporary thinkers and movers and shakers. Up until recently many academics fought valiantly to exclude folklore, oral culture, American Studies, Popular Culture, Ethnic Studies and Black Studies as impure and irrelevant invasions of holy terrain. Many still resent the sociologist who wants to examine the object, the fact, the thinking, the event in its social and cultural matrix.

Academics slip easily into complacency, and complacency breeds arrogance as well as contempt. Academia frequently becomes the list for tilts in one-up-man-ship. Aping the Cabots who spoke only to the Lodges who spoke only to God, Thoreauvians speak only to Emersonians, or directly to God; Miltonians speak only to Miltonians, or only to God. The most useful put-down is the type attributed to Henry James: "If you haven't read— — — I can't talk with you." Up until recently the high priests in Academic humanities were the nineteenth century Englishman Matthew Arnold and America's Dwight MacDonald because they taught what the majority of Humanities academics want to hear, that most Americans can be taught to act but not think, can only appreciate on a gut and money level, therefore can never be "cultured" in any true sense of the word. What kind of teaching could bring a broader and happier smile to the face of the Humanities professor, who by his own definition has already entered into Valhalla and wants to keep others out?

Though there are thousands of academics today voicing this philosophy, perhaps the extreme latest statement was that of Maynard Mack, currently director of the National Humanities Institute at Yale University, who while being supported by the taxpayers of this country could voice the ultimate elitist view, "The humanities are not really something you can democratize. It's like democratizing surgery. Who wants someone picked up off the street to operate on him? Well, its the same thing in the humanities." Mack is apparently admitting that the principle held so dear that the humanities enrich life is a sham. Thus — again — following this philosophy, the humanities will be denied to humanity — who are considered perhaps, in Edmund Burke's term, still "the swinish multitude."

Such academics are interested in "Main Currents," "Major Trends," "Great Writers," the full picture, the overall view, the "verities." They are not interested in ideas unless, in the words of A.O. Lovejoy in *The Great Chain of Being* "they come dressed in full warpaint." As such they miss the beauty and importance of the trees while admiring the forest. If this is correct, the word Humanities should be labeled a term more benefitting its masquerading role.

The philosophical icon on which the other two legs in the Trinity lean is the cry of "standards." Academics believe that they are the salt of the earth, the first, the last, and only, great hope of man, and they therefore must keep their product pure and high, like Caesar's wife above reproach. Their battle cry against all critics who would change the curriculum or make the institution more attuned to contemporary life is "Maintain our high standards forever." With such sentiment, were it really honest, few people would want to argue. To paraphrase Whitman's feeling about the need for critics, before one can have education, we must have true standards. But such is the insular, self-perpetuating, unexamined nature of Academia that the cry of high standards might well be merely the burly euphonious way of saying "Wrong Standards forever!"

In our world each generation has to rewrite its history and its reinterpretations. It is foolish to think that standards, whatever they really are, are a constant in a world otherwise filled with change. Just as the literary student's evaluation of the literary masters matures and changes, so should one's concepts of the criteria of excellence. It is obviously unwise to judge American standards of the 1970's by those of Victorian England, when Matthew Arnold intoned that culture is the best thoughts stated in the best way. Such a judgment, if it were ever valid, simply carries no weight today. It is pitiable but true that although America has now celebrated its political Bicentennial, despite Emerson's plea over a century and a quarter ago in "The American Scholar" it has yet to declare its cultural independence.

New standards are not necessarily inferior; they are merely different. In some — minor and late — ways this concept is recognized as valid. For example, the standard IQ tests, after generations of incalculable harm that they have done, are recognized as improper tests for judging intelligence. They were designed by middle class educators for middle class people and were weighed against other — minority and unacculturated — groups. These tests thus excluded thousands of promising minds by condemning them to jobs reserved for people with low IQ's. Nowadays we are concerned with the illiteracy rife in society, where people graduating from high school have only a ninth grade reading ability. Before we condemn all youngsters today to Siberia, however, we should consider if our testing is correct. Or are we merely applying other tests as invalid as the old IQ tests? Academic testers are likely to be the dragging edge of literacy, testing today's children by yesterday's White, middle-class literary standards.

So it has always been, apparently. When moveable type was invented, monks in the monasteries — those that could read — undoubtedly cried out that ugliness would curse mankind as illuminated manuscripts disappeared and nobody any longer appreciated beautiful writing. It just might be that we are using a monkish approach to the literacy test today. Academics are very likely to do this because generally speaking they all read fairly well, but are not adept in the other media. The printed word they have mastered but the electronics media intimidates them.

Test the literate academic against the electronic literate kid and we discover that both are speaking different languages, one a conventional printed linear language, the other a visual collage. The trouble with the kid's language is that of the visitor in a new land, a Columbus among the Indians of the New World. The Indians were forced to adapt to the language of the majority. Electronic kids are forced to speak their language in a society that still predominately uses printed words. The situation is analogous to the introduction of the metric standard of measurement in America today. Although the resistance is high, eventually the metric standard, or modification of it, will become standard. And eventually electronic communication will modify one way or another and one degree or another the conventional linear language.

It probably is therefore foolish and backward looking to insist on the word literacy in an electronic, picture age. If so, this is yet another example of the academic who marches into the future backward, admiring the good old ways and wishing not for the utopia of tomorrow but for the Eden of yesterday. They will use any cry to try to frighten their critics away. They are overly zealous, overly defensive and undoubtedly do both themselves and society a great disservice. One suspects that one can say about academics in their fervor a paraphrase of what Dr. Samuel Johnson said about patriotism, "the cry of 'standards' is the last refuge of the academic scoundrel."

A major fortress of this god of standards is, characteristically, promulgated in negative terms, that is, "Publish or Perish." Though stated in negative terms by its enemies, these words voice one of the finer traditions in academia, that is, that academics, in addition to their teaching duties, should be publishing scholars. The thinking behind this impulse was the realization that no graduate school can teach anyone everything, that therefore teachers will learn things on their own and they should communicate these discoveries to their colleagues at large. By and large such thinking has great merit. One can safely say that individual academics have only begun to understand and appreciate materials in their purview and the only way their colleagues can learn these things is through the printed word. Further, there can be great benefit to the teacher, who grows a little everytime he publishes something that gains the attention and respect of his colleagues, and the student, who surely benefits from the growing dimensions of his professor as long as those dimensions are directed toward better teaching and greater understanding.

But academics tend to become absolutionists instead of relativists, to think that a philosophy that is noble and useful when kept in perspective is even nobler and more useful when carried to its logical extreme. Like most extremes this can do great damage. Scholars often begin to publish because they have something to say, continue to publish when they *might* have something worth saying but persist in publishing long after their minds have gone bad merely because it is the thing to do. Such activity is foolish perversion. The lack of respect for the whole process is echoed in the cry of the excluded and abused lament, "Publish or Perish," where in its proper perspective the shout should be "Publish and Prosper."

The remarkable thing about academics today is that despite the fact that most of us have some knowledge of, though not necessarily any feel for, history and though we know Santayana's injunction that unless we learn from the mistakes of history we will be doomed to relive them, we in fact have learned little from history. Historians squeezed out of the curriculum their commendable course in Western Civilization because it was not sufficently specialized to please the faculty, who were rushing toward and continue to prefer specialization. English professors do not like to teach composition or general courses, when they are much better prepared to handle and much prefer to teach specialized courses. But it is becoming more and more clear that the trend toward specialized courses in the Humanities must be reversed into general courses with different purposes and thrusts.

And some method must be devised whereby rewards in prestige and salary must be given to those truly imaginative and energetic individuals who have nothing to publish, don't want to publish and therefore should be encouraged not to publish. These individuals must somehow be distinguished from their colleagues who because they have nothing to say, have other interests or are too lazy, have nothing to publish and nothing in fact to contribute to academia. These people, when separated, should be tagged. Just as there should be merit raises for the meritorious, there should be demerit cuts for the demeritous. Like Alice in Wonderland we have to run hard just to keep up.

Academics should be able to clean house and place merit where it belongs. The trend now, as the financial crunch tightens in academia, is to seek out the prestigious professor for the diminishing faculty. Such is a natural and noble impulse. But perhaps new gauges to measure prestige should be developed. There are foolish articles and books as well as wise ones. There are publications that should have been published and publications that should not have been brought out. There are fools who publish as well as wise people who don't. The trick is to distinguish between them. As a beginning a bright light should be focused on the icon as a prelude to its examination. Perhaps it cannot any longer justify its continuance.

All the icons of standards, like all others associated with academia, should be living organisms, changing as the times change, not what is in effect stuffed animals which when squeezed emit programmed sounds. In life, developing biologically or socially pure strains though seemingly attractive and useful at the beginning, ultimately refines the breed out of existence. Royalty has always reinvigorated its line by interbreeding with commoners. American academia generally allows the outsider in but has usually succeeded in metamorphosing him from the larvae to the butterfly, in convincing the stripling academic saint to deny his old gods and take up the new religion with its new icons. But the trend is being slowly reversed. There are too many commoners now in academia who insist that the old sacred cows of the Humanities are scrawny relics that spread pollution on the streets. Joshua is again at the walls of Jericho, the walls will come tumbling down, and the invader, armed with his new purpose will reveal that the academicons, like the Emperor who was perpetuating a fraud about his new clothes, will stand naked without justification and will change or will crumble and pass away.